# Illuminating Realities: The Theory of Real-Time Ray Tracing

Kameron Hussain and Frahaan Hussain

Published by Sonar Publishing, 2024.

While every precaution has been taken in the preparation of this book, the publisher assumes no responsibility for errors or omissions, or for damages resulting from the use of the information contained herein.

ILLUMINATING REALITIES: THE THEORY OF REAL-TIME RAY TRACING

**First edition. July 23, 2024.**

Copyright © 2024 Kameron Hussain and Frahaan Hussain.

ISBN: 979-8227555137

Written by Kameron Hussain and Frahaan Hussain.

# Table of Contents

Chapter 1: Introduction to Ray Tracing

    1.1. The Evolution of Ray Tracing

    1.2. Basic Principles of Ray Tracing

    Ray-Object Intersection

    Shading and Lighting Models

    Anti-Aliasing and Sampling

    1.3. Real-Time Ray Tracing vs. Traditional Methods

    Rasterization: Strengths and Limitations

    Real-Time Ray Tracing: Bridging the Gap

    Examples of Real-Time Ray Tracing

    Performance Considerations

    1.4. Applications of Ray Tracing in Modern Computing

    Video Games and Interactive Media

    Film and Animation

    Virtual Reality and Augmented Reality

    Architectural Visualization

    Scientific Visualization

    Automotive and Industrial Design

Education and Training

Medical Imaging and Visualization

1.5. Overview of the Book Structure

Chapter 2: Foundations of Real-Time Ray Tracing

Chapter 3: The Ray Tracing Pipeline

Chapter 4: Optimizing for Real-Time Performance

Chapter 5: Light and Material Interaction

Chapter 6: Shadows and Illumination

Chapter 7: Color and Perception

Chapter 8: Reflections and Refractions

Chapter 9: Advanced Lighting Techniques

Chapter 10: Ray Tracing in Gaming

Chapter 11: Ray Tracing in Film and Animation

Chapter 12: Real-Time Ray Tracing in Virtual Reality

Chapter 13: Acoustics and Ray Tracing

Chapter 14: AI and Machine Learning in Ray Tracing

Chapter 15: Hardware and Ray Tracing

Chapter 16: Software and Tools for Ray Tracing

Chapter 17: Real-Time Ray Tracing in Design and Architecture

Chapter 18: Ethical and Environmental Considerations

# ILLUMINATING REALITIES: THE THEORY OF REAL-TIME RAY TRACING

Chapter 19: The Future of Real-Time Ray Tracing

Chapter 20: Case Studies and Practical Applications

Chapter 2: Foundations of Real-Time Ray Tracing

2.1. Understanding Light and Optics

Nature of Light

Reflection and Refraction

Optical Properties of Materials

Color and Wavelength

Light Sources

Shadows and Penumbra

Global Illumination

Caustics

Polarization and Interference

Absorption and Scattering

Conclusion

2.2. Mathematical Foundations: Rays and Surfaces

Ray Representation

Vector Algebra

Intersection Tests

Transformations

Normals and Surface Properties

Parametric Surfaces

Differential Geometry

Monte Carlo Integration

Linear Algebra and Systems of Equations

Conclusion

2.3. Algorithmic Basics of Ray Tracing

Ray Generation

Ray-Object Intersection

Shading and Lighting

Reflection and Refraction

Acceleration Structures

Recursive Ray Tracing

Anti-Aliasing and Sampling

Denoising

Conclusion

2.4. The Role of Hardware in Ray Tracing

Graphics Processing Units (GPUs)

Ray Tracing Cores

Tensor Cores and AI Denoising

# ILLUMINATING REALITIES: THE THEORY OF REAL-TIME RAY TRACING

Field-Programmable Gate Arrays (FPGAs)

Central Processing Units (CPUs)

Hybrid Rendering Systems

Memory Bandwidth and Management

Advanced Memory Technologies

Real-Time Constraints and Optimization

Case Studies: Hardware-Accelerated Ray Tracing

Future Trends in Hardware

Conclusion

2.5. Introduction to Real-Time Constraints

Frame Rate and Latency

Performance Optimization

Acceleration Structures

Parallel Processing

Memory Management

Level of Detail (LOD)

Denoising and Image Quality

Adaptive Sampling

Hybrid Rendering Techniques

Real-Time Ray Tracing in Games

Virtual Reality Constraints

Case Studies: Real-Time Ray Tracing

Conclusion

Chapter 3: The Ray Tracing Pipeline

3.1. The Architecture of a Ray Tracing Engine

Scene Representation

Ray Generation

Intersection Testing

Shading

Rendering

Optimization Techniques

Example of a Simple Ray Tracing Loop

Conclusion

3.2. Scene Setting and Object Modeling

Geometric Primitives

Sphere Modeling

Plane Modeling

Triangle Meshes

Material Properties

Texture Mapping

Scene Graphs

Example of a Scene Graph Node

Instancing

Lighting Setup

Example of a Simple Lighting Setup

Environment Mapping

Conclusion

3.3. Ray Generation and Propagation

Camera Model

Perspective Projection

Orthographic Projection

Ray Generation Algorithm

Ray Propagation

Intersection Testing

Recursive Ray Tracing

Reflection and Refraction

Shadow Rays

Example of Shadow Ray Calculation

Global Illumination

Path Tracing

Monte Carlo Integration

Importance Sampling

Conclusion

3.4. Intersection Tests and Calculations

Sphere Intersection

Plane Intersection

Triangle Intersection

Möller–Trumbore Algorithm

Bounding Volume Hierarchies (BVH)

K-D Trees

Spatial Partitioning

Intersection Test Optimization

Ray Coherence

Example of BVH Intersection

Conclusion

3.5. Shading and Rendering Techniques

Phong Shading Model

Blinn-Phong Shading Model

Physically-Based Rendering (PBR)

Microfacet Models

Fresnel Effect

Subsurface Scattering

Ambient Occlusion

Screen-Space Ambient Occlusion (SSAO)

Global Illumination

Path Tracing

Importance Sampling

Tone Mapping

Anti-Aliasing

Denoising

Example of Path Tracing Loop

Conclusion

Chapter 4: Optimizing for Real-Time Performance

    4.1. Acceleration Structures: BVH and K-D Trees

    Bounding Volume Hierarchies (BVH)

    K-D Trees

    Spatial Partitioning

    Uniform Grids

    Octrees

    Example of K-D Tree Traversal

Conclusion

4.2. Parallel Processing and Ray Tracing

Graphics Processing Units (GPUs)

Multi-Core CPUs

SIMD and SIMT

Distributed Ray Tracing

Load Balancing

Task Parallelism

Data Parallelism

Example of Data Parallelism in Ray Tracing

Performance Metrics

Conclusion

4.3. Memory Management in Ray Tracing

Data Structures

Texture Mapping

Scene Graphs

Instancing

Memory Allocation

Example of Memory Pooling

Cache Optimization

Data Locality

Prefetching

Memory Bandwidth

Asynchronous Memory Transfers

Example of Double Buffering

Virtual Memory

Conclusion

4.4. Optimizing Ray Tracing Algorithms

Ray Generation Optimization

Example of SIMD Ray Generation

Intersection Test Optimization

Early Termination

Bounding Volume Tests

Shading Optimization

Precomputed Lighting

Lookup Tables

Importance Sampling

Example of Importance Sampling in Path Tracing

Adaptive Sampling

Example of Adaptive Sampling

Denoising

Temporal Denoising

Spatial Denoising

Conclusion

4.5. Case Studies in Efficient Ray Tracing

Case Study 1: NVIDIA RTX Technology

Case Study 2: Quake II RTX

Case Study 3: Pixar's RenderMan

Case Study 4: Real-Time Ray Tracing in Unreal Engine

Case Study 5: Blender's Cycles Renderer

Lessons Learned

Conclusion

Chapter 5: Light and Material Interaction

5.1. Simulating Light Behavior

Light Sources

Light Intensity and Attenuation

Reflection

Specular Reflection

Diffuse Reflection

Refraction

Fresnel Effect

Absorption and Scattering

Volume Rendering

Photon Mapping

Conclusion

5.2. Material Properties and Ray Interaction

Basic Material Properties

Diffuse Materials

Specular Materials

Glossy Materials

Translucent Materials

Transparent Materials

Composite Materials

BRDF Models

Example of a Cook-Torrance BRDF

Texture Mapping

Bump Mapping

Displacement Mapping

Example of Bump Mapping

Conclusion

## 5.3. Reflection, Refraction, and Transparency

Reflection

Specular Reflection

Glossy Reflection

Refraction

Total Internal Reflection

Fresnel Effect

Example of Fresnel Effect Calculation

Transparency

Beer-Lambert Law

Caustics

Simulating Caustics

Conclusion

## 5.4. Texturing and Bump Mapping

Texture Mapping

UV Mapping

Example of UV Mapping

Procedural Textures

Example of a Simple Procedural Texture

Normal Mapping

Example of Normal Mapping

Bump Mapping

Example of Bump Mapping

Displacement Mapping

Parallax Mapping

Example of Parallax Mapping

Conclusion

5.5. Advanced Lighting Models

Global Illumination

Radiosity

Photon Mapping

Path Tracing

Bidirectional Path Tracing

Subsurface Scattering

Example of Subsurface Scattering Calculation

Volumetric Lighting

Example of Volumetric Lighting

Ambient Occlusion

Screen-Space Ambient Occlusion (SSAO)

Example of SSAO Calculation

Caustics

Simulating Caustics

Conclusion

## Chapter 6: Shadows and Illumination

6.1. The Science of Shadows in Ray Tracing

Shadow Formation

Types of Shadows

Penumbra and Umbra

Ray Traced Shadows

Example of Shadow Ray Calculation

Soft Shadows

Example of Soft Shadow Calculation

Shadow Maps

Example of Shadow Map Usage

Ray Traced vs. Shadow Maps

Volumetric Shadows

Simulating Volumetric Shadows

Example of Volumetric Shadow Calculation

Conclusion

6.2. Soft Shadows and Hard Shadows

# ILLUMINATING REALITIES: THE THEORY OF REAL-TIME RAY TRACING

Hard Shadows

Characteristics of Hard Shadows

Example of Hard Shadow Calculation

Soft Shadows

Characteristics of Soft Shadows

Example of Soft Shadow Calculation

Area Lights and Soft Shadows

Sampling Techniques

Stratified Sampling

Example of Stratified Sampling

Monte Carlo Sampling

Comparison of Hard and Soft Shadows

Conclusion

6.3. Global Illumination Techniques

Direct vs. Indirect Lighting

Radiosity

Radiosity Method

Photon Mapping

Photon Emission

Photon Gathering

Example of Photon Mapping

Path Tracing

Monte Carlo Integration

Example of Path Tracing

Bidirectional Path Tracing

Example of Bidirectional Path Tracing

Metropolis Light Transport

Voxel-Based GI

Light Propagation Volumes

Example of Light Propagation Volumes

Conclusion

6.4. Ambient Occlusion in Real-Time Ray Tracing

Basics of Ambient Occlusion

Types of Ambient Occlusion

Screen-Space Ambient Occlusion (SSAO)

Example of SSAO Calculation

Horizon-Based Ambient Occlusion (HBAO)

Example of HBAO Calculation

Distance-Based AO

Example of Distance-Based AO

Volumetric Ambient Occlusion

Example of Volumetric AO

Optimizing AO for Real-Time Rendering

Example of Optimized AO

Conclusion

6.5. Practical Applications and Examples

Video Games

Film and Animation

Architectural Visualization

Automotive Design

Scientific Visualization

Virtual Reality

Product Visualization

Interactive Simulations

Conclusion

Chapter 7: Color and Perception

7.1. Color Theory in Digital Imaging

The Nature of Color

RGB Color Model

CMYK Color Model

HSV and HSL Models

Color Spaces

Gamma Correction

Color Matching and Conversion

Perception of Color

Metamerism

Color Blindness

Use of Color in Design

Example of Color Blending

Conclusion

7.2. Implementing Color in Ray Tracing

Color Representation

Example of Color Representation

Shading Models

Lambertian Shading

Phong Shading

Global Illumination

Path Tracing

Photon Mapping

Example of Photon Mapping

Texture Mapping

Example of Texture Mapping

Tone Mapping

Example of Tone Mapping

Conclusion

7.3. High Dynamic Range Imaging (HDRI)

The Concept of HDRI

Creating HDR Images

Example of HDR Image Creation

HDR File Formats

Tone Mapping

Example of Tone Mapping

Applications of HDRI

HDRI in Photography

HDRI in Film and Animation

Example of HDRI Environment Lighting

HDRI in Video Games

Dynamic Range Compression

Example of Reinhard Tone Mapping

Challenges in HDRI

Conclusion

7.4. Color Grading and Post-Processing

The Purpose of Color Grading

Basic Color Adjustments

Example of Basic Color Adjustment

Advanced Color Grading

Example of Selective Color Correction

Color Grading in Film and Video

LUTs (Look-Up Tables)

Example of Applying a LUT

Post-Processing Effects

Example of Bloom Effect

Vignetting

Example of Vignetting Effect

Chromatic Aberration

Example of Chromatic Aberration Effect

HDR Tone Mapping

Conclusion

7.5. Perception and Human Vision Considerations

The Human Visual System

Rods and Cones

Color Perception

Tristimulus Theory

Example of Tristimulus Calculation

Color Adaptation

Simulating Color Adaptation

Depth Perception

Techniques to Enhance Depth Perception

Example of Depth Cue Calculation

Visual Acuity

Simulating Visual Acuity

Example of Depth of Field

Color Blindness Considerations

Simulating Color Blindness

Example of Simulating Deuteranopia

Conclusion

Chapter 8: Reflections and Refractions

8.1. Mirrors and Reflective Surfaces

Reflection Principles

Specular Reflection

Example of Specular Reflection Calculation

Reflective Materials

Example of Reflective Material

Rendering Reflective Surfaces

Example of Recursive Reflection

Importance of Reflection

Glossy Reflection

Example of Glossy Reflection

Reflectance Models

Fresnel Effect

Example of Fresnel Calculation

Combining Reflection with Other Effects

Example of Combined Reflection and Refraction

Conclusion

8.2. Water and Glass: Realistic Refractions

Refraction Principles

Snell's Law

Example of Refraction Calculation

Refractive Materials

Rendering Refractive Surfaces

Example of Recursive Refraction

Importance of Refraction

Caustics

Simulating Caustics

Example of Caustic Calculation

Dispersion

Example of Dispersion Calculation

Conclusion

8.3. Complex Refractive Phenomena

Total Internal Reflection

Example of Total Internal Reflection Calculation

Multiple Scattering

Simulating Multiple Scattering

Example of Multiple Scattering Calculation

Subsurface Scattering

Example of Subsurface Scattering Calculation

Combining Refraction with Scattering

Example of Combined Refraction and Scattering

Birefringence

Example of Birefringence Calculation

Chromatic Aberration

Example of Chromatic Aberration Calculation

Conclusion

8.4. Reflection and Refraction Optimization

Acceleration Structures

Example of BVH Traversal

Adaptive Sampling

Example of Adaptive Sampling

Importance Sampling

Example of Importance Sampling

Russian Roulette Termination

Example of Russian Roulette

Caching and Reusing Results

Example of Result Caching

Hybrid Rendering Techniques

Example of Hybrid Rendering

Conclusion

8.5. Case Studies: Reflections and Refractions in Games and Films

Case Study 1: Ray-Traced Reflections in "Battlefield V"

Implementation Details

# ILLUMINATING REALITIES: THE THEORY OF REAL-TIME RAY TRACING

- Example of Hybrid Reflection Rendering
- Case Study 2: Realistic Water Refraction in "Finding Nemo"
- Implementation Details
- Example of Water Refraction Calculation
- Case Study 3: Reflective Surfaces in "Spider-Man: Miles Morales"
- Implementation Details
- Example of Reflective Surface Rendering
- Case Study 4: Underwater Refractions in "Avatar"
- Implementation Details
- Example of Underwater Refraction Simulation
- Case Study 5: Glass and Reflections in "Frozen"
- Implementation Details
- Example of Ice Reflection and Refraction
- Conclusion

Chapter 9: Advanced Lighting Techniques
- 9.1. Photon Mapping in Ray Tracing
- The Photon Mapping Process
- Photon Emission Phase
- Photon Gathering Phase

Importance of Photon Mapping

Advantages of Photon Mapping

Challenges of Photon Mapping

Optimizations in Photon Mapping

Example of Photon Map Hierarchy

Conclusion

9.2. Caustics: Simulation of Light Through Transparent Media

Understanding Caustics

Types of Caustics

Photon Mapping for Caustics

Example of Caustic Photon Mapping

Rendering Caustics

Example of Caustic Rendering

Caustic Texture Mapping

Example of Caustic Texture Application

Optimizations for Caustics

Example of Adaptive Photon Emission

Conclusion

9.3. Subsurface Scattering for Realistic Skin

Understanding Subsurface Scattering

The BSSRDF Model

Example of BSSRDF Implementation

Multi-Layered Skin Model

Example of Multi-Layered Skin

Precomputed Scattering Profiles

Example of Applying Scattering Profile

Real-Time Subsurface Scattering

Example of Screen-Space Subsurface Scattering

Combining SSS with Other Effects

Example of Combined Effects

Conclusion

9.4. Volumetric Lighting Effects

Understanding Volumetric Lighting

The Volume Rendering Equation

Example of Volume Rendering Equation

Light Shafts and God Rays

Example of Light Shaft Simulation

Volumetric Fog

Example of Volumetric Fog Calculation

Real-Time Volumetric Lighting

Example of Screen-Space Volumetric Lighting

Voxel-Based Volumetrics

Example of Voxel-Based Volumetric Lighting

Combining Volumetric Lighting with Other Effects

Example of Combined Volumetric Effects

Conclusion

9.5. Implementing Advanced Lighting in Real-Time Systems

Deferred Shading

Example of Deferred Shading

Real-Time Ray Tracing

Example of Real-Time Ray Tracing

Hybrid Rendering Techniques

Example of Hybrid Rendering

Dynamic Lighting and Shadows

Example of Dynamic Shadow Mapping

Temporal Accumulation

Example of Temporal Accumulation

Conclusion

Chapter 10: Ray Tracing in Gaming

10.1. The Impact of Ray Tracing on Video Game Graphics

Enhanced Lighting and Shadows

Example of Ray-Traced Shadows

Realistic Reflections

Example of Ray-Traced Reflections

Global Illumination

Example of Global Illumination

Increased Realism in Game Environments

Example of Enhanced Game Environment

Improved Material Representation

Example of Material Representation

The Role of Hardware

Example of Hardware Utilization

Future Prospects

Conclusion

10.2. Challenges of Implementing Ray Tracing in Games

Performance Constraints

Optimization Techniques

Example of Adaptive Sampling

Integration with Existing Pipelines

Hybrid Rendering Approaches

Example of Hybrid Rendering Integration

Maintaining Visual Consistency

Ensuring Consistent Shading Models

Example of Consistent Shading Model

Managing Resource Constraints

Example of Resource Management

Handling Dynamic Scenes

Example of Dynamic Scene Handling

Future Directions

Conclusion

10.3. Case Studies: Games that Utilize Ray Tracing

Case Study 1: "Control" by Remedy Entertainment

Ray-Traced Reflections in "Control"

Example of Reflection Rendering

Global Illumination in "Control"

Example of Global Illumination Rendering

Case Study 2: "Metro Exodus" by 4A Games

Ray-Traced Ambient Occlusion in "Metro Exodus"

Example of Ambient Occlusion Rendering

Global Illumination in "Metro Exodus"

Example of Global Illumination Rendering

Case Study 3: "Cyberpunk 2077" by CD Projekt Red

Ray-Traced Shadows in "Cyberpunk 2077"

Example of Shadow Rendering

Reflections and Global Illumination in "Cyberpunk 2077"

Example of Reflection and GI Rendering

Conclusion

10.4. Future Trends in Ray Tracing for Gaming

Advancements in GPU Technology

Example of GPU Utilization

Real-Time Path Tracing

Example of Real-Time Path Tracing

AI and Machine Learning Integration

Example of AI-Optimized Ray Tracing

Hybrid Rendering Techniques

Example of Advanced Hybrid Rendering

Cloud-Based Ray Tracing

Example of Cloud-Based Ray Tracing

Conclusion

### 10.5. Integrating Ray Tracing with Traditional Rendering Techniques

Hybrid Rendering Approaches

Example of Hybrid Rendering

Deferred Shading with Ray Tracing

Example of Deferred Shading with Ray Tracing

Screen-Space Reflections

Example of Screen-Space Reflections with Ray Tracing

Combining Ray Tracing and Rasterization for Shadows

Example of Combined Shadow Rendering

Volumetric Lighting with Ray Tracing

Example of Volumetric Lighting with Ray Tracing

Conclusion

## Chapter 11: Ray Tracing in Film and Animation

### 11.1. Historical Use of Ray Tracing in Movies

Early Beginnings

The Rise of CGI

Example of Early Ray Tracing

Major Milestones

The 2000s and Beyond

Example of Advanced Ray Tracing

Photorealism in Modern Films

Ray Tracing in Animation

Example of Animation Ray Tracing

The Future of Ray Tracing in Film

Conclusion

11.2. Real-Time Ray Tracing in Modern Animation

Real-Time vs. Offline Rendering

Benefits of Real-Time Ray Tracing

Example of Real-Time Ray Tracing Workflow

Hardware Acceleration

Example of GPU-Accelerated Ray Tracing

Real-Time Ray Tracing in Game Engines

Example of Ray Tracing in Unreal Engine

Virtual Production

Example of Virtual Production Workflow

Challenges and Solutions

Example of Hybrid Rendering

Future of Real-Time Ray Tracing

Conclusion

11.3. Bridging the Gap: Real-Time and Offline Rendering

Real-Time Rendering

Example of Real-Time Rendering

Offline Rendering

Example of Offline Rendering

Hybrid Rendering Techniques

Example of Hybrid Rendering Workflow

Use Cases for Hybrid Rendering

Example of Previsualization Workflow

Advantages of Hybrid Rendering

Challenges of Hybrid Rendering

Example of Resource Management

Future Directions

Conclusion

11.4. Visual Effects and Ray Tracing

Realistic Lighting and Shadows

Example of Realistic Lighting

Accurate Reflections and Refractions

Example of Reflection and Refraction

Complex Material Properties

Example of Subsurface Scattering

Particle and Fluid Simulations

Example of Particle Simulation

Integration with Compositing

Example of Compositing Workflow

Real-Time Previsualization

Example of Real-Time Previsualization

Challenges in VFX

Example of Acceleration Structures

Future of Ray Tracing in VFX

Conclusion

11.5. Case Studies: Iconic Films Using Ray Tracing

Case Study 1: "Avatar" (2009)

Use of Ray Tracing in "Avatar"

Example of Lighting in "Avatar"

Case Study 2: "The Lion King" (2019)

Use of Ray Tracing in "The Lion King"

Example of Fur Rendering

Case Study 3: "Blade Runner 2049" (2017)

Use of Ray Tracing in "Blade Runner 2049"

Example of Neon Lighting

Case Study 4: "Finding Dory" (2016)

Use of Ray Tracing in "Finding Dory"

Example of Underwater Caustics

Case Study 5: "Gravity" (2013)

Use of Ray Tracing in "Gravity"

Example of Space Reflections

Conclusion

## Chapter 12: Real-Time Ray Tracing in Virtual Reality

### 12.1. The Unique Demands of VR on Ray Tracing

Performance Requirements

Example of Real-Time Performance Optimization

Latency Considerations

Example of Asynchronous Reprojection

Field of View and Resolution

Example of FOV and Resolution Handling

Real-Time Interaction

Example of Interactive Ray Tracing

Eye Tracking and Foveated Rendering

Example of Foveated Rendering

Challenges in VR Ray Tracing

Example of Resource Management

Future Directions

Conclusion

12.2. Achieving Realism in Virtual Environments

Realistic Lighting

Example of Realistic Lighting

Dynamic Shadows

Example of Dynamic Shadows

Realistic Reflections and Refractions

Example of Reflections and Refractions

Realistic Material Properties

Example of Material Properties

Volumetric Effects

Example of Volumetric Effects

Realistic Animation and Movement

Example of Motion Blur

High Dynamic Range Imaging (HDRI)

Example of HDRI

Challenges in Achieving Realism

Example of Balancing Performance and Realism

Future Directions

Conclusion

12.3. Performance Optimization for VR

Hardware Acceleration

Example of Hardware-Accelerated Rendering

Adaptive Sampling

Example of Adaptive Sampling

Level of Detail (LOD)

Example of LOD Rendering

Parallel Processing

Example of Parallel Processing

Temporal Accumulation

Example of Temporal Accumulation

Foveated Rendering

Example of Foveated Rendering

Optimizing Shaders

Example of Optimized Shader

Resource Management

# ILLUMINATING REALITIES: THE THEORY OF REAL-TIME RAY TRACING

Example of Resource Management

Future Directions

Conclusion

12.4. Immersive Experiences and Ray Tracing

Realistic Lighting and Shadows

Example of Realistic Lighting

Dynamic Reflections and Refractions

Example of Dynamic Reflections and Refractions

Detailed Material Properties

Example of Material Properties

Volumetric Effects

Example of Volumetric Effects

High Dynamic Range Imaging (HDRI)

Example of HDRI

Realistic Animation and Movement

Example of Motion Blur

Interactive and Responsive Environments

Example of Interactive Ray Tracing

Spatial Audio Integration

Example of Spatial Audio

Challenges in Creating Immersive Experiences

Example of Balancing Performance and Immersion

Future Directions

Conclusion

12.5. Future of VR and Ray Tracing Technologies

Advancements in Hardware

Example of Future Hardware Utilization

Software Innovations

Example of Software Optimization

Real-Time Path Tracing

Example of Real-Time Path Tracing

AI and Machine Learning Integration

Example of AI-Optimized Ray Tracing

Hybrid Rendering Techniques

Example of Advanced Hybrid Rendering

Cloud-Based Ray Tracing

Example of Cloud-Based Ray Tracing

Augmented Reality (AR) Integration

Example of AR Ray Tracing

Cross-Platform Compatibility

Example of Cross-Platform Rendering

Conclusion

Chapter 13: Acoustics and Ray Tracing

13.1. The Concept of Acoustic Ray Tracing

Principles of Acoustic Ray Tracing

Basic Algorithm

Reflection and Refraction

Example of Reflection Calculation

Absorption and Scattering

Example of Absorption

Simulation Accuracy

Real-Time Acoustic Ray Tracing

Example of Real-Time Optimization

Applications

Architectural Acoustics

Audio Engineering

Virtual Reality

Conclusion

13.2. Simulating Sound in Three-Dimensional Spaces

The Basics of Sound Propagation

Emission and Reception

Example of Sound Emission

Reflection and Diffusion

Example of Reflection

Refraction and Transmission

Example of Refraction

Absorption and Attenuation

Example of Absorption

Environmental Effects

Example of Reverberation

Real-Time Sound Simulation

Example of Real-Time Optimization

Spatial Audio

Example of Spatial Audio Processing

Applications

Conclusion

13.3. Applications in Architectural Acoustics

Importance of Acoustic Design

Example of Acoustic Design

Sound Isolation

# ILLUMINATING REALITIES: THE THEORY OF REAL-TIME RAY TRACING

Example of Sound Isolation

Reverberation Control

Example of Reverberation Control

Noise Control

Example of Noise Control

Diffusion and Scattering

Example of Diffusion

Acoustic Simulation Software

Example of Acoustic Simulation

Case Studies

Example of Case Study

Future Trends

Conclusion

13.4. Ray Tracing in Audio for Games and VR

Importance of Audio in Immersion

Example of Sound Localization

Environmental Effects

Example of Environmental Reverb

Occlusion and Obstruction

Example of Occlusion

Spatial Audio and HRTF

Example of HRTF Processing

Real-Time Audio Ray Tracing

Example of Real-Time Optimization

Integration with Game Engines

Example of Game Engine Integration

VR Audio Considerations

Example of VR Audio

Challenges and Solutions

Example of Hybrid Approach

Future Trends

Conclusion

13.5. Future Directions in Acoustic Ray Tracing

Enhanced Realism

Example of Enhanced Realism

Real-Time Performance

Example of Real-Time Optimization

AI and Machine Learning

Example of AI-Driven Acoustic Simulation

Integration with Other Technologies

Example of AR Integration

Improved Material Models

Example of Improved Material Modeling

Hybrid Simulation Approaches

Example of Hybrid Simulation

Personalized Acoustic Experiences

Example of Personalized Acoustics

Collaborative Simulations

Example of Collaborative Simulation

Education and Training

Example of Educational Simulation

Conclusion

## Chapter 14: AI and Machine Learning in Ray Tracing

### 14.1. The Role of AI in Optimizing Ray Tracing

Enhancing Performance

Example of AI-Enhanced Ray Tracing

Noise Reduction

Example of AI Denoising

Adaptive Sampling

Example of Adaptive Sampling

Predictive Rendering

Example of Predictive Rendering

Scene Analysis

Example of Scene Analysis

Light Path Optimization

Example of Light Path Optimization

Material Prediction

Example of Material Prediction

Real-Time Rendering

Example of Real-Time AI Rendering

Future Prospects

Conclusion

14.2. Machine Learning Algorithms for Real-Time Rendering

Supervised Learning for Denoising

Example of Supervised Learning for Denoising

Reinforcement Learning for Path Tracing

Example of Reinforcement Learning for Path Tracing

Generative Adversarial Networks (GANs)

Example of GAN-Based Image Generation

Transfer Learning for Material Prediction

Example of Transfer Learning for Materials

Neural Networks for Global Illumination

Example of Neural Network for Global Illumination

Adaptive Sampling with Machine Learning

Example of Adaptive Sampling

Bayesian Optimization for Rendering Parameters

Example of Bayesian Optimization

Inverse Rendering with Machine Learning

Example of Inverse Rendering

Real-Time Rendering in Games and VR

Example of Real-Time Rendering

Future Directions

Conclusion

14.3. Predictive Rendering and Intelligent Sampling

Predictive Rendering Techniques

Example of Predictive Rendering

Intelligent Sampling Methods

Example of Intelligent Sampling

Adaptive Path Tracing

Example of Adaptive Path Tracing

AI-Driven Importance Sampling

Example of Importance Sampling

Light Transport Prediction

Example of Light Transport Prediction

Scene Complexity Analysis

Example of Scene Analysis

Data-Driven Rendering

Example of Data-Driven Rendering

Error Prediction and Correction

Example of Error Prediction

Hybrid Rendering Techniques

Example of Hybrid Rendering

Future Trends

Conclusion

14.4. AI-Assisted Denoising Techniques

Supervised Denoising

Example of Supervised Denoising

Unsupervised Denoising

Example of Unsupervised Denoising

Denoising Autoencoders

Example of Denoising Autoencoder

Generative Adversarial Networks (GANs)

Example of GAN-Based Denoising

Variational Autoencoders (VAEs)

Example of VAE-Based Denoising

Recurrent Neural Networks (RNNs)

Example of RNN-Based Denoising

Hybrid Denoising Techniques

Example of Hybrid Denoising

Real-Time Denoising

Example of Real-Time Denoising

Training Denoising Models

Example of Training Process

Evaluating Denoising Quality

Example of Evaluation Metrics

Future Directions

Conclusion

14.5. Future of AI in Ray Tracing Development

AI-Enhanced Realism

Example of AI-Enhanced Realism

Fully AI-Driven Rendering

Example of Fully AI-Driven Rendering

Integration with Augmented and Virtual Reality

Example of AR/VR Integration

Intelligent Scene Understanding

Example of Scene Understanding

Predictive Maintenance and Optimization

Example of Predictive Maintenance

Personalized Rendering

Example of Personalized Rendering

Collaborative AI Models

Example of Collaborative AI

Quantum Computing Integration

Example of Quantum Computing Integration

Autonomous Creative AI

Example of Creative AI

Future Research Directions

Conclusion

Chapter 15: Hardware and Ray Tracing

15.1. GPUs and Their Role in Ray Tracing

Evolution of GPUs for Ray Tracing

GPU Architecture

Ray Tracing Cores

Example of Ray Tracing Core Usage

Performance Optimization

Real-Time Ray Tracing with GPUs

Programming GPUs for Ray Tracing

Example of CUDA Ray Tracing Kernel

Future Directions for GPUs

Conclusion

15.2. Custom Hardware for Ray Tracing

FPGA and ASIC Solutions

Custom Ray Tracing Chips

Performance and Efficiency

Example of Custom Ray Tracing Chip Architecture

Integration with Existing Systems

Case Studies

Future Prospects

Conclusion

15.3. The Evolution of Ray Tracing Hardware

Historical Perspective

Milestones in Hardware Development

Impact on Visual Computing

Current Trends

Example of Hybrid Rendering

Future Innovations

Conclusion

15.4. Comparing Different Hardware Solutions

GPUs vs. CPUs

Example of GPU Ray Tracing

Example of CPU Ray Tracing

FPGA vs. ASIC

Example of FPGA Ray Tracing

Example of ASIC Ray Tracing

Performance Benchmarks

Use Cases

Cost and Efficiency

Conclusion

15.5. Future Hardware Trends in Ray Tracing

Emerging Technologies

Example of Quantum Computing

Integration with AI

Example of AI Integration

Quantum Computing

Example of Quantum Ray Tracing

Energy Efficiency

Example of Energy-Efficient Ray Tracing

Industry Impact

Example of Industry Impact

Conclusion

Chapter 16: Software and Tools for Ray Tracing

16.1. Overview of Ray Tracing Software

Introduction to Ray Tracing Software

Popular Ray Tracing Libraries

Example of Using PBRT

Features of Ray Tracing Software

Example of Scene Description

Integration with Graphics APIs

Example of Vulkan Integration

Customizable Shading Models

Example of Custom Shading

Distributed Rendering

Example of Distributed Rendering

AI Integration

Example of AI Denoising

Conclusion

16.2. Programming Languages and APIs for Ray Tracing

C++ for Ray Tracing

Example of C++ Ray Tracing

Python for Rapid Prototyping

Example of Python Ray Tracing

CUDA and OpenCL for GPU Acceleration

Example of CUDA Ray Tracing

Vulkan and DirectX Raytracing (DXR)

Example of Vulkan Ray Tracing

OpenGL for Cross-Platform Development

Example of OpenGL Ray Tracing

Metal for Apple Ecosystem

Example of Metal Ray Tracing

WebGL for Web-Based Applications

Example of WebGL Ray Tracing

Conclusion

16.3. Integrating Ray Tracing into Existing Engines

Unreal Engine

Example of Unreal Engine Ray Tracing Integration

Unity

Example of Unity Ray Tracing Integration

OpenSceneGraph

Example of OpenSceneGraph Ray Tracing Integration

CryEngine

Example of CryEngine Ray Tracing Integration

Godot Engine

Example of Godot Ray Tracing Integration

Custom Engines

Example of Custom Engine Ray Tracing Integration

Conclusion

16.4. Tools and Libraries for Developers

PBRT (Physically Based Rendering Toolkit)

Example of Using PBRT

Embree

Example of Using Embree

OptiX

Example of Using OptiX

OSPRay

Example of Using OSPRay

Radeon ProRender

Example of Using Radeon ProRender

Mitsuba

Example of Using Mitsuba

LuxCoreRender

Example of Using LuxCoreRender

Conclusion

16.5. Open Source vs. Proprietary Solutions

Advantages of Open Source Solutions

Example of Open Source Solution: PBRT

Advantages of Proprietary Solutions

Example of Proprietary Solution: OptiX

Cost Considerations

Example of Cost Comparison

Flexibility and Customization

Example of Customization

Support and Community

Example of Community Support

Performance and Optimization

Example of Performance Optimization

Conclusion

Chapter 17: Real-Time Ray Tracing in Design and Architecture

17.1. Applications in Interior and Architectural Design

Enhancing Design Visualization

Example of Design Visualization

Interactive Design Adjustments

Example of Interactive Adjustments

Accurate Lighting Simulation

Example of Lighting Simulation

Material and Texture Realism

Example of Material Realism

Client Presentations

Example of Client Presentation

Virtual Reality Integration

Example of VR Integration

Efficient Design Iterations

Example of Efficient Iterations

Conclusion

17.2. Real-Time Visualization in Urban Planning

Large-Scale Visualization

Example of Urban Visualization

Impact Analysis

Example of Impact Analysis

Public Engagement

Example of Public Engagement

Interactive Urban Planning

Example of Interactive Planning

Sustainable Design

Example of Sustainable Analysis

Traffic Simulation

Example of Traffic Simulation

Pedestrian Flow

Example of Pedestrian Flow Analysis

Conclusion

17.3. Lighting Simulation for Architectural Spaces

Accurate Daylighting Simulation

Example of Daylighting Simulation

Artificial Lighting Design

Example of Artificial Lighting Design

Light Interaction with Materials

Example of Material Interaction

Energy Efficiency Analysis

Example of Energy Efficiency Analysis

Visual Comfort

Example of Visual Comfort Evaluation

Dynamic Lighting Scenarios

Example of Dynamic Lighting

Conclusion

17.4. Interactive Design Tools

Real-Time Feedback

Example of Real-Time Feedback

Collaborative Design

Example of Collaborative Design

Design Exploration

Example of Design Exploration

Parametric Design

Example of Parametric Design

Conclusion

17.5. Future of Design with Ray Tracing Technologies

Enhanced Realism

Example of Enhanced Realism

AI Integration

Example of AI Integration

Virtual and Augmented Reality

Example of VR/AR Integration

Real-Time Collaboration

Example of Real-Time Collaboration

Automated Design Optimization

Example of Design Optimization

Sustainable Design

Example of Sustainable Design

Conclusion

Chapter 18: Ethical and Environmental Considerations

18.1. Energy Consumption in High-Performance Ray Tracing

Energy Demands of Ray Tracing

Example of Energy Consumption Analysis

Environmental Impact

Example of Environmental Impact Evaluation

Optimization Techniques

Example of Optimization

Renewable Energy Sources

Example of Renewable Energy Integration

Future Directions

Example of Future Innovations

Conclusion

18.2. Ethical Implications of Photorealism

Misinformation and Deepfakes

Example of Deepfake Detection

Copyright and Intellectual Property

Example of Copyright Management

Privacy Concerns

Example of Privacy Protection

Responsible Use of Technology

Example of Responsible Content Creation

Conclusion

18.3. Sustainable Practices in Ray Tracing Technology

Energy-Efficient Hardware

Example of Energy-Efficient Hardware

Optimized Algorithms

Example of Algorithm Optimization

Cloud Rendering

Example of Cloud Rendering

Recycling and Reuse

Example of Hardware Recycling

Conclusion

18.4. The Role of Ray Tracing in Deepfakes

Creating Realistic Deepfakes

Example of Deepfake Creation

Detecting Deepfakes

Example of Deepfake Detection

Ethical Considerations

Example of Ethical Guidelines

Conclusion

18.5. Balancing Innovation with Responsibility

Responsible Innovation

Example of Responsible Innovation

Ethical Design

Example of Ethical Design

Environmental Sustainability

Example of Environmental Sustainability

Social Impact

Example of Social Impact Assessment

Conclusion

Chapter 19: The Future of Real-Time Ray Tracing

19.1. Emerging Trends in Ray Tracing

AI and Machine Learning Integration

Example of AI-Driven Denoising

Real-Time Global Illumination

Example of Voxel Cone Tracing

Hybrid Rendering Techniques

Example of Hybrid Rendering

Cloud-Based Ray Tracing

Example of Cloud-Based Rendering

Real-Time Ray Tracing in VR and AR

Example of VR Integration

Conclusion

## 19.2. The Convergence of Real-Time and Offline Rendering

Bridging the Gap

Example of Convergent Techniques

Unified Rendering Pipelines

Example of Unified Pipeline

Real-Time Ray Tracing Hardware

Example of Using Dedicated Hardware

AI-Driven Enhancements

Example of AI-Driven Upscaling

Case Studies

Example of a Case Study

Conclusion

## 19.3. Next-Generation Ray Tracing Technologies

Quantum Computing

Example of Quantum Ray Tracing

Neuromorphic Computing

Example of Neuromorphic Processing

Photonic Computing

Example of Photonic Computing

Advanced Shading Models

Example of Advanced Shading

Real-Time Path Tracing

Example of Real-Time Path Tracing

Conclusion

19.4. Predictions for the Next Decade

Ubiquity of Real-Time Ray Tracing

Example of Industry Adoption

Enhanced AI Integration

Example of AI Optimization

Increased Accessibility

Example of User-Friendly Tools

Sustainable Practices

Example of Sustainable Rendering

Cross-Platform Integration

Example of Cross-Platform Rendering

Conclusion

19.5. The Long-Term Impact of Ray Tracing on Digital Media

Transforming Visual Storytelling

Example of Enhanced Storytelling

Redefining Design and Architecture

Example of Architectural Visualization

Enabling New Art Forms

Example of Digital Art Creation

Enhancing Virtual Reality

Example of VR Enhancement

Conclusion

Chapter 20: Case Studies and Practical Applications

20.1. In-Depth Analysis of Notable Real-Time Ray Tracing Projects

Case Study: NVIDIA RTX Games

Example of RTX Implementation

Case Study: Unreal Engine Ray Tracing

Example of Unreal Engine Ray Tracing

Case Study: Quake II RTX

Example of Quake II RTX

Conclusion

20.2. Comparative Study of Rendering Techniques

Rasterization

# ILLUMINATING REALITIES: THE THEORY OF REAL-TIME RAY TRACING

Example of Rasterization

Ray Tracing

Example of Ray Tracing

Hybrid Rendering

Example of Hybrid Rendering

Comparative Analysis

Example of Comparative Evaluation

Conclusion

20.3. Lessons from Failed Ray Tracing Implementations

Overestimating Hardware Capabilities

Example of Hardware Limitation

Insufficient Optimization

Example of Optimization

Ignoring Scene Complexity

Example of Scene Simplification

Conclusion

20.4. Inspirational Success Stories in Ray Tracing

Pixar's RenderMan

Example of RenderMan Usage

Cyberpunk 2077

Example of Game Ray Tracing

Architectural Visualization by DBOX

Example of Architectural Visualization

Conclusion

20.5. Guided Tutorial for a Basic Ray Tracing Project

Setting Up the Project

Example of Project Setup

Defining the Scene

Example of Scene Definition

Implementing Ray Tracing

Example of Ray Tracing Implementation

Adding Shading and Lighting

Example of Shading and Lighting

Rendering the Final Image

Example of Final Rendering

Conclusion

# Chapter 1: Introduction to Ray Tracing

## 1.1. The Evolution of Ray Tracing

Ray tracing is a rendering technique for generating realistic images by tracing the path of light as pixels in an image plane. This technique simulates the effects of interactions between light and objects, including reflections, refractions, and shadows. The history of ray tracing dates back to the 1960s when it was first conceptualized for use in optics.

In the early stages, ray tracing was computationally expensive and impractical for real-time applications. It was primarily used in scientific visualization and high-quality image generation, where rendering time was not a critical factor. The seminal work by Turner Whitted in 1980 marked a significant milestone, introducing recursive ray tracing to simulate global illumination effects such as reflections and refractions.

Throughout the 1980s and 1990s, advancements in algorithms and increasing computational power made ray tracing more accessible. The introduction of acceleration structures like Bounding Volume Hierarchies (BVH) and K-D Trees significantly improved the efficiency of ray-object intersection tests, reducing the computational overhead.

With the advent of modern GPUs and the development of dedicated ray tracing hardware by companies like NVIDIA, real-time ray tracing became feasible. The release of NVIDIA's RTX series in 2018 was a game-changer, providing hardware support for ray tracing and making it possible to achieve real-time performance in interactive applications like video games and virtual reality.

Despite these advancements, achieving real-time ray tracing remains a challenging task due to the sheer computational complexity involved. Researchers and engineers continue to explore new algorithms, hardware optimizations, and hybrid rendering techniques to push the boundaries of what is possible.

The evolution of ray tracing is a testament to the relentless pursuit of realism in computer graphics. From its humble beginnings in academic research to its current status as a cornerstone of modern rendering, ray tracing has transformed the way we generate and perceive digital images.

Understanding the historical context of ray tracing helps appreciate the technological breakthroughs that have shaped its development. It also provides insights into the future directions of this ever-evolving field, where innovations in artificial intelligence, hardware acceleration, and software optimization will continue to drive progress.

As we delve deeper into the principles and applications of ray tracing, it becomes evident that this technique is more than just a method for rendering images. It is a fundamental tool for visualizing complex interactions of light, enabling the creation of immersive and photorealistic experiences.

## 1.2. Basic Principles of Ray Tracing

At its core, ray tracing involves simulating the paths that rays of light take as they interact with surfaces in a scene. The fundamental principle is based on tracing the path of rays from the eye (or camera) to the light sources, although the actual computation is often done in reverse, from the light source to the eye, to optimize performance.

The process begins with generating rays from the camera through each pixel in the image plane. These primary rays traverse the scene, testing for intersections with objects. When a ray intersects an object, the algorithm calculates the color and intensity of the pixel based on the material properties and lighting conditions at the point of intersection.

The recursive nature of ray tracing allows for the simulation of various optical effects. For example, when a ray hits a reflective surface, a secondary ray is generated in the direction of reflection. Similarly, rays can be refracted through transparent materials, leading to complex light interactions such as caustics.

A key challenge in ray tracing is managing the vast number of rays and intersection tests required to produce high-quality images. Acceleration structures like BVH and K-D Trees are employed to organize the scene geometry and reduce the number of intersection tests, significantly improving performance.

## Ray-Object Intersection

The efficiency of ray tracing largely depends on the speed of ray-object intersection tests. These tests determine whether and where a ray intersects an object in the scene. Different geometric primitives, such as spheres, triangles, and planes, have specific intersection algorithms optimized for their shapes.

For example, the intersection of a ray with a sphere involves solving a quadratic equation. Given a ray defined by its origin $o$ and direction $d$, and a sphere with center $c$ and radius $r$, the intersection test can be formulated as:

$$(o + td - c) \cdot (o + td - c) = r^2$$

Solving this equation for $t$ gives the points of intersection along the ray. If $t$ is positive, the intersection is in front of the ray origin, and the corresponding point is considered for further calculations.

## Shading and Lighting Models

Once intersections are determined, shading models are applied to compute the color of each pixel. Shading involves evaluating the light contributions from various sources, including direct illumination, reflections, and ambient light. Common shading models include Phong shading, Blinn-Phong shading, and physically-based rendering (PBR) models.

PBR models have gained popularity due to their ability to produce highly realistic images by simulating the physical properties of materials and light interactions. These models account for factors such as microfacet distributions, Fresnel effects, and energy conservation, resulting in more accurate and visually appealing renderings.

## Anti-Aliasing and Sampling

Ray tracing inherently produces high-frequency details, which can lead to aliasing artifacts in the rendered image. To mitigate this, anti-aliasing techniques are employed. One common approach is supersampling, where multiple rays are traced per pixel, and their results are averaged to produce a smoother image.

Adaptive sampling techniques further optimize performance by focusing computational resources on areas with high detail or contrast. By dynamically adjusting the number of samples based on local image characteristics, these methods achieve a balance between image quality and rendering speed.

## 1.3. Real-Time Ray Tracing vs. Traditional Methods

Traditional rendering methods, such as rasterization, have been the backbone of real-time graphics for decades. Rasterization involves projecting 3D objects onto a 2D screen and determining the color of each pixel based on the objects' attributes and lighting conditions. This method is highly efficient and well-suited for real-time applications, but it has limitations in simulating complex optical effects.

Ray tracing, on the other hand, excels in producing realistic images with accurate reflections, refractions, and shadows. However, the computational cost has historically made it impractical for real-time use. With advancements in hardware and algorithms, real-time ray tracing has become feasible, offering a hybrid approach that combines the strengths of both methods.

### Rasterization: Strengths and Limitations

Rasterization is highly efficient due to its simplicity and the ability to leverage hardware acceleration. Graphics Processing Units (GPUs) are designed to perform rasterization tasks quickly, making it possible to render complex scenes at high frame rates. Techniques like Z-buffering, texture mapping, and shading models have been optimized for rasterization, contributing to its performance.

However, rasterization struggles with effects that require global illumination, such as accurate reflections, refractions, and complex shadows. Approximations and screen-space techniques can simulate some of these effects, but they often fall short of the quality achievable with ray tracing.

## Real-Time Ray Tracing: Bridging the Gap

Real-time ray tracing aims to bridge the gap between rasterization and offline ray tracing by leveraging modern hardware and optimized algorithms. The introduction of NVIDIA's RTX technology, featuring dedicated ray tracing cores, marked a significant step towards this goal. These cores accelerate the computation of ray-scene intersections, enabling real-time performance.

Hybrid rendering techniques combine rasterization and ray tracing to achieve high performance and realism. For instance, rasterization can be used for the primary rendering pass, while ray tracing is employed for specific effects like reflections and shadows. This approach balances the strengths of both methods, providing a practical solution for real-time applications.

## Examples of Real-Time Ray Tracing

Several high-profile video games and applications have demonstrated the potential of real-time ray tracing. Titles like "Battlefield V," "Control," and "Cyberpunk 2077" have incorporated ray tracing for enhanced visual fidelity. These games showcase realistic reflections, accurate shadows, and lifelike lighting, elevating the immersive experience.

Real-time ray tracing is also making inroads in other domains, such as virtual reality, architectural visualization, and interactive simulations. The ability to render photorealistic scenes in real-time opens up new possibilities for design, entertainment, and scientific research.

## Performance Considerations

Achieving real-time performance with ray tracing requires careful optimization of both hardware and software. Modern GPUs with dedicated ray tracing cores, such as the NVIDIA RTX series, provide the necessary computational power. In addition, efficient algorithms and data structures, such as BVH, are crucial for managing ray-scene intersections.

Software optimizations include techniques like denoising, where machine learning algorithms are used to reduce noise in the rendered image. Temporal and spatial upscaling methods also play a role in enhancing performance, allowing for high-quality visuals without compromising frame rates.

# 1.4. Applications of Ray Tracing in Modern Computing

Ray tracing's ability to produce highly realistic images has led to its adoption across various fields, from entertainment to scientific visualization. The technique's versatility and accuracy make it an invaluable tool for professionals and researchers alike.

## Video Games and Interactive Media

The gaming industry has embraced ray tracing to enhance visual realism and immersion. Real-time ray tracing enables accurate reflections, shadows, and global illumination, creating more lifelike environments. Games like "Minecraft" and "Fortnite" have introduced ray tracing options, showcasing the technology's potential to transform the gaming experience.

## Film and Animation

In the film industry, ray tracing has long been used for rendering high-quality visual effects. Movies like "Toy Story" and "Avatar" employed ray tracing for their photorealistic imagery. The ability to simulate complex lighting interactions and produce realistic shadows and reflections is crucial for achieving cinematic quality.

## Virtual Reality and Augmented Reality

Ray tracing plays a significant role in virtual and augmented reality, where realism is essential for immersion. Real-time ray tracing enhances the visual fidelity of VR/AR experiences, providing more convincing lighting, shadows, and reflections. This is particularly important for applications in training, simulation, and interactive design.

## Architectural Visualization

Architects and designers use ray tracing to create accurate visualizations of buildings and interiors. The ability to simulate natural light and material properties helps in evaluating design choices and presenting concepts to clients. Real-time ray tracing enables interactive walkthroughs and real-time modifications, enhancing the design process.

## Scientific Visualization

In scientific research, ray tracing is used to visualize complex data and simulations. Fields such as astrophysics, medical imaging, and fluid dynamics benefit from the technique's ability to render detailed and accurate representations of phenomena. For example, ray tracing can visualize light propagation in optical systems or simulate particle interactions in physics simulations.

## Automotive and Industrial Design

The automotive industry leverages ray tracing for designing and visualizing vehicles. Accurate rendering of materials, lighting, and reflections helps designers evaluate aesthetics and functionality. Industrial designers also use ray tracing to visualize products, prototypes, and manufacturing processes, facilitating better design decisions.

## Education and Training

Ray tracing is used in educational tools and training simulations to create realistic environments. Flight simulators, medical training systems, and virtual laboratories benefit from the technique's ability to provide lifelike visuals. This enhances the learning experience by immersing students and trainees in realistic scenarios.

## Medical Imaging and Visualization

Medical imaging technologies, such as CT and MRI, use ray tracing algorithms to reconstruct detailed images from scan data. These images provide crucial information for diagnosis and treatment planning. Ray tracing's precision and ability to handle complex geometries make it well-suited for medical applications.

## 1.5. Overview of the Book Structure

This book is structured to provide a comprehensive understanding of real-time ray tracing, from fundamental principles to advanced applications. Each chapter builds on the previous ones, gradually introducing more complex concepts and techniques.

## Chapter 2: Foundations of Real-Time Ray Tracing

Chapter 2 delves into the basic principles of light and optics, mathematical foundations, and the role of hardware in ray tracing. It provides the groundwork necessary for understanding the subsequent chapters.

## Chapter 3: The Ray Tracing Pipeline

Chapter 3 explores the architecture of a ray tracing engine, covering scene setting, ray generation, intersection tests, and shading techniques. It provides a detailed overview of the ray tracing pipeline and its components.

## Chapter 4: Optimizing for Real-Time Performance

Chapter 4 focuses on optimization techniques, including acceleration structures, parallel processing, memory management, and algorithmic optimizations. It presents case studies to illustrate efficient ray tracing implementations.

## Chapter 5: Light and Material Interaction

Chapter 5 examines the interaction of light with different materials, covering reflection, refraction, transparency, texturing, and advanced lighting models. It provides insights into simulating realistic material properties.

## Chapter 6: Shadows and Illumination

Chapter 6 discusses the science of shadows, including soft and hard shadows, global illumination, and ambient occlusion. It presents practical applications and examples to demonstrate these concepts.

## Chapter 7: Color and Perception

Chapter 7 explores color theory, high dynamic range imaging (HDRI), color grading, and the role of human vision in perception. It discusses how to implement and manage color in ray tracing.

## Chapter 8: Reflections and Refractions

Chapter 8 covers the simulation of reflective and refractive surfaces, including complex phenomena and optimization techniques. It presents case studies from games and films to illustrate these concepts.

## Chapter 9: Advanced Lighting Techniques

Chapter 9 introduces advanced lighting techniques such as photon mapping, caustics, subsurface scattering, and volumetric lighting. It discusses their implementation in real-time systems.

## Chapter 10: Ray Tracing in Gaming

Chapter 10 examines the impact of ray tracing on video game graphics, challenges of implementation, case studies, and future trends. It explores the integration of ray tracing with traditional rendering techniques.

## Chapter 11: Ray Tracing in Film and Animation

Chapter 11 discusses the historical use of ray tracing in movies, real-time applications in animation, visual effects, and case studies of iconic films. It bridges the gap between real-time and offline rendering.

## Chapter 12: Real-Time Ray Tracing in Virtual

## Reality

Chapter 12 addresses the unique demands of VR on ray tracing, achieving realism, performance optimization, and immersive experiences. It looks at the future of VR and ray tracing technologies.

## Chapter 13: Acoustics and Ray Tracing

Chapter 13 explores acoustic ray tracing, simulating sound in 3D spaces, applications in architectural acoustics, audio for games and VR, and future directions in acoustic ray tracing.

## Chapter 14: AI and Machine Learning in Ray Tracing

Chapter 14 discusses the role of AI in optimizing ray tracing, machine learning algorithms for rendering, predictive rendering, AI-assisted denoising, and the future of AI in ray tracing development.

## Chapter 15: Hardware and Ray Tracing

Chapter 15 examines the role of GPUs, custom hardware, the evolution of ray tracing hardware, comparisons of different solutions, and future hardware trends in ray tracing.

## Chapter 16: Software and Tools for Ray Tracing

Chapter 16 provides an overview of ray tracing software, programming languages, APIs, integration into existing engines, tools and libraries, and open-source vs. proprietary solutions.

## Chapter 17: Real-Time Ray Tracing in Design and Architecture

Chapter 17 discusses applications in interior and architectural design, real-time visualization in urban planning, lighting simulation, interactive design tools, and the future of design with ray tracing.

## Chapter 18: Ethical and Environmental Considerations

Chapter 18 addresses energy consumption, ethical implications of photorealism, sustainable practices, the role of ray tracing in deep fakes, and balancing innovation with responsibility.

## Chapter 19: The Future of Real-Time Ray Tracing

Chapter 19 explores emerging trends, the convergence of real-time and offline rendering, next-generation technologies, predictions for the next decade, and the long-term impact on digital media.

## Chapter 20: Case Studies and Practical Applications

Chapter 20 presents in-depth analyses of notable projects, comparative studies of rendering techniques, lessons from failed implementations, success stories, and a guided tutorial for a basic ray tracing project.

# Chapter 2: Foundations of Real-Time Ray Tracing

## 2.1. Understanding Light and Optics

Light and optics form the foundation of ray tracing, as the technique simulates the behavior of light to create realistic images.

Understanding how light interacts with objects, materials, and surfaces is crucial for accurate rendering.

## Nature of Light

Light is an electromagnetic wave, characterized by its wavelength and frequency. It behaves both as a wave and a particle, a duality described by quantum mechanics. In ray tracing, light is typically modeled as rays traveling in straight lines until they interact with surfaces.

## Reflection and Refraction

When light encounters a surface, it can be reflected, refracted, or absorbed. The behavior of light at the interface between two media is governed by the laws of reflection and refraction. The law of reflection states that the angle of incidence is equal to the angle of reflection. The law of refraction, described by Snell's law, relates the angles of incidence and refraction to the refractive indices of the media.

$$n_1 \sin\theta_1 = n_2 \sin\theta_2$$

## Optical Properties of Materials

Materials have intrinsic optical properties, such as reflectivity, refractivity, and absorption. These properties determine how light interacts with the material. For example, metals reflect most of the light, while transparent materials like glass and water refract light, causing it to bend as it passes through.

## Color and Wavelength

The color of light is determined by its wavelength. When light interacts with a surface, the perceived color depends on the wavelengths that are reflected or transmitted. In ray tracing, simulating the spectral properties of light and materials is essential for producing accurate colors.

## Light Sources

Light sources in ray tracing can be modeled in various ways, such as point lights, directional lights, and area lights. Each type of light source has different characteristics and effects on the scene. For example, point lights emit light uniformly in all directions from a single point, while directional lights simulate distant light sources like the sun, with parallel rays.

## Shadows and Penumbra

Shadows are an important aspect of realistic rendering. They provide depth cues and enhance the perception of spatial relationships in a scene. Ray tracing can accurately simulate hard shadows, where the light is completely blocked by an object, and soft shadows, where the light is partially blocked, creating a penumbra.

## Global Illumination

Global illumination refers to the comprehensive simulation of light interactions in a scene, including direct and indirect lighting. Indirect lighting, such as light bouncing off surfaces, contributes to the overall illumination and realism of the scene. Ray tracing inherently supports global illumination by tracing multiple rays and simulating light bounces.

## Caustics

Caustics are patterns of light formed when light rays are focused by reflective or refractive surfaces. Examples include the bright patterns seen at the bottom of a swimming pool or the light concentrated by a magnifying glass. Ray tracing can accurately simulate caustics, enhancing the realism of scenes involving water, glass, and other materials.

## Polarization and Interference

Advanced ray tracing techniques may also account for polarization and interference effects. Polarization refers to the orientation of light waves, which can affect reflection and transmission properties. Interference occurs when light waves interact, leading to phenomena such as thin-film interference, which is responsible for the colorful patterns seen on soap bubbles and oil films.

## Absorption and Scattering

As light travels through a medium, it can be absorbed or scattered. Absorption reduces the intensity of light, while scattering redirects it. These effects are important for simulating realistic lighting in materials like fog, smoke, and translucent objects. Volume rendering techniques in ray tracing handle these interactions, providing lifelike representations of participating media.

## Conclusion

Understanding light and optics is essential for mastering ray tracing. The principles discussed in this section form the basis for simulating realistic light interactions, enabling the creation of photorealistic images. As we move forward, these concepts will be applied and expanded upon to develop a deeper understanding of ray tracing and its applications.

## 2.2. Mathematical Foundations: Rays and Surfaces

Mathematics plays a crucial role in ray tracing, providing the tools and frameworks necessary to describe and manipulate rays, surfaces, and their interactions. This section covers the essential mathematical concepts and techniques used in ray tracing.

### Ray Representation

A ray in 3D space is defined by its origin $o$ and direction $d$. The equation of a ray can be written as:

$$r(t) = o + td$$

where $t$ is a parameter representing the distance along the ray. The origin and direction are typically represented as vectors.

### Vector Algebra

Vector algebra is fundamental to ray tracing, as it allows for the representation and manipulation of geometric entities. Key operations include vector addition, subtraction, scalar multiplication, dot product, and cross product.

- **Dot Product**: The dot product of two vectors $a$ and $b$ is given by $a \cdot b$. It measures the projection of one vector onto another and is used to compute angles and determine perpendicularity.

- **Cross Product**: The cross product of two vectors $a$ and $b$ is given by $a \times b$. It produces a vector perpendicular to both $a$ and $b$ and is used to compute normals to surfaces.

## Intersection Tests

Intersection tests determine whether and where a ray intersects a surface. Different geometric primitives, such as spheres, planes, and triangles, have specific intersection algorithms.

- **Sphere Intersection**: The intersection of a ray with a sphere involves solving a quadratic equation. Given a sphere with center $c$ and radius $r$, the intersection test is:

$$(o + td - c) \cdot (o + td - c) = r^2$$

Solving for $t$ gives the intersection points along the ray.

- **Plane Intersection**: The intersection of a ray with a plane can be found using the plane's normal $n$ and a point $p$ on the plane. The intersection test is:

$$t = \frac{(p - o) \cdot n}{d \cdot n}$$

- **Triangle Intersection**: The intersection of a ray with a triangle can be computed using barycentric coordinates.

The Möller–Trumbore algorithm is a common method for this test.

## Transformations

Geometric transformations, such as translation, rotation, and scaling, are used to position and orient objects in a scene. Transformations can be represented using matrices, which allow for efficient computation and composition of multiple transformations.

- **Translation**: Moving an object by a vector $t$ is represented by adding $t$ to the object's coordinates.

- **Rotation**: Rotating an object by an angle $\theta$ around an axis can be represented by a rotation matrix.

- **Scaling**: Scaling an object by a factor $s$ is represented by multiplying the object's coordinates by $s$.

## Normals and Surface Properties

Normals are vectors perpendicular to a surface at a given point. They are crucial for shading calculations, as they determine how light interacts with the surface. The normal at a point on a surface can be computed using partial derivatives or cross products of tangent vectors.

## Parametric Surfaces

Parametric surfaces, such as Bézier surfaces and NURBS, are defined by mathematical equations that describe their shape. These surfaces are commonly used in modeling and require specific techniques for intersection tests and shading.

## Differential Geometry

Differential geometry provides the framework for understanding and manipulating curved surfaces. Concepts such as curvature, geodesics, and differential operators are used to describe the properties and behavior of surfaces.

## Monte Carlo Integration

Monte Carlo integration is a statistical method used to approximate integrals, particularly in the context of global illumination and sampling. It involves randomly sampling points and averaging the results, which is useful for simulating complex lighting interactions.

## Linear Algebra and Systems of Equations

Linear algebra is essential for solving systems of equations that arise in ray tracing, such as intersection tests and transformations. Techniques like matrix inversion and eigenvalue decomposition are commonly used.

## Conclusion

The mathematical foundations of ray tracing provide the tools and techniques necessary to model and manipulate rays, surfaces, and their interactions. A solid understanding of these concepts is crucial for implementing efficient and accurate ray tracing algorithms. As we progress through the book, these mathematical principles will be applied to develop more advanced techniques and optimizations.

## 2.3. Algorithmic Basics of Ray Tracing

The core of ray tracing lies in its algorithms, which determine how rays are traced, intersected with objects, and used to compute shading. This section covers the fundamental algorithms that form the backbone of ray tracing.

### Ray Generation

Ray generation is the first step in the ray tracing pipeline. Rays are typically generated from the camera through each pixel in the image plane. The direction of each ray is determined by the camera's position, orientation, and field of view.

#### Perspective Projection

In perspective projection, rays diverge from a single point (the camera) and pass through the image plane. The direction of each ray can be computed using the camera's position $c$, the image plane dimensions, and the pixel coordinates.

### Ray-Object Intersection

Intersection tests are critical for determining which objects a ray intersects. Efficient intersection algorithms are essential for real-time performance. Each geometric primitive has specific intersection tests optimized for its shape.

#### Sphere Intersection Algorithm

The intersection of a ray with a sphere is found by solving a quadratic equation. Given a ray $r(t) = o + td$ and a sphere with center $c$ and radius $r$, the equation is:

$$(o + td - c) \cdot (o + td - c) = r^2$$

Solving for $t$ gives the intersection points.

*Plane Intersection Algorithm*

For a plane defined by a point $p$ and a normal $n$, the intersection with a ray is found using:

$$t = \frac{(p - o) \cdot n}{d \cdot n}$$

## Shading and Lighting

Shading models determine the color and intensity of light at the intersection point. Common shading models include Phong shading, Blinn-Phong shading, and physically-based rendering (PBR).

*Phong Shading Model*

The Phong shading model consists of three components: ambient, diffuse, and specular reflection. The total color $C$ is given by:

$$C = C_{ambient} + C_{diffuse} + C_{specular}$$

# Illuminating Realities: The Theory of Real-Time Ray Tracing

## Reflection and Refraction

Reflection and refraction are simulated by generating secondary rays. Reflection rays follow the law of reflection, while refraction rays are computed using Snell's law.

### Reflection Ray

The direction of a reflection ray $r_{reflect}$ is given by:

$$r_{reflect} = d - 2(d \cdot n)n$$

where $d$ is the incident ray direction and $n$ is the surface normal.

### Refraction Ray

The direction of a refraction ray $r_{refract}$ is given by Snell's law:

$$r_{refract} = \frac{n_1}{n_2}(d - (d \cdot n)n) - n\sqrt{1 - \left(\frac{n_1}{n_2}\right)^2 (1 - (d \cdot n)^2)}$$

## Acceleration Structures

Acceleration structures, such as BVH and K-D Trees, organize scene geometry to reduce the number of intersection tests. These structures improve the efficiency of ray tracing by quickly eliminating large portions of the scene from consideration.

*Bounding Volume Hierarchy (BVH)*

BVH is a tree structure where each node represents a bounding volume that contains a subset of objects. Intersection tests are performed hierarchically, starting from the root node and proceeding to the leaves.

*K-D Tree*

A K-D Tree is a binary space partitioning structure that recursively subdivides space into axis-aligned regions. It is particularly effective for scenes with non-uniformly distributed geometry.

## Recursive Ray Tracing

Ray tracing is inherently recursive, as rays generate secondary rays upon intersecting surfaces. This recursion allows for the simulation of multiple bounces of light, enabling realistic effects like reflections and refractions.

## Anti-Aliasing and Sampling

Anti-aliasing techniques, such as supersampling and adaptive sampling, reduce visual artifacts. Supersampling traces multiple rays per pixel and averages the results, while adaptive sampling focuses computational resources on areas with high detail.

*Supersampling*

In supersampling, rays are jittered within each pixel, and the results are averaged to produce a smoother image. This technique helps mitigate aliasing artifacts caused by high-frequency details.

### Denoising

Denoising algorithms, often based on machine learning, reduce noise in the rendered image. These algorithms analyze the image and apply filters to smooth out noise while preserving details.

### Conclusion

The algorithmic basics of ray tracing encompass ray generation, intersection tests, shading, and optimization techniques. Mastering these algorithms is essential for implementing efficient and realistic ray tracing systems. As we advance to more complex topics, these foundational algorithms will be built upon and refined to achieve higher levels of performance and realism.

## 2.4. The Role of Hardware in Ray Tracing

Hardware plays a crucial role in the performance and efficiency of ray tracing. The advent of specialized hardware, such as GPUs and dedicated ray tracing cores, has revolutionized the field, enabling real-time ray tracing in applications like video games and virtual reality.

### Graphics Processing Units (GPUs)

GPUs are designed to handle parallel processing tasks, making them ideal for ray tracing. Modern GPUs contain thousands of cores that can execute many threads simultaneously, significantly accelerating ray tracing computations.

#### *NVIDIA RTX Technology*

NVIDIA's RTX series introduced hardware-accelerated ray tracing through dedicated RT cores. These cores perform ray-triangle intersection tests and BVH traversal, offloading these tasks from the main GPU cores and improving performance.

### *AMD Radeon Rays*

AMD's Radeon Rays is an open-source ray tracing library optimized for AMD GPUs. It leverages the compute capabilities of modern AMD graphics cards to accelerate ray tracing computations.

## Ray Tracing Cores

Dedicated ray tracing cores, like NVIDIA's RT cores, are specialized hardware units designed to accelerate specific ray tracing tasks. These cores handle BVH traversal and ray-object intersection tests, freeing up the main GPU cores for other tasks.

## Tensor Cores and AI Denoising

Tensor cores, initially introduced for AI computations, are now used in ray tracing for denoising. Machine learning algorithms running on tensor cores can effectively reduce noise in the rendered image, improving visual quality without a significant performance hit.

## Field-Programmable Gate Arrays (FPGAs)

FPGAs offer customizable hardware acceleration for ray tracing. They can be programmed to perform specific ray tracing tasks efficiently, making them suitable for specialized applications where flexibility and performance are critical.

## Central Processing Units (CPUs)

While GPUs dominate ray tracing, CPUs also play a role, especially in tasks that require complex logic or less parallelism. Multi-core CPUs can perform ray tracing efficiently for certain workloads, such as BVH construction and scene management.

## Hybrid Rendering Systems

Hybrid rendering systems combine the strengths of CPUs and GPUs to achieve high performance. GPUs handle the parallelizable tasks, such as ray tracing computations, while CPUs manage scene logic, data structures, and other tasks that benefit from sequential processing.

## Memory Bandwidth and Management

Ray tracing is memory-intensive, requiring efficient management of large datasets, such as scene geometry, textures, and acceleration structures. High memory bandwidth and advanced memory management techniques are essential for maintaining performance.

## Advanced Memory Technologies

Technologies like High Bandwidth Memory (HBM) and GDDR6 provide the necessary memory bandwidth for real-time ray tracing. These memory types are optimized for high-speed data transfer, reducing bottlenecks and improving overall performance.

## Real-Time Constraints and Optimization

Real-time ray tracing imposes strict performance constraints, requiring optimizations at both the hardware and software levels. Techniques like ray bundling, packet tracing, and efficient data structures help achieve real-time performance.

## Case Studies: Hardware-Accelerated Ray Tracing

Several applications and games have demonstrated the capabilities of hardware-accelerated ray tracing. Titles like "Battlefield V" and "Cyberpunk 2077" leverage NVIDIA's RTX technology to deliver stunning visuals with real-time ray tracing.

## Future Trends in Hardware

The future of ray tracing hardware lies in continued advancements in GPU architecture, specialized cores, and memory technologies. Emerging trends include the integration of ray tracing capabilities into mobile devices and cloud-based rendering solutions.

## Conclusion

Hardware advancements have been pivotal in making real-time ray tracing a reality. The combination of powerful GPUs, dedicated ray tracing cores, and advanced memory technologies enables the efficient execution of ray tracing algorithms. As hardware continues to evolve, the potential for even more realistic and immersive real-time rendering will expand, driving innovation across various fields.

# 2.5. Introduction to Real-Time Constraints

Real-time ray tracing introduces specific constraints that must be addressed to achieve interactive frame rates. These constraints involve performance optimization, efficient resource management, and balancing visual quality with computational requirements.

## Frame Rate and Latency

Real-time applications, such as video games and virtual reality, require high frame rates (typically 60 frames per second or higher) and low latency to ensure a smooth and responsive experience. Achieving these metrics with ray tracing poses significant challenges due to the computational complexity involved.

## Performance Optimization

Optimizing ray tracing algorithms for real-time performance involves several strategies, including acceleration structures, parallel processing, and efficient memory management. These optimizations aim to reduce the number of computations and minimize bottlenecks.

## Acceleration Structures

Acceleration structures, such as BVH and K-D Trees, are crucial for optimizing ray tracing performance. These structures organize scene geometry to quickly eliminate large portions of the scene from intersection tests, reducing the computational load.

### BVH Optimization

Optimizing BVH involves techniques like tree balancing, spatial splits, and refitting. These methods enhance the efficiency of BVH traversal and intersection tests, improving overall performance.

## Parallel Processing

Leveraging parallel processing capabilities of modern GPUs is essential for real-time ray tracing. Techniques such as SIMD (Single Instruction, Multiple Data) and SIMT (Single Instruction, Multiple Threads) enable efficient execution of ray tracing tasks across multiple cores.

## Memory Management

Efficient memory management is critical for handling the large datasets required by ray tracing. Techniques like texture compression, mipmapping, and efficient data structures help manage memory usage and bandwidth.

## Level of Detail (LOD)

Level of Detail (LOD) techniques reduce the complexity of rendering distant objects by using simplified models. This approach conserves computational resources, allowing more detailed rendering of closer objects.

## Denoising and Image Quality

Denoising algorithms play a vital role in real-time ray tracing by reducing noise in the rendered image. Machine learning-based denoising techniques can achieve high-quality results with minimal performance impact.

### Temporal Denoising

Temporal denoising leverages information from previous frames to reduce noise. This technique is particularly effective in real-time applications, where consecutive frames share similarities.

## Adaptive Sampling

Adaptive sampling techniques dynamically adjust the number of samples per pixel based on local image characteristics. This approach focuses computational resources on areas with high detail or noise, improving efficiency.

## Hybrid Rendering Techniques

Hybrid rendering combines rasterization and ray tracing to balance performance and visual quality. For instance, rasterization can be used for primary rendering passes, while ray tracing handles specific effects like reflections and shadows.

## Real-Time Ray Tracing in Games

Several games have implemented real-time ray tracing, showcasing its potential for enhancing visual fidelity. Titles like "Control" and "Metro Exodus" demonstrate the practical application of ray tracing in real-time environments.

## Virtual Reality Constraints

Virtual reality imposes additional constraints on real-time ray tracing, including higher frame rate requirements and stereoscopic rendering. Achieving real-time performance in VR requires further optimization and efficient use of resources.

## Case Studies: Real-Time Ray Tracing

Case studies of successful real-time ray tracing implementations provide insights into effective optimization strategies. These examples highlight the challenges and solutions in achieving interactive frame rates with ray tracing.

## Conclusion

Meeting real-time constraints in ray tracing requires a combination of performance optimization, efficient resource management, and advanced rendering techniques. By addressing these challenges, it is possible to achieve interactive frame rates and deliver immersive experiences with high visual fidelity. As technology advances, the ability to balance real-time constraints with the demands of ray tracing will continue to improve, driving innovation in interactive applications.

# Chapter 3: The Ray Tracing Pipeline

## 3.1. The Architecture of a Ray Tracing Engine

The architecture of a ray tracing engine is designed to efficiently manage the complex calculations required to trace rays through a scene. This involves handling scene data, generating rays, performing intersection tests, shading, and finally, rendering the image. A well-designed ray tracing engine ensures that these tasks are executed optimally to achieve high performance and visual quality.

### Scene Representation

A scene in a ray tracing engine consists of geometric objects, light sources, and materials. These elements are stored in data structures that allow for efficient access and manipulation. Commonly used data structures include lists, arrays, and spatial partitioning structures like BVH (Bounding Volume Hierarchies) and K-D Trees.

### Ray Generation

Ray generation is the process of creating rays that originate from the camera and pass through each pixel on the image plane. This step is crucial for determining the color and intensity of each pixel based on the interactions of these rays with the scene.

```
Ray generateRay(int x, int y, Camera& camera) {
```

```
float u = (x + 0.5) / width;

float v = (y + 0.5) / height;

Vector3 direction = camera.lowerLeftCorner + u * camera.horizontal + v * camera.vertical - camera.origin;

return Ray(camera.origin, direction);
}
```

## Intersection Testing

Intersection testing involves determining whether and where rays intersect with objects in the scene. Efficient intersection algorithms are critical for performance, as each ray may need to be tested against many objects.

## Shading

Shading calculates the color of a point on an object based on the material properties, light sources, and viewing direction. This step involves evaluating various shading models, such as Phong or PBR (Physically-Based Rendering).

## Rendering

Rendering is the final step, where the calculated colors of all pixels are assembled into an image. This process involves handling tasks such as anti-aliasing, tone mapping, and post-processing to enhance visual quality.

## Optimization Techniques

Various optimization techniques are employed in the ray tracing pipeline to improve performance. These include the use of acceleration structures, parallel processing, and efficient memory management.

## Example of a Simple Ray Tracing Loop

```
for (int y = 0; y < height; ++y) {

for (int x = 0; x < width; ++x) {

Ray ray = generateRay(x, y, camera);

Color color = traceRay(ray, scene);

image.setPixel(x, y, color);

}

}
```

## Conclusion

The architecture of a ray tracing engine is designed to handle the complex computations required to produce high-quality images. By efficiently managing scene data, ray generation, intersection testing, shading, and rendering, a well-designed engine can achieve real-time performance while maintaining visual fidelity.

## 3.2. Scene Setting and Object Modeling

Scene setting and object modeling are fundamental steps in the ray tracing pipeline. These processes involve defining the geometry, materials, and spatial arrangement of objects within the scene. Accurate and efficient modeling is crucial for realistic rendering and performance optimization.

## Geometric Primitives

Geometric primitives are the basic building blocks of a scene. Common primitives include spheres, planes, and triangles. Each primitive has specific mathematical representations and intersection algorithms.

## Sphere Modeling

A sphere is defined by its center and radius. The intersection of a ray with a sphere involves solving a quadratic equation.

```
struct Sphere {

Vector3 center;

float radius;

};

bool intersect(const Ray& ray, const Sphere& sphere, float& t) {

Vector3 oc = ray.origin - sphere.center;

float a = dot(ray.direction, ray.direction);

float b = 2.0 * dot(oc, ray.direction);

float c = dot(oc, oc) - sphere.radius * sphere.radius;

float discriminant = b * b - 4 * a * c;

if (discriminant > 0) {

t = (-b - sqrt(discriminant)) / (2.0 * a);

return true;

}
```

return false;

}

## Plane Modeling

A plane is defined by a point and a normal vector. The intersection of a ray with a plane is computed using the plane equation.

## Triangle Meshes

Triangle meshes are used to represent complex objects. A mesh consists of vertices and faces, where each face is a triangle. Efficient data structures like vertex buffers and index buffers are used to store and manipulate mesh data.

## Material Properties

Materials define how objects interact with light. Common properties include color, reflectivity, refractivity, and texture. Physically-Based Rendering (PBR) models use parameters like albedo, roughness, and metallic to simulate realistic materials.

## Texture Mapping

Textures add detail to objects by mapping 2D images onto their surfaces. UV mapping coordinates are used to associate points on the object with points on the texture image.

## Scene Graphs

Scene graphs are hierarchical data structures that represent the spatial relationships between objects. Nodes in a scene graph can represent transformations, geometric objects, or groupings of objects. This structure allows for efficient scene management and traversal.

## Example of a Scene Graph Node

**struct** SceneNode {

Matrix4 transform;

std::vector<SceneNode*> children;

GeometricPrimitive* geometry;

};

## Instancing

Instancing allows multiple copies of an object to be rendered efficiently. Instead of storing separate data for each instance, transformations are applied to a single set of geometry data.

## Lighting Setup

Lighting setup involves defining the types and positions of light sources. Common light types include point lights, directional lights, and area lights. The lighting setup significantly impacts the appearance of the scene.

## Example of a Simple Lighting Setup

**struct** PointLight {

Vector3 position;

Color intensity;

};

PointLight light = { Vector3(10, 10, 10), Color(1, 1, 1) };

## Environment Mapping

Environment mapping uses a surrounding image, such as a skybox or HDRI, to simulate complex lighting conditions. This technique enhances realism by providing accurate reflections and ambient light.

## Conclusion

Scene setting and object modeling are essential for creating realistic and efficient ray-traced images. By accurately defining geometric primitives, materials, textures, and lighting, a well-constructed scene can be rendered with high visual fidelity and performance.

# 3.3. Ray Generation and Propagation

Ray generation and propagation are critical steps in the ray tracing pipeline. These processes involve creating rays from the camera, tracing their paths through the scene, and calculating the interactions with objects and light sources.

## Camera Model

The camera model defines the viewpoint and projection of the scene. Parameters such as position, orientation, field of view, and aspect ratio determine how rays are generated.

## Perspective Projection

In perspective projection, rays originate from the camera and pass through each pixel on the image plane. This creates a frustum, with rays diverging from the camera position.

## Orthographic Projection

In orthographic projection, rays are parallel and orthogonal to the image plane. This projection is used for technical and architectural visualizations where perspective distortion is undesirable.

## Ray Generation Algorithm

Ray generation involves calculating the direction of rays for each pixel. This process takes into account the camera parameters and image resolution.

Ray generateRay(int x, int y, Camera& camera) {

float u = (x + 0.5) / width;

float v = (y + 0.5) / height;

Vector3 direction = camera.lowerLeftCorner + u * camera.horizontal + v * camera.vertical - camera.origin;

**return** Ray(camera.origin, direction);

}

## Ray Propagation

Ray propagation involves tracing the path of rays through the scene. This step includes intersection tests, calculating reflections and refractions, and handling interactions with light sources.

## Intersection Testing

Intersection testing determines whether and where a ray intersects with objects in the scene. Efficient intersection algorithms are crucial for performance, as each ray may intersect multiple objects.

## Recursive Ray Tracing

Ray tracing is inherently recursive, as rays generate secondary rays upon intersecting surfaces. This recursion allows for the simulation of multiple bounces of light, enabling realistic effects like reflections and refractions.

## Reflection and Refraction

Reflection and refraction are simulated by generating secondary rays. Reflection rays follow the law of reflection, while refraction rays are computed using Snell's law.

## Shadow Rays

Shadow rays are used to determine whether a point is in shadow. A shadow ray is traced from the intersection point to each light source. If the ray is obstructed, the point is in shadow.

## Example of Shadow Ray Calculation

bool isInShadow(const Vector3& point, const Light& light, const Scene& scene) {

Vector3 direction = light.position - point;

Ray shadowRay(point, direction);

**for** (const **auto**& object : scene.objects) {

**if** (object->intersect(shadowRay)) {

**return true;**

}

}

**return false;**

}

## Global Illumination

Global illumination refers to the comprehensive simulation of light interactions in a scene, including direct and indirect lighting. Ray tracing inherently supports global illumination by tracing multiple rays and simulating light bounces.

## Path Tracing

Path tracing is a global illumination algorithm that traces random paths from the camera through the scene. It simulates complex lighting interactions by sampling multiple light paths and averaging the results.

## Monte Carlo Integration

Monte Carlo integration is a statistical method used to approximate integrals, particularly in the context of global illumination and sampling. It involves randomly sampling points and averaging the results, which is useful for simulating complex lighting interactions.

## Importance Sampling

Importance sampling improves the efficiency of Monte Carlo integration by focusing samples on the most significant parts of the integrand. This reduces variance and improves convergence.

## Conclusion

Ray generation and propagation are essential for simulating realistic light interactions in a scene. By accurately generating rays from the camera and tracing their paths through the scene, a ray tracing engine can produce high-quality images with realistic lighting and shading.

## 3.4. Intersection Tests and Calculations

Intersection tests and calculations are fundamental components of the ray tracing pipeline. These processes determine where rays intersect with objects in the scene, which is crucial for shading and rendering.

### Sphere Intersection

A sphere is defined by its center and radius. The intersection of a ray with a sphere involves solving a quadratic equation.

**struct** Sphere {

Vector3 center;

float radius;

};

bool intersect(const Ray& ray, const Sphere& sphere, float& t) {

Vector3 oc = ray.origin - sphere.center;

float a = dot(ray.direction, ray.direction);

float b = 2.0 * dot(oc, ray.direction);

float c = dot(oc, oc) - sphere.radius * sphere.radius;

```
float discriminant = b * b - 4 * a * c;

if (discriminant > 0) {

t = (-b - sqrt(discriminant)) / (2.0 * a);

return true;

}

return false;

}
```

## Plane Intersection

A plane is defined by a point and a normal vector. The intersection of a ray with a plane is computed using the plane equation.

```
struct Plane {

Vector3 point;

Vector3 normal;

};

bool intersect(const Ray& ray, const Plane& plane, float& t) {

float denom = dot(plane.normal, ray.direction);

if (abs(denom) > 1e-6) {

Vector3 p0l0 = plane.point - ray.origin;

t = dot(p0l0, plane.normal) / denom;

return (t >= 0);
```

}

**return false;**

}

## Triangle Intersection

Triangles are commonly used in mesh representations. The intersection of a ray with a triangle can be computed using barycentric coordinates or the Möller–Trumbore algorithm.

## Möller–Trumbore Algorithm

The Möller–Trumbore algorithm is an efficient method for testing ray-triangle intersections.

**struct** Triangle {

Vector3 v0, v1, v2;

};

bool intersect(const Ray& ray, const Triangle& triangle, float& t, float& u, float& v) {

Vector3 edge1 = triangle.v1 - triangle.v0;

Vector3 edge2 = triangle.v2 - triangle.v0;

Vector3 h = cross(ray.direction, edge2);

float a = dot(edge1, h);

**if** (a > -1e-6 && a < 1e-6) **return false;**

float f = 1.0 / a;

```
Vector3 s = ray.origin - triangle.v0;

u = f * dot(s, h);

if (u < 0.0 || u > 1.0) return false;

Vector3 q = cross(s, edge1);

v = f * dot(ray.direction, q);

if (v < 0.0 || u + v > 1.0) return false;

t = f * dot(edge2, q);

return (t > 1e-6);

}
```

## Bounding Volume Hierarchies (BVH)

BVH is a tree structure where each node represents a bounding volume that contains a subset of objects. Intersection tests are performed hierarchically, starting from the root node and proceeding to the leaves.

## K-D Trees

A K-D Tree is a binary space partitioning structure that recursively subdivides space into axis-aligned regions. It is particularly effective for scenes with non-uniformly distributed geometry.

## Spatial Partitioning

Spatial partitioning divides the scene into regions to accelerate intersection tests. Techniques like uniform grids, octrees, and BVH are used to organize scene geometry.

## Intersection Test Optimization

Optimizing intersection tests involves reducing the number of calculations and improving the efficiency of algorithms. Techniques like early termination, bounding volume tests, and SIMD (Single Instruction, Multiple Data) are employed.

## Ray Coherence

Ray coherence refers to the similarity of rays in terms of origin and direction. Exploiting ray coherence can improve performance by reducing redundant calculations and leveraging data locality.

## Example of BVH Intersection

```
bool intersect(const Ray& ray, const BVHNode& node, float& t)
{

if (!node.bounds.intersect(ray)) return false;

if (node.isLeaf()) {

return node.object->intersect(ray, t);

}

float tLeft, tRight;

bool hitLeft = intersect(ray, *node.left, tLeft);

bool hitRight = intersect(ray, *node.right, tRight);

if (hitLeft && hitRight) {

t = min(tLeft, tRight);

return true;
```

}

**if** (hitLeft) {

t = tLeft;

**return true;**

}

**if** (hitRight) {

t = tRight;

**return true;**

}

**return false;**

}

## Conclusion

Intersection tests and calculations are essential for determining where rays interact with objects in a scene. Efficient algorithms and optimization techniques are crucial for achieving high performance in ray tracing, enabling realistic rendering in real-time applications.

## 3.5. Shading and Rendering Techniques

Shading and rendering techniques determine the final appearance of objects in a ray-traced scene. These processes involve calculating the color, intensity, and effects of light at each point of intersection based on material properties and lighting conditions.

## Phong Shading Model

The Phong shading model is a widely used method for calculating surface illumination. It consists of three components: ambient, diffuse, and specular reflection.

Color phongShading(const Intersection& hit, const Light& light, const Camera& camera) {

Vector3 lightDir = normalize(light.position - hit.position);

Vector3 viewDir = normalize(camera.position - hit.position);

Vector3 reflectDir = reflect(-lightDir, hit.normal);

float ambientStrength = 0.1;

Color ambient = ambientStrength * light.color;

float diff = max(dot(hit.normal, lightDir), 0.0);

Color diffuse = diff * light.color;

float spec = pow(max(dot(viewDir, reflectDir), 0.0), 32);

Color specular = spec * light.color;

**return** (ambient + diffuse + specular) * hit.material.color;

}

## Blinn-Phong Shading Model

The Blinn-Phong shading model is a variation of Phong shading that uses a halfway vector for specular reflection calculations, improving performance and visual quality.

## Physically-Based Rendering (PBR)

PBR models simulate the physical properties of materials and light interactions. Parameters such as albedo, roughness, and metallic are used to achieve realistic shading.

## Microfacet Models

Microfacet models simulate the roughness of surfaces by considering the distribution of microfacets. The Cook-Torrance model is a popular microfacet model used in PBR.

## Fresnel Effect

The Fresnel effect describes how the reflectance of a surface varies with the angle of incidence. This effect is crucial for realistic rendering of materials like glass and water.

## Subsurface Scattering

Subsurface scattering simulates the diffusion of light within translucent materials, such as skin and marble. This effect is essential for rendering realistic human skin and other organic materials.

## Ambient Occlusion

Ambient occlusion simulates the occlusion of ambient light in crevices and corners, enhancing the perception of depth and realism.

## Screen-Space Ambient Occlusion (SSAO)

SSAO is a real-time approximation of ambient occlusion that operates in screen space. It improves performance by avoiding complex geometry calculations.

## Global Illumination

Global illumination accounts for both direct and indirect lighting, simulating the full complexity of light interactions in a scene.

## Path Tracing

Path tracing is a global illumination algorithm that traces random paths from the camera through the scene, sampling multiple light paths to achieve realistic lighting.

## Importance Sampling

Importance sampling improves the efficiency of Monte Carlo integration by focusing samples on the most significant parts of the integrand, reducing variance and improving convergence.

## Tone Mapping

Tone mapping converts high dynamic range (HDR) images to low dynamic range (LDR) for display on standard monitors, preserving detail and contrast.

## Anti-Aliasing

Anti-aliasing techniques reduce visual artifacts caused by high-frequency details. Supersampling and multisampling are common methods used to achieve smoother images.

## Denoising

Denoising algorithms reduce noise in the rendered image, particularly in path tracing and other Monte Carlo methods. Machine learning-based denoising techniques can achieve high-quality results with minimal performance impact.

## Example of Path Tracing Loop

Color pathTrace(const Ray& ray, const Scene& scene, int depth) {

**if** (depth <= 0) **return** Color(0, 0, 0);

Intersection hit;

**if** (scene.intersect(ray, hit)) {

Ray scattered;

Color attenuation;

**if** (hit.material.scatter(ray, hit, attenuation, scattered)) {

**return** attenuation * pathTrace(scattered, scene, depth - 1);

}

**return** Color(0, 0, 0);

}

Vector3 unitDirection = normalize(ray.direction);

float t = 0.5 * (unitDirection.y + 1.0);

**return** (1.0 - t) * Color(1.0, 1.0, 1.0) + t * Color(0.5, 0.7, 1.0);

}

## Conclusion

Shading and rendering techniques are essential for determining the final appearance of objects in a ray-traced scene. By accurately simulating light interactions and material properties, these techniques enable the creation of realistic and visually appealing images.

# Chapter 4: Optimizing for Real-Time Performance

## 4.1. Acceleration Structures: BVH and K-D Trees

Acceleration structures are critical for optimizing the performance of ray tracing algorithms. They organize scene geometry to reduce the number of intersection tests, improving efficiency and enabling real-time performance.

### Bounding Volume Hierarchies (BVH)

BVH is a tree structure where each node represents a bounding volume that contains a subset of objects. The primary advantage of BVH is its ability to quickly eliminate large portions of the scene from intersection tests.

*BVH Construction*

Constructing a BVH involves recursively splitting the scene into smaller bounding volumes. Various heuristics, such as the surface area heuristic (SAH), can be used to optimize the splitting process.

```
struct BVHNode {
```

```cpp
BoundingBox bounds;

BVHNode* left;

BVHNode* right;

GeometricPrimitive* object;

};

BVHNode* buildBVH(std::vector<GeometricPrimitive*>& objects, int start, int end) {

BVHNode* node = new BVHNode();

if (start == end) {

node->bounds = objects[start]->boundingBox();

node->object = objects[start];

} else {

int mid = (start + end) / 2;

node->left = buildBVH(objects, start, mid);

node->right = buildBVH(objects, mid + 1, end);

node->bounds = union(node->left->bounds, node->right->bounds);

}

return node;

}
```

## BVH Traversal

Traversal of a BVH involves descending the tree and testing rays against bounding volumes. Early termination can be achieved by intersecting the closest objects first.

```cpp
bool intersect(const Ray& ray, const BVHNode& node, float& t)
{
    if (!node.bounds.intersect(ray)) return false;
    if (node.isLeaf()) {
        return node.object->intersect(ray, t);
    }
    float tLeft, tRight;
    bool hitLeft = intersect(ray, *node.left, tLeft);
    bool hitRight = intersect(ray, *node.right, tRight);
    if (hitLeft && hitRight) {
        t = min(tLeft, tRight);
        return true;
    }
    if (hitLeft) {
        t = tLeft;
        return true;
    }
```

**if** (hitRight) {

t = tRight;

**return true**;

}

**return false**;

}

# K-D Trees

A K-D Tree is a binary space partitioning structure that recursively subdivides space into axis-aligned regions. It is particularly effective for scenes with non-uniformly distributed geometry.

### K-D Tree Construction

Constructing a K-D Tree involves choosing a splitting plane and recursively dividing the space. The choice of splitting plane can be optimized using heuristics such as SAH.

### K-D Tree Traversal

Traversal of a K-D Tree involves recursively testing rays against the split planes and descending into the relevant child nodes.

# Spatial Partitioning

Spatial partitioning divides the scene into regions to accelerate intersection tests. Techniques like uniform grids and octrees are used to organize scene geometry.

## Uniform Grids

Uniform grids divide the scene into a regular grid of cells. Each cell contains a list of objects that intersect it, allowing for efficient intersection tests.

## Octrees

Octrees recursively subdivide space into eight octants. Each node in an octree represents a bounding volume, and the subdivision continues until a predefined condition is met.

## Example of K-D Tree Traversal

bool intersect(const Ray& ray, const KDTreeNode& node, float& t) {

**if** (!node.bounds.intersect(ray)) **return false**;

**if** (node.isLeaf()) {

**return** node.object->intersect(ray, t);

}

float tLeft, tRight;

bool hitLeft = intersect(ray, *node.left, tLeft);

bool hitRight = intersect(ray, *node.right, tRight);

**if** (hitLeft && hitRight) {

t = min(tLeft, tRight);

**return true**;

}

```
if (hitLeft) {

t = tLeft;

return true;

}

if (hitRight) {

t = tRight;

return true;

}

return false;

}
```

## Conclusion

Acceleration structures like BVH and K-D Trees are essential for optimizing the performance of ray tracing algorithms. By organizing scene geometry to reduce the number of intersection tests, these structures enable efficient rendering and real-time performance.

## 4.2. Parallel Processing and Ray Tracing

Parallel processing is a key technique for achieving real-time performance in ray tracing. By leveraging the parallel nature of modern hardware, such as GPUs and multi-core CPUs, ray tracing computations can be significantly accelerated.

## Graphics Processing Units (GPUs)

GPUs are designed for parallel processing, with thousands of cores capable of executing many threads simultaneously. This architecture is ideal for ray tracing, where each ray can be processed independently.

### CUDA and OpenCL

CUDA and OpenCL are parallel computing platforms and APIs that allow developers to write programs that execute on GPUs. CUDA is specific to NVIDIA GPUs, while OpenCL is an open standard that supports a wide range of hardware.

### Example of a Simple CUDA Kernel for Ray Tracing

```
__global__ void traceRays(Ray* rays, Color* colors, int numRays, Scene* scene) {

int idx = blockIdx.x * blockDim.x + threadIdx.x;

if (idx < numRays) {

Ray ray = rays[idx];

colors[idx] = traceRay(ray, scene);

}

}
```

## Multi-Core CPUs

Modern CPUs feature multiple cores that can execute tasks in parallel. Multi-threading and parallel algorithms can be used to distribute ray tracing computations across all available cores.

### OpenMP

OpenMP is an API that supports multi-platform shared memory multiprocessing programming in C, C++, and Fortran. It simplifies the development of parallel applications by providing compiler directives and library routines.

### Example of Parallel Ray Tracing with OpenMP

```
void renderScene(Scene& scene, Image& image) {

#pragma omp parallel for schedule(dynamic)

for (int y = 0; y < image.height(); ++y) {

for (int x = 0; x < image.width(); ++x) {

Ray ray = generateRay(x, y, camera);

Color color = traceRay(ray, scene);

image.setPixel(x, y, color);

}

}

}
```

## SIMD and SIMT

SIMD (Single Instruction, Multiple Data) and SIMT (Single Instruction, Multiple Threads) are parallel computing paradigms that execute a single instruction on multiple data points simultaneously. These paradigms are well-suited for ray tracing, where many rays follow similar computational paths.

## Distributed Ray Tracing

Distributed ray tracing involves distributing the ray tracing workload across multiple machines or nodes in a cluster. This approach can handle large scenes and high-resolution images by leveraging the combined computational power of the cluster.

## Load Balancing

Load balancing ensures that the computational workload is evenly distributed across all available processing units. This prevents bottlenecks and maximizes the utilization of hardware resources.

## Task Parallelism

Task parallelism involves dividing the ray tracing pipeline into independent tasks that can be executed concurrently. For example, ray generation, intersection tests, and shading can be performed in parallel.

## Data Parallelism

Data parallelism involves dividing the data into smaller chunks and processing each chunk independently. This approach is particularly effective for ray tracing, where each ray can be processed independently of others.

## Example of Data Parallelism in Ray Tracing

```
void        traceRays(const        std::vector<Ray>&        rays,
std::vector<Color>& colors, const Scene& scene) {

#pragma omp parallel for schedule(dynamic)

for (size_t i = 0; i < rays.size(); ++i) {

colors[i] = traceRay(rays[i], scene);

}

}
```

## Performance Metrics

Performance metrics, such as frame rate, latency, and throughput, are used to evaluate the efficiency of parallel ray tracing implementations. Optimizing these metrics is crucial for achieving real-time performance.

## Conclusion

Parallel processing is essential for achieving real-time performance in ray tracing. By leveraging the parallel nature of modern hardware, such as GPUs and multi-core CPUs, and employing techniques like SIMD, SIMT, and distributed ray tracing, it is possible to accelerate ray tracing computations and render complex scenes efficiently.

## 4.3. Memory Management in Ray Tracing

Efficient memory management is crucial for achieving high performance in ray tracing. This involves optimizing data storage, access patterns, and memory usage to reduce bottlenecks and ensure smooth rendering.

## Data Structures

Choosing the right data structures is essential for efficient memory management. Common data structures in ray tracing include arrays, lists, and spatial partitioning structures like BVH and K-D Trees.

## Texture Mapping

Textures are used to add detail to objects in a scene. Efficient texture mapping and storage techniques, such as mipmapping and texture compression, help manage memory usage and improve performance.

*Mipmapping*

Mipmapping involves creating multiple levels of detail for a texture, with each level being a progressively lower resolution version of the original. This technique improves rendering performance and reduces aliasing.

*Texture Compression*

Texture compression reduces the amount of memory required to store textures. Compressed textures are decompressed on-the-fly during rendering, balancing memory usage and performance.

## Scene Graphs

Scene graphs are hierarchical data structures that represent the spatial relationships between objects. Efficient scene graph traversal and management help optimize memory usage and access patterns.

## Instancing

Instancing allows multiple copies of an object to be rendered efficiently. Instead of storing separate data for each instance, transformations are applied to a single set of geometry data, reducing memory usage.

## Memory Allocation

Efficient memory allocation and deallocation are crucial for maintaining performance. Techniques such as memory pooling and custom allocators help manage memory usage and reduce fragmentation.

## Example of Memory Pooling

**class** MemoryPool {

std::vector<void*> pool;

**public**:

void* allocate(size_t size) {

**if** (pool.empty()) {

**return** std::malloc(size);

} **else** {

void* ptr = pool.back();

pool.pop_back();

```
return ptr;
    }
}
void deallocate(void* ptr) {
    pool.push_back(ptr);
}
};
```

## Cache Optimization

Optimizing data access patterns to take advantage of CPU and GPU caches improves performance. Techniques such as data locality and prefetching help reduce cache misses and improve memory access speed.

## Data Locality

Data locality involves organizing data so that frequently accessed elements are stored close together in memory. This improves cache efficiency and reduces memory access latency.

## Prefetching

Prefetching involves loading data into cache before it is needed, reducing the wait time for memory accesses. This technique is particularly effective for predictable access patterns in ray tracing.

## Memory Bandwidth

High memory bandwidth is essential for handling the large datasets required by ray tracing. Modern GPUs and memory technologies, such as HBM (High Bandwidth Memory) and GDDR6, provide the necessary bandwidth for efficient rendering.

## Asynchronous Memory Transfers

Asynchronous memory transfers allow data to be transferred between the CPU and GPU without stalling the rendering pipeline. Techniques such as double buffering and overlapping computation with data transfers help maximize resource utilization.

## Example of Double Buffering

void renderFrame() {

// Swap buffers

std::swap(currentBuffer, nextBuffer);

// Start asynchronous data transfer

startDataTransfer(nextBuffer);

// Perform rendering using current buffer

renderScene(currentBuffer);

// Wait for data transfer to complete

waitForDataTransfer();

}

## Virtual Memory

Virtual memory provides an abstraction layer that allows applications to use more memory than physically available.

Efficient management of virtual memory and page faults is crucial for maintaining performance in large scenes.

## Conclusion

Efficient memory management is crucial for achieving high performance in ray tracing. By optimizing data structures, texture mapping, scene graphs, and memory allocation, and employing techniques such as cache optimization, prefetching, and asynchronous memory transfers, it is possible to manage memory usage effectively and ensure smooth rendering.

## 4.4. Optimizing Ray Tracing Algorithms

Optimizing ray tracing algorithms involves improving the efficiency of ray generation, intersection tests, shading, and other components of the pipeline. These optimizations aim to reduce computational overhead and enhance performance.

### Ray Generation Optimization

Efficient ray generation reduces the computational cost of creating rays from the camera. Techniques such as ray coherence and SIMD (Single Instruction, Multiple Data) can be employed.

### Example of SIMD Ray Generation

```
void generateRays(const Camera& camera, Ray* rays, int width, int height) {

#pragma omp parallel for

for (int y = 0; y < height; ++y) {

for (int x = 0; x < width; ++x) {
```

```
float u = (x + 0.5) / width;

float v = (y + 0.5) / height;

Vector3 direction = camera.lowerLeftCorner + u * camera.horizontal + v * camera.vertical - camera.origin;

rays[y * width + x] = Ray(camera.origin, direction);
}
}
}
```

## Intersection Test Optimization

Optimizing intersection tests involves reducing the number of calculations and improving the efficiency of algorithms. Techniques like early termination, bounding volume tests, and SIMD are employed.

## Early Termination

Early termination stops intersection tests as soon as a hit is found, reducing unnecessary calculations.

## Bounding Volume Tests

Bounding volume tests quickly eliminate large portions of the scene from intersection tests, reducing the computational load.

## Shading Optimization

Shading calculations can be optimized by precomputing values, using lookup tables, and employing efficient mathematical techniques.

## Precomputed Lighting

Precomputed lighting involves calculating lighting information in advance and storing it in lookup tables. This reduces the computational cost during rendering.

## Lookup Tables

Lookup tables store precomputed values for functions that are expensive to compute, such as trigonometric functions and Fresnel equations.

## Importance Sampling

Importance sampling improves the efficiency of Monte Carlo integration by focusing samples on the most significant parts of the integrand, reducing variance and improving convergence.

## Example of Importance Sampling in Path Tracing

Color sampleLight(const Light& light, const Intersection& hit, const Scene& scene) {

Vector3 lightDir = normalize(light.position - hit.position);

Ray shadowRay(hit.position, lightDir);

**if** (!isInShadow(shadowRay, scene)) {

float pdf = max(dot(hit.normal, lightDir), 0.0) / (4 * PI);

**return** light.intensity * hit.material.color / pdf;

}

**return** Color(0, 0, 0);

}

## Adaptive Sampling

Adaptive sampling techniques dynamically adjust the number of samples per pixel based on local image characteristics. This approach focuses computational resources on areas with high detail or noise, improving efficiency.

## Example of Adaptive Sampling

```
void renderScene(Scene& scene, Image& image) {
#pragma omp parallel for
for (int y = 0; y < image.height(); ++y) {
for (int x = 0; x < image.width(); ++x) {
int samples = determineSampleCount(x, y, image);
Color color(0, 0, 0);
for (int i = 0; i < samples; ++i) {
Ray ray = generateRay(x, y, camera);
color += traceRay(ray, scene);
}
image.setPixel(x, y, color / samples);
}
}
}
```

## Denoising

Denoising algorithms reduce noise in the rendered image, particularly in path tracing and other Monte Carlo methods. Machine learning-based denoising techniques can achieve high-quality results with minimal performance impact.

## Temporal Denoising

Temporal denoising leverages information from previous frames to reduce noise. This technique is particularly effective in real-time applications, where consecutive frames share similarities.

## Spatial Denoising

Spatial denoising analyzes the spatial characteristics of an image to reduce noise. Techniques like bilateral filtering and wavelet-based denoising are commonly used.

## Conclusion

Optimizing ray tracing algorithms is essential for achieving high performance and visual quality. By improving the efficiency of ray generation, intersection tests, shading, and other components of the pipeline, and employing techniques like importance sampling, adaptive sampling, and denoising, it is possible to reduce computational overhead and enhance performance.

# 4.5. Case Studies in Efficient Ray Tracing

Case studies provide valuable insights into the practical implementation and optimization of ray tracing algorithms. By examining successful projects and their optimization strategies, we can learn effective techniques for achieving real-time performance and high visual quality.

# ILLUMINATING REALITIES: THE THEORY OF REAL-TIME RAY TRACING

## Case Study 1: NVIDIA RTX Technology

NVIDIA's RTX technology revolutionized real-time ray tracing by introducing hardware-accelerated ray tracing cores. These dedicated cores perform ray-triangle intersection tests and BVH traversal, significantly improving performance.

*Key Optimizations*

- **Dedicated Ray Tracing Cores**: Specialized hardware units accelerate ray tracing tasks, offloading them from the main GPU cores.

- **Hybrid Rendering**: Combines rasterization and ray tracing to balance performance and visual quality.

- **DLSS (Deep Learning Super Sampling)**: Uses machine learning to upscale lower resolution images, improving performance while maintaining visual fidelity.

## Case Study 2: Quake II RTX

Quake II RTX is a remaster of the classic game Quake II, incorporating real-time ray tracing to enhance visual quality. The project demonstrates the potential of ray tracing in real-time applications and the importance of optimization techniques.

*Key Optimizations*

- **Efficient BVH Construction**: Optimized BVH structures reduce the computational cost of intersection tests.

- **Dynamic Light Source Management**: Efficient handling of dynamic light sources ensures real-time performance.

- **Adaptive Sampling**: Focuses computational resources on areas with high detail, improving efficiency.

## Case Study 3: Pixar's RenderMan

Pixar's RenderMan has been a pioneer in ray tracing for feature films. The renderer has evolved over the years to incorporate advanced ray tracing techniques and optimizations.

*Key Optimizations*

- **Efficient Shading Algorithms**: Uses precomputed lighting and lookup tables to reduce shading calculations.

- **Importance Sampling**: Improves the efficiency of Monte Carlo integration, reducing noise and improving convergence.

- **Denoising**: Advanced denoising techniques enhance the visual quality of rendered images.

## Case Study 4: Real-Time Ray Tracing in Unreal Engine

Unreal Engine is a popular game engine that has integrated real-time ray tracing to enhance the visual quality of games and interactive experiences.

*Key Optimizations*

- **Hybrid Rendering**: Combines rasterization and ray tracing to achieve real-time performance.

- **Efficient Memory Management**: Uses texture compression and instancing to optimize memory usage.

- **Dynamic BVH Updates**: Efficiently updates BVH structures for dynamic scenes, ensuring real-time performance.

## Case Study 5: Blender's Cycles Renderer

Blender's Cycles renderer is an open-source path tracing engine used for creating high-quality visual effects and animations.

*Key Optimizations*

- **GPU Acceleration**: Leverages the parallel processing power of GPUs to accelerate rendering.

- **Adaptive Sampling**: Dynamically adjusts the number of samples per pixel based on image characteristics, improving efficiency.

- **Denoising**: Uses advanced denoising algorithms to reduce noise and enhance visual quality.

## Lessons Learned

The case studies highlight several key optimization strategies that are essential for efficient ray tracing:

- **Hardware Acceleration**: Leveraging specialized hardware, such as ray tracing cores and GPUs, significantly improves performance.

- **Hybrid Rendering**: Combining rasterization and ray tracing balances performance and visual quality.

- **Efficient Data Structures**: Using optimized data structures, such as BVH and K-D Trees, reduces the computational cost of intersection tests.

- **Adaptive Sampling and Denoising**: These techniques enhance the efficiency of Monte Carlo integration and improve visual quality.

## Conclusion

Case studies provide valuable insights into the practical implementation and optimization of ray tracing algorithms. By examining successful projects and their optimization strategies, we can learn effective techniques for achieving real-time performance and high visual quality. These lessons can be applied to future projects to push the boundaries of what is possible with ray tracing technology.

# Chapter 5: Light and Material Interaction

# 5.1. Simulating Light Behavior

Simulating light behavior is fundamental to creating realistic images in ray tracing. Understanding how light interacts with surfaces, materials, and the environment allows for accurate rendering of scenes.

## Light Sources

Light sources in ray tracing can be modeled in various ways, including point lights, directional lights, and area lights. Each type of light source has unique characteristics and influences the appearance of the scene differently.

- **Point Lights**: Emit light uniformly in all directions from a single point. Useful for simulating light bulbs or candles.

- **Directional Lights**: Emit parallel rays of light, simulating distant sources like the sun.

- **Area Lights**: Emit light from a defined area, producing soft shadows and more realistic lighting.

## Light Intensity and Attenuation

Light intensity determines the brightness of a light source. Attenuation models how light intensity decreases with distance. The common attenuation model includes constant, linear, and quadratic terms.

```
float calculateAttenuation(float distance, float constant, float linear, float quadratic) {

return 1.0 / (constant + linear * distance + quadratic * distance * distance);

}
```

## Reflection

Reflection occurs when light bounces off a surface. The law of reflection states that the angle of incidence equals the angle of reflection. Reflection can be specular (mirror-like) or diffuse (scattered).

## Specular Reflection

Specular reflection produces sharp, mirror-like reflections. The reflection direction can be calculated using the incident direction and the surface normal.

Vector3 calculateReflection(Vector3 incident, Vector3 normal) {

**return** incident - 2 * dot(incident, normal) * normal;

}

## Diffuse Reflection

Diffuse reflection scatters light uniformly in all directions. The Lambertian model is commonly used to simulate diffuse reflection, where the intensity depends on the angle between the light direction and the surface normal.

float calculateDiffuseIntensity(Vector3 lightDir, Vector3 normal) {

**return** max(dot(lightDir, normal), 0.0);

}

## Refraction

Refraction occurs when light passes through a transparent material and bends due to a change in its speed. Snell's law describes the

# ILLUMINATING REALITIES: THE THEORY OF REAL-TIME RAY TRACING

relationship between the angles of incidence and refraction and the refractive indices of the materials.

Vector3 calculateRefraction(Vector3 incident, Vector3 normal, float ior) {

float cosi = clamp(dot(incident, normal), -1.0, 1.0);

float etai = 1, etat = ior;

Vector3 n = normal;

**if** (cosi < 0) { cosi = -cosi; }

**else** { swap(etai, etat); n = -normal; }

float eta = etai / etat;

float k = 1 - eta * eta * (1 - cosi * cosi);

**return** k < 0 ? Vector3(0, 0, 0) : eta * incident + (eta * cosi - sqrt(k)) * n;

}

## Fresnel Effect

The Fresnel effect describes how light reflectance varies with the angle of incidence. This effect is significant for realistic rendering of reflective and refractive materials.

## Absorption and Scattering

Light can be absorbed or scattered as it passes through a medium. Absorption reduces light intensity, while scattering changes its direction. These effects are important for simulating materials like fog, smoke, and translucent objects.

## Volume Rendering

Volume rendering techniques handle the interactions of light with participating media, such as smoke and fog. This involves solving the radiative transfer equation to account for absorption, emission, and scattering within the volume.

## Photon Mapping

Photon mapping is a two-pass algorithm used to simulate global illumination. The first pass traces photons from the light source and stores their interactions in a photon map. The second pass uses this map to estimate illumination at points in the scene.

## Conclusion

Simulating light behavior is essential for creating realistic images in ray tracing. By understanding and accurately modeling the interactions between light and materials, it is possible to achieve photorealistic rendering.

# 5.2. Material Properties and Ray Interaction

Material properties define how rays of light interact with surfaces, influencing the appearance of objects in a rendered scene. Accurately modeling these interactions is crucial for realistic rendering.

## Basic Material Properties

- **Albedo**: The base color of the material, which reflects diffuse light.

- **Specular**: The reflectivity of the material, determining how much light is reflected in a mirror-like fashion.

# ILLUMINATING REALITIES: THE THEORY OF REAL-TIME RAY TRACING

- **Roughness**: Controls the sharpness of reflections; lower roughness results in sharper reflections.

- **Metallic**: Determines if the material behaves like a metal, affecting its reflectance and appearance.

## Diffuse Materials

Diffuse materials scatter light uniformly in all directions. The Lambertian reflectance model is commonly used to simulate diffuse reflection, where the intensity depends on the cosine of the angle between the light direction and the surface normal.

Color calculateDiffuseColor(const Material& material, const Vector3& lightDir, const Vector3& normal) {

float intensity = max(dot(lightDir, normal), 0.0);

**return** material.albedo * intensity;

}

## Specular Materials

Specular materials reflect light in a specific direction, creating sharp highlights. The Phong reflection model is often used to simulate specular reflection, with the intensity depending on the view direction and the reflection direction.

Color calculateSpecularColor(const Material& material, const Vector3& lightDir, const Vector3& viewDir, const Vector3& normal) {

Vector3 reflectDir = calculateReflection(lightDir, normal);

float intensity = pow(max(dot(viewDir, reflectDir), 0.0), material.shininess);

**return** material.specular * intensity;

}

## Glossy Materials

Glossy materials have both diffuse and specular components. The reflectance varies based on the roughness of the surface. Microfacet models, such as the Cook-Torrance model, are used to simulate glossy reflections.

## Translucent Materials

Translucent materials allow light to pass through them, with some scattering occurring inside the material. Subsurface scattering models simulate this effect, important for rendering materials like skin, marble, and wax.

## Transparent Materials

Transparent materials refract light as it passes through them. The refraction direction is calculated using Snell's law, and the Fresnel effect determines the proportion of light reflected versus refracted.

## Composite Materials

Composite materials combine multiple properties, such as a base diffuse layer with a specular coat. Layered models simulate these interactions, providing realistic rendering of complex materials.

## BRDF Models

Bidirectional Reflectance Distribution Function (BRDF) models describe how light is reflected at an opaque surface. Common BRDF models include Lambertian, Phong, Blinn-Phong, and Cook-Torrance.

## Example of a Cook-Torrance BRDF

float calculateCookTorranceBRDF(const Material& material, const Vector3& lightDir, const Vector3& viewDir, const Vector3& normal) {

Vector3 halfVec = normalize(lightDir + viewDir);

float D = calculateNormalDistribution(material.roughness, normal, halfVec);

float G = calculateGeometryFunction(material.roughness, normal, lightDir, viewDir);

float F = calculateFresnel(viewDir, halfVec, material.specular);

**return** (D * G * F) / (4 * max(dot(normal, lightDir), 0.0) * max(dot(normal, viewDir), 0.0));

}

## Texture Mapping

Textures add detail to materials by mapping 2D images onto 3D surfaces. UV coordinates associate points on the surface with points on the texture image.

## Bump Mapping

Bump mapping simulates surface detail without altering the actual geometry. It uses a normal map to perturb the surface normals, creating the illusion of depth and detail.

## Displacement Mapping

Displacement mapping modifies the actual geometry of the surface based on a height map, creating realistic surface details and silhouettes.

## Example of Bump Mapping

Vector3 calculateBumpedNormal(const Vector3& normal, const Vector3& tangent, const Vector3& bitangent, const Vector3& bumpMapValue) {

**return** normalize(normal + bumpMapValue.x * tangent + bumpMapValue.y * bitangent);

}

## Conclusion

Material properties and their interaction with rays of light are essential for realistic rendering in ray tracing. By accurately modeling these properties, it is possible to achieve a wide range of visual effects and realistic appearances.

# 5.3. Reflection, Refraction, and Transparency

Reflection, refraction, and transparency are critical phenomena in ray tracing, allowing for the realistic rendering of materials like glass, water, and metals. These interactions are governed by physical laws and are essential for creating lifelike images.

## Reflection

Reflection occurs when light bounces off a surface. The law of reflection states that the angle of incidence equals the angle of reflection. This principle is used to calculate the direction of reflected rays in ray tracing.

Vector3 calculateReflection(const Vector3& incident, const Vector3& normal) {

**return** incident - 2 * dot(incident, normal) * normal;

}

## Specular Reflection

Specular reflection produces mirror-like reflections. The intensity and sharpness of the reflection depend on the material properties, such as specular coefficient and roughness.

## Glossy Reflection

Glossy reflection is a combination of specular and diffuse reflection. It creates soft reflections with a blurred appearance, simulating materials like brushed metal or frosted glass.

## Refraction

Refraction occurs when light passes through a transparent material and bends due to a change in its speed. Snell's law describes the relationship between the angles of incidence and refraction and the refractive indices of the materials.

```
Vector3 calculateRefraction(const Vector3& incident, const Vector3& normal, float ior) {

    float cosi = clamp(dot(incident, normal), -1.0, 1.0);

    float etai = 1, etat = ior;

    Vector3 n = normal;

    if (cosi < 0) { cosi = -cosi; }

    else { swap(etai, etat); n = -normal; }

    float eta = etai / etat;

    float k = 1 - eta * eta * (1 - cosi * cosi);

    return k < 0 ? Vector3(0, 0, 0) : eta * incident + (eta * cosi - sqrt(k)) * n;

}
```

## Total Internal Reflection

Total internal reflection occurs when light attempts to move from a medium with a higher refractive index to one with a lower refractive index at a steep angle. The light is completely reflected within the material, creating effects seen in diamonds and fiber optics.

## Fresnel Effect

The Fresnel effect describes how the reflectance of a surface varies with the angle of incidence. This effect is significant for realistic rendering of reflective and refractive materials.

## Example of Fresnel Effect Calculation

float calculateFresnel(const Vector3& viewDir, const Vector3& halfVec, float ior) {

float cosTheta = dot(viewDir, halfVec);

float F0 = pow((ior - 1) / (ior + 1), 2);

return F0 + (1 - F0) * pow(1 - cosTheta, 5);

}

## Transparency

Transparency allows light to pass through a material. Transparent materials are modeled using both refraction and absorption properties, influencing how light is transmitted and attenuated.

## Beer-Lambert Law

The Beer-Lambert law describes the attenuation of light as it passes through an absorbing medium. It is used to simulate the reduction in light intensity for transparent materials.

float calculateTransmission(float distance, float absorptionCoefficient) {

return exp(-absorptionCoefficient * distance);

}

## Caustics

Caustics are patterns of light formed when light rays are focused by reflective or refractive surfaces. They are commonly seen as bright patches on surfaces adjacent to water or glass.

## Simulating Caustics

Simulating caustics involves tracing additional rays from the light source to capture the focused light patterns. Photon mapping and bidirectional path tracing are techniques used to simulate caustics.

## Conclusion

Reflection, refraction, and transparency are fundamental to realistic rendering in ray tracing. By accurately modeling these interactions, it is possible to create lifelike images of materials like glass, water, and metals.

# 5.4. Texturing and Bump Mapping

Texturing and bump mapping are techniques used to add detail and realism to 3D surfaces without increasing the geometric complexity. These methods simulate surface details such as color variations, patterns, and small-scale deformations.

## Texture Mapping

Texture mapping involves applying a 2D image (texture) to a 3D surface. UV coordinates are used to map points on the texture to points on the surface.

## UV Mapping

UV mapping defines how a 2D texture is wrapped around a 3D object. Each vertex of the object is assigned UV coordinates that correspond to points on the texture image.

## Example of UV Mapping

```
struct Vertex {
```

Vector3 position;

Vector2 uv;

};

void applyTexture(const Texture& texture, const Vertex& vertex) {

Color color = texture.getPixel(vertex.uv);

// Apply color to the vertex or fragment

}

## Procedural Textures

Procedural textures are generated algorithmically rather than being derived from images. These textures can create patterns such as wood grain, marble, or noise, which are often difficult to capture in images.

## Example of a Simple Procedural Texture

Color generateCheckerboardTexture(const Vector2& uv, int numSquares) {

int checker = (int(floor(uv.x * numSquares)) + int(floor(uv.y * numSquares))) % 2;

**return** checker == 0 ? Color(1, 1, 1) : Color(0, 0, 0);

}

## Normal Mapping

Normal mapping is a technique used to simulate small-scale surface details by perturbing the surface normals. A normal map stores these perturbations as RGB values, which are interpreted as vectors.

## Example of Normal Mapping

Vector3 applyNormalMap(const Vector3& normal, const Vector3& tangent, const Vector3& bitangent, const Vector3& normalMapValue) {

Matrix3 TBN(tangent, bitangent, normal);

**return** normalize(TBN * (2.0 * normalMapValue - 1.0));

}

## Bump Mapping

Bump mapping is similar to normal mapping but uses a height map to perturb the surface normals. The height map defines the displacement at each point, creating the illusion of depth.

## Example of Bump Mapping

Vector3 calculateBumpedNormal(const Vector3& normal, const Vector3& tangent, const Vector3& bitangent, float height) {

Vector3 perturbedNormal = normal + height * (tangent + bitangent);

**return** normalize(perturbedNormal);

}

## Displacement Mapping

Displacement mapping physically displaces the vertices of the surface based on a height map, creating actual geometric variations.

This method is more computationally intensive but produces highly realistic details.

## Parallax Mapping

Parallax mapping is an approximation of displacement mapping that adjusts texture coordinates based on the view angle. It creates the illusion of depth without modifying the geometry.

### Example of Parallax Mapping

Vector2 applyParallaxMapping(const Vector2& uv, const Vector3& viewDir, const Texture& heightMap) {

float height = heightMap.getPixel(uv).r;

**return** uv + viewDir.xy * (height * parallaxScale);

}

### Conclusion

Texturing and bump mapping techniques add detail and realism to 3D surfaces without increasing geometric complexity. By applying textures, normal maps, bump maps, and displacement maps, it is possible to create rich and detailed visual effects.

## 5.5. Advanced Lighting Models

Advanced lighting models enhance the realism of rendered scenes by simulating complex light interactions. These models account for effects such as global illumination, subsurface scattering, and volumetric lighting.

## Global Illumination

Global illumination (GI) models the indirect lighting in a scene, including light that bounces off surfaces. It captures the complex interplay of light and color, resulting in more realistic images.

## Radiosity

Radiosity is a global illumination method that divides the scene into patches and calculates the light exchange between them. It is particularly effective for scenes with diffuse interreflections.

## Photon Mapping

Photon mapping is a two-pass algorithm used to simulate global illumination. The first pass traces photons from the light source and stores their interactions in a photon map. The second pass uses this map to estimate illumination at points in the scene.

## Path Tracing

Path tracing is a global illumination algorithm that traces random paths from the camera through the scene. It simulates complex lighting interactions by sampling multiple light paths and averaging the results.

## Bidirectional Path Tracing

Bidirectional path tracing traces paths from both the camera and the light sources, connecting them to simulate light transport more efficiently. It improves convergence and reduces noise in scenes with difficult lighting conditions.

## Subsurface Scattering

Subsurface scattering (SSS) simulates the diffusion of light within translucent materials, such as skin, marble, and wax. It accounts for light entering the material, scattering beneath the surface, and exiting at a different point.

## Example of Subsurface Scattering Calculation

Color calculateSubsurfaceScattering(const Vector3& point, const Vector3& normal, const Light& light, const Material& material) {

float scatterRadius = material.scatterRadius;

Vector3 lightDir = normalize(light.position - point);

float distance = length(light.position - point);

float scatter = exp(-distance / scatterRadius);

**return** material.subsurfaceColor * light.intensity * scatter;

}

## Volumetric Lighting

Volumetric lighting models the interaction of light with participating media, such as fog, smoke, and clouds. It captures the scattering and absorption of light within the volume, creating realistic atmospheric effects.

## Example of Volumetric Lighting

Color calculateVolumetricLighting(const Vector3& point, const Vector3& lightDir, const Light& light, const Volume& volume) {

float density = volume.getDensity(point);

float scatter = exp(-density * length(lightDir));

**return** light.intensity * scatter * volume.color;

}

## Ambient Occlusion

Ambient occlusion (AO) simulates the occlusion of ambient light in crevices and corners, enhancing the perception of depth and realism. It calculates how exposed each point in a scene is to ambient lighting.

## Screen-Space Ambient Occlusion (SSAO)

SSAO is a real-time approximation of ambient occlusion that operates in screen space. It improves performance by avoiding complex geometry calculations.

## Example of SSAO Calculation

float calculateSSAO(const Vector3& position, const Vector3& normal, const Scene& scene) {

float occlusion = 0.0;

**for** (int i = 0; i < numSamples; ++i) {

Vector3 sample = generateSampleSphere();

**if** (!scene.intersect(position + sample * aoRadius)) {

occlusion += max(dot(normal, sample), 0.0);

}

}

**return** 1.0 - occlusion / numSamples;

}

## Caustics

Caustics are patterns of light formed when light rays are focused by reflective or refractive surfaces. They are commonly seen as bright patches on surfaces adjacent to water or glass.

## Simulating Caustics

Simulating caustics involves tracing additional rays from the light source to capture the focused light patterns. Photon mapping and bidirectional path tracing are techniques used to simulate caustics.

## Conclusion

Advanced lighting models enhance the realism of rendered scenes by simulating complex light interactions. By incorporating global illumination, subsurface scattering, volumetric lighting, ambient occlusion, and caustics, it is possible to achieve highly realistic and visually appealing images.

# Chapter 6: Shadows and Illumination

## 6.1. The Science of Shadows in Ray Tracing

Shadows are an essential component of realistic rendering in ray tracing, providing depth and context to a scene. Understanding the science behind shadows involves exploring their formation, types, and the techniques used to simulate them.

## Shadow Formation

Shadows are formed when an object blocks light from reaching a surface. The region behind the object that does not receive direct light is in shadow. The characteristics of shadows depend on the light source, the object's shape, and the distance between them.

## Types of Shadows

- **Hard Shadows**: Produced by point light sources, resulting in sharp and well-defined edges.

- **Soft Shadows**: Created by area light sources, leading to gradual transitions between light and shadow.

## Penumbra and Umbra

Shadows consist of two main regions:

- **Umbra**: The fully shaded area where the light source is completely blocked.

- **Penumbra**: The partially shaded area where the light source is partially blocked.

## Ray Traced Shadows

In ray tracing, shadows are typically calculated by tracing shadow rays from the intersection point to the light source. If the shadow ray intersects any object before reaching the light source, the point is in shadow.

## Example of Shadow Ray Calculation

```cpp
bool isInShadow(const Vector3& point, const Light& light, const Scene& scene) {

Vector3 direction = normalize(light.position - point);

Ray shadowRay(point, direction);

for (const auto& object : scene.objects) {

if (object->intersect(shadowRay)) {

return true;

}

}

return false;

}
```

## Soft Shadows

Soft shadows are simulated by sampling multiple shadow rays across the area light source. The percentage of rays blocked determines the shadow's softness and intensity.

## Example of Soft Shadow Calculation

```cpp
float calculateSoftShadow(const Vector3& point, const AreaLight& light, const Scene& scene) {

int numSamples = 16;

float shadow = 0.0;
```

```cpp
for (int i = 0; i < numSamples; ++i) {
    Vector3 samplePosition = light.samplePosition();
    Vector3 direction = normalize(samplePosition - point);
    Ray shadowRay(point, direction);
    if (isInShadow(shadowRay, scene)) {
        shadow += 1.0 / numSamples;
    }
}
return shadow;
}
```

## Shadow Maps

Shadow maps are a technique used to create shadows in real-time rendering. They involve rendering the scene from the light's perspective and storing the depth information in a texture. During the final render, this texture is used to determine whether points are in shadow.

## Example of Shadow Map Usage

```cpp
void renderShadowMap(const Light& light, const Scene& scene, ShadowMap& shadowMap) {
    for (const auto& object : scene.objects) {
        object->renderToShadowMap(light, shadowMap);
    }
}
```

```
}

bool isInShadowWithShadowMap(const Vector3& point, const
Light& light, const ShadowMap& shadowMap) {

    Vector3 lightSpacePosition =
light.transformToLightSpace(point);

    float shadowDepth =
shadowMap.getDepth(lightSpacePosition.xy);

    return lightSpacePosition.z > shadowDepth;

}
```

## Ray Traced vs. Shadow Maps

Ray traced shadows provide higher accuracy and realism but are computationally expensive. Shadow maps are more efficient and suitable for real-time applications but can suffer from artifacts like aliasing and shadow acne.

## Volumetric Shadows

Volumetric shadows, or god rays, occur when light is scattered by particles in the atmosphere. These shadows create beams of light that add depth and atmosphere to a scene.

## Simulating Volumetric Shadows

Simulating volumetric shadows involves tracing rays through a volume and accounting for scattering and absorption. Techniques like ray marching are used to approximate these effects.

### Example of Volumetric Shadow Calculation

```
Color calculateVolumetricShadow(const Vector3& point, const Light& light, const Volume& volume, const Scene& scene) {
    Vector3 direction = normalize(light.position - point);
    float density = volume.getDensity(point);
    float scatter = exp(-density * length(direction));
    return light.intensity * scatter * volume.color;
}
```

### Conclusion

Understanding the science of shadows is crucial for realistic rendering in ray tracing. By accurately simulating hard and soft shadows, shadow maps, and volumetric shadows, it is possible to create lifelike and immersive scenes.

## 6.2. Soft Shadows and Hard Shadows

Shadows play a vital role in enhancing the realism of a scene by providing depth and context. The nature of the shadows—whether soft or hard—depends on the light source and the interaction with objects.

### Hard Shadows

Hard shadows are produced by point light sources, resulting in sharp, well-defined edges. These shadows occur when there is a single, small light source, and there is no gradual transition between light and dark areas.

## Characteristics of Hard Shadows

- **Sharp Edges**: Hard shadows have clear and distinct boundaries.

- **Defined Umbra**: The umbra, or the fully shaded area, is well-defined and lacks any transition.

- **Simple Calculation**: Easier to compute in ray tracing as it involves tracing a single shadow ray per light source.

## Example of Hard Shadow Calculation

bool calculateHardShadow(const Vector3& point, const Light& light, const Scene& scene) {

Vector3 direction = normalize(light.position - point);

Ray shadowRay(point, direction);

**for** (const **auto**& object : scene.objects) {

**if** (object->intersect(shadowRay)) {

**return true**;

}

}

**return false**;

}

## Soft Shadows

Soft shadows are created by area light sources, resulting in shadows with gradual transitions between light and dark areas. These shadows occur when the light source has a finite size, causing some parts of the shadow to be partially illuminated.

## Characteristics of Soft Shadows

- **Gradual Edges**: Soft shadows have smooth transitions between the light and dark regions.

- **Penumbra**: The presence of a penumbra, or partially shaded area, creates a gradient effect.

- **Complex Calculation**: Requires multiple shadow rays to sample different points on the area light source.

## Example of Soft Shadow Calculation

```
float calculateSoftShadow(const Vector3& point, const AreaLight& light, const Scene& scene) {

int numSamples = 16;

float shadow = 0.0;

for (int i = 0; i < numSamples; ++i) {

Vector3 samplePosition = light.samplePosition();

Vector3 direction = normalize(samplePosition - point);

Ray shadowRay(point, direction);

if (isInShadow(shadowRay, scene)) {

shadow += 1.0 / numSamples;

}
```

}

**return** shadow;

}

## Area Lights and Soft Shadows

Area lights emit light from a finite area rather than a single point. This results in softer, more natural shadows with gradual transitions. The size and shape of the area light influence the appearance of the shadows.

## Sampling Techniques

To accurately simulate soft shadows, multiple shadow rays are sampled across the area light source. The average of these samples determines the shadow's softness and intensity.

## Stratified Sampling

Stratified sampling divides the area light source into a grid and samples each cell, reducing variance and producing smoother shadows.

## Example of Stratified Sampling

float calculateStratifiedSoftShadow(const Vector3& point, const AreaLight& light, const Scene& scene) {

int gridSize = 4;

float shadow = 0.0;

**for** (int i = 0; i < gridSize; ++i) {

**for** (int j = 0; j < gridSize; ++j) {

```
Vector3 samplePosition = light.samplePosition(i, j, gridSize);
Vector3 direction = normalize(samplePosition - point);
Ray shadowRay(point, direction);
if (isInShadow(shadowRay, scene)) {
shadow += 1.0 / (gridSize * gridSize);
}
}
}
return shadow;
}
```

## Monte Carlo Sampling

Monte Carlo sampling randomly selects points on the area light source, providing a more accurate representation of soft shadows at the cost of increased computational effort.

## Comparison of Hard and Soft Shadows

- **Hard Shadows**: Easier to compute, but less realistic for large or diffuse light sources.

- **Soft Shadows**: More realistic for natural lighting, but computationally expensive due to multiple samples required.

## Conclusion

Both hard and soft shadows are essential for realistic rendering in ray tracing. Hard shadows are simpler to compute and provide sharp boundaries, while soft shadows require more complex calculations but result in more natural and visually appealing scenes.

## 6.3. Global Illumination Techniques

Global illumination (GI) techniques simulate the complex interactions of light within a scene, capturing both direct and indirect lighting. These techniques are essential for achieving realistic and visually rich renderings.

### Direct vs. Indirect Lighting

- **Direct Lighting**: Light that travels directly from a light source to a surface.

- **Indirect Lighting**: Light that reflects off one or more surfaces before reaching the final surface.

### Radiosity

Radiosity is a GI method that calculates the diffuse transfer of light between surfaces. It is particularly effective for scenes with diffuse interreflections.

### Radiosity Method

- Divide the scene into patches.

- Calculate the form factors, representing the fraction of light transferred between patches.

- Solve the radiosity equation iteratively to determine the steady-state distribution of light.

## Photon Mapping

Photon mapping is a two-pass algorithm used to simulate global illumination. It involves storing photons emitted from light sources in a photon map and using this map to estimate illumination during rendering.

## Photon Emission

- Emit photons from the light source.

- Trace the photons through the scene, storing their interactions in the photon map.

## Photon Gathering

- Gather photons from the photon map to estimate the illumination at a given point.

- Use techniques like nearest-neighbor search to find relevant photons.

## Example of Photon Mapping

```
void emitPhotons(const Light& light, PhotonMap& photonMap)
{
for (int i = 0; i < numPhotons; ++i) {
Photon photon = light.emitPhoton();
tracePhoton(photon, photonMap);
```

}

}

Color gatherPhotons(const PhotonMap& photonMap, const Vector3& point, const Vector3& normal) {

std::vector<Photon> nearbyPhotons = photonMap.getPhotons(point, gatherRadius);

Color illumination(0, 0, 0);

**for** (const Photon& photon : nearbyPhotons) {

illumination += photon.color * max(dot(photon.direction, normal), 0.0);

}

**return** illumination / nearbyPhotons.size();

}

## Path Tracing

Path tracing is a GI algorithm that traces random paths from the camera through the scene, sampling multiple light paths to simulate complex lighting interactions.

## Monte Carlo Integration

Path tracing uses Monte Carlo integration to estimate the illumination by sampling random light paths and averaging the results.

## Example of Path Tracing

```
Color tracePath(const Ray& ray, const Scene& scene, int depth) {
    if (depth <= 0) return Color(0, 0, 0);
    Intersection hit;
    if (scene.intersect(ray, hit)) {
        Vector3 newDirection = sampleDirection(hit.normal);
        Ray newRay(hit.position, newDirection);
        Color incoming = tracePath(newRay, scene, depth - 1);
        return hit.material.color * incoming * max(dot(newDirection, hit.normal), 0.0);
    }
    return scene.backgroundColor;
}
```

## Bidirectional Path Tracing

Bidirectional path tracing traces paths from both the camera and the light sources, connecting them to simulate light transport more efficiently. It improves convergence and reduces noise in scenes with difficult lighting conditions.

## Example of Bidirectional Path Tracing

```
Color traceBidirectionalPath(const Ray& cameraRay, const Scene& scene, int depth) {
```

Path cameraPath = generateCameraPath(cameraRay, scene, depth);

Path lightPath = generateLightPath(scene, depth);

Color illumination = connectPaths(cameraPath, lightPath, scene);

**return** illumination;

}

## Metropolis Light Transport

Metropolis Light Transport (MLT) is a Monte Carlo method that focuses on exploring important light paths. It uses a random walk to sample paths and a mutation strategy to explore the path space efficiently.

## Voxel-Based GI

Voxel-based GI divides the scene into a 3D grid of voxels, storing lighting information in each voxel. This technique allows for efficient indirect lighting calculations, especially in real-time applications.

## Light Propagation Volumes

Light Propagation Volumes (LPV) use a grid of volumes to propagate light through the scene. It approximates global illumination by iteratively spreading light across the grid.

## Example of Light Propagation Volumes

void propagateLight(LightPropagationVolume& lpv, const Scene& scene) {

```
for (int iteration = 0; iteration < numIterations; ++iteration) {
    for (int x = 0; x < lpv.size(); ++x) {
        for (int y = 0; y < lpv.size(); ++y) {
            for (int z = 0; z < lpv.size(); ++z) {
                lpv.propagate(x, y, z);
            }
        }
    }
}
```

## Conclusion

Global illumination techniques are essential for simulating the complex interactions of light within a scene. By using methods such as radiosity, photon mapping, path tracing, and light propagation volumes, it is possible to achieve realistic and visually rich renderings.

## 6.4. Ambient Occlusion in Real-Time Ray Tracing

Ambient occlusion (AO) is a shading technique used to simulate the soft shadows that occur in crevices, corners, and other areas where light is occluded. It enhances the perception of depth and realism in a scene.

## Basics of Ambient Occlusion

Ambient occlusion calculates how exposed each point in a scene is to ambient lighting. Points that are more occluded receive less ambient light, resulting in darker shading.

## Types of Ambient Occlusion

- **Static AO**: Precomputed for static scenes and stored in textures or vertex data.

- **Dynamic AO**: Calculated in real-time for dynamic scenes and moving objects.

## Screen-Space Ambient Occlusion (SSAO)

SSAO is a real-time approximation of ambient occlusion that operates in screen space. It uses the depth buffer to estimate occlusion, making it suitable for real-time applications.

## Example of SSAO Calculation

float calculateSSAO(const Vector3& position, const Vector3& normal, const Scene& scene) {

float occlusion = 0.0;

int numSamples = 16;

**for** (int i = 0; i < numSamples; ++i) {

Vector3 sample = generateSampleSphere();

Vector3 samplePos = position + sample * sampleRadius;

**if** (scene.isOccluded(samplePos)) {

```
occlusion += max(dot(normal, sample), 0.0);
}
}
return 1.0 - occlusion / numSamples;
}
```

## Horizon-Based Ambient Occlusion (HBAO)

HBAO is an advanced AO technique that improves accuracy by considering the horizon angle around each pixel. It provides better quality occlusion at the cost of increased computational effort.

## Example of HBAO Calculation

```
float calculateHBAO(const Vector3& position, const Vector3& normal, const Scene& scene) {

float occlusion = 0.0;

int numSamples = 16;

for (int i = 0; i < numSamples; ++i) {

Vector3 sample = generateSampleHemisphere(normal);

Vector3 samplePos = position + sample * sampleRadius;

if (scene.isOccluded(samplePos)) {

float horizonAngle = acos(dot(normal, sample));

occlusion += (1.0 - horizonAngle / PI);

}
```

}

**return** 1.0 - occlusion / numSamples;

}

## Distance-Based AO

Distance-based AO calculates occlusion based on the distance between the point and occluding geometry. It provides a more physically accurate representation of occlusion.

## Example of Distance-Based AO

float calculateDistanceBasedAO(const Vector3& position, const Vector3& normal, const Scene& scene) {

float occlusion = 0.0;

int numSamples = 16;

**for** (int i = 0; i < numSamples; ++i) {

Vector3 sample = generateSampleSphere();

Vector3 samplePos = position + sample * sampleRadius;

float distance = length(samplePos - position);

**if** (scene.isOccluded(samplePos)) {

occlusion += (1.0 - distance / maxDistance) * max(dot(normal, sample), 0.0);

}

}

return 1.0 - occlusion / numSamples;

}

## Volumetric Ambient Occlusion

Volumetric ambient occlusion calculates occlusion within a 3D volume, providing a more accurate representation of AO for scenes with complex geometry and volumetric effects.

## Example of Volumetric AO

```
float calculateVolumetricAO(const Vector3& position, const Vector3& normal, const Volume& volume) {

float occlusion = 0.0;

int numSamples = 16;

for (int i = 0; i < numSamples; ++i) {

Vector3 sample = generateSampleSphere();

Vector3 samplePos = position + sample * sampleRadius;

float density = volume.getDensity(samplePos);

occlusion += density * max(dot(normal, sample), 0.0);

}

return 1.0 - occlusion / numSamples;

}
```

## Optimizing AO for Real-Time Rendering

Optimizing AO for real-time rendering involves reducing the number of samples, using efficient data structures, and leveraging parallel processing capabilities of modern hardware.

## Example of Optimized AO

```
float calculateOptimizedAO(const Vector3& position, const Vector3& normal, const Scene& scene) {

float occlusion = 0.0;

int numSamples = 8; // Reduced number of samples

for (int i = 0; i < numSamples; ++i) {

Vector3 sample = generateSampleHemisphere(normal);

Vector3 samplePos = position + sample * sampleRadius;

if (scene.isOccluded(samplePos)) {

occlusion += max(dot(normal, sample), 0.0);

}

}

return 1.0 - occlusion / numSamples;

}
```

## Conclusion

Ambient occlusion enhances the perception of depth and realism in a scene by simulating the soft shadows in occluded areas. Techniques like SSAO, HBAO, distance-based AO, and volumetric AO provide various approaches to calculating AO in real-time ray tracing.

## 6.5. Practical Applications and Examples

Understanding shadows and illumination in ray tracing is essential, but seeing practical applications and examples helps solidify these concepts. This section will explore real-world uses and detailed examples of how shadows and illumination enhance rendering.

### Video Games

In video games, realistic shadows and illumination contribute significantly to immersion. Techniques like soft shadows, global illumination, and ambient occlusion are used extensively to create visually stunning environments.

*Example: Real-Time Shadows in Games*

Games like "Shadow of the Tomb Raider" use advanced shadow techniques to enhance realism. Real-time ray-traced shadows allow for accurate and dynamic shadow casting, adapting to changing light conditions and environments.

### Film and Animation

In the film industry, ray tracing is used to create lifelike visual effects and animations. Accurate shadowing and global illumination are crucial for achieving photorealism.

*Example: Animated Films*

Pixar's "Toy Story 4" utilizes global illumination and ray-traced shadows to create rich and believable scenes. The interplay of light and shadow enhances the storytelling by adding depth and mood to each frame.

## Architectural Visualization

Architects use ray tracing to visualize buildings and interiors with realistic lighting and shadows. This helps in evaluating design choices and presenting concepts to clients.

*Example: Interior Design*

Architectural visualization software like Autodesk 3ds Max uses global illumination and ambient occlusion to simulate natural and artificial lighting. This provides clients with a realistic preview of how their spaces will look under different lighting conditions.

## Automotive Design

Ray tracing is used in automotive design to create realistic renderings of vehicles. Accurate reflections, refractions, and shadows are essential for evaluating aesthetics and functionality.

*Example: Car Renderings*

Software like Blender and V-Ray is used to create high-quality renderings of cars, showcasing their design and materials. Realistic lighting and shadows help in highlighting the vehicle's features and design elements.

## Scientific Visualization

In scientific research, ray tracing is used to visualize complex data and simulations. Accurate lighting and shadowing are crucial for interpreting and presenting scientific results.

*Example: Medical Imaging*

Ray tracing techniques are used in medical imaging to visualize structures within the human body. Volume rendering and global illumination help create detailed and informative images from MRI and CT scans.

## Virtual Reality

In virtual reality (VR), realistic lighting and shadows enhance the immersive experience. Techniques like real-time ray tracing and ambient occlusion are used to create believable virtual environments.

*Example: VR Training Simulations*

VR training simulations for fields like medicine and engineering use advanced lighting techniques to create realistic and interactive environments. Accurate shadows and illumination help in making the simulations more convincing and effective.

## Product Visualization

Product designers use ray tracing to create realistic renderings of their products. This helps in evaluating the design and materials before manufacturing.

### Example: Consumer Electronics

Companies like Apple use ray tracing to create photorealistic renderings of their products for marketing and promotional materials. Realistic lighting and shadows help in showcasing the product's design and features effectively.

## Interactive Simulations

Interactive simulations, such as those used in education and training, benefit from realistic lighting and shadows. These visual elements enhance the learning experience by making the simulations more engaging.

### Example: Flight Simulators

Flight simulators use advanced lighting techniques to create realistic environments for pilot training. Accurate shadows and global illumination help in simulating different times of day and weather conditions.

## Conclusion

Practical applications of shadows and illumination in ray tracing span various industries, including video games, film, architecture, automotive design, scientific visualization, virtual reality, product visualization, and interactive simulations. These techniques enhance realism and provide valuable insights, making ray tracing an indispensable tool in modern rendering.

# Chapter 7: Color and Perception

## 7.1. Color Theory in Digital Imaging

Color theory in digital imaging is foundational for understanding how colors are represented, perceived, and manipulated in digital environments. It involves the study of how different colors interact, how they are produced, and how they affect human perception.

### The Nature of Color

Color is a visual perceptual property derived from the spectrum of light interacting with the photoreceptor cells in our eyes. The human eye can perceive millions of colors, each corresponding to a different wavelength of light.

### RGB Color Model

The RGB color model is the most common color model used in digital imaging. It stands for Red, Green, and Blue, the primary colors of light. By combining these three colors at various intensities, a broad spectrum of colors can be created.

```
struct Color {

float red;

float green;

float blue;

Color(float r, float g, float b) : red(r), green(g), blue(b) {}

Color operator+(const Color& other) const {
```

```
    return Color(red + other.red, green + other.green, blue + other.blue);

}

Color operator*(float scalar) const {

    return Color(red * scalar, green * scalar, blue * scalar);

}
};
```

## CMYK Color Model

The CMYK color model is used in color printing and stands for Cyan, Magenta, Yellow, and Key (Black). This model works by subtracting light from white, which is why it's often referred to as a subtractive color model.

## HSV and HSL Models

HSV (Hue, Saturation, Value) and HSL (Hue, Saturation, Lightness) are color models that describe colors in terms of their appearance. These models are often more intuitive for humans to use because they align more closely with how we perceive and describe colors.

## Color Spaces

Color spaces are specific organizations of colors. Common color spaces include sRGB, Adobe RGB, and ProPhoto RGB. Each color space defines a range of colors (gamut) that can be represented within it.

## Gamma Correction

Gamma correction adjusts the luminance of colors to account for the non-linear way in which humans perceive light and color. This correction ensures that colors are represented accurately on various devices.

```
float applyGammaCorrection(float value, float gamma) {
    return pow(value, 1.0 / gamma);
}
```

## Color Matching and Conversion

Color matching ensures that colors appear the same across different devices. This involves converting colors between different color spaces using color profiles and transformation algorithms.

## Perception of Color

Human perception of color is influenced by several factors, including lighting conditions, surrounding colors, and individual differences in vision. Understanding these factors is crucial for accurate color reproduction in digital imaging.

## Metamerism

Metamerism is the phenomenon where colors appear the same under one lighting condition but different under another. This can be challenging in color matching and requires careful management of lighting and color profiles.

## Color Blindness

Color blindness affects how certain individuals perceive colors, typically due to deficiencies in one or more types of cone cells in the retina. Digital imaging must account for this to ensure accessibility.

## Use of Color in Design

Color is a powerful tool in design, used to evoke emotions, convey information, and create aesthetic appeal. Effective use of color requires understanding both the technical aspects of color theory and the psychological impact of colors.

## Example of Color Blending

Color blendColors(const Color& color1, const Color& color2, float alpha) {

**return** color1 * (1.0 - alpha) + color2 * alpha;

}

## Conclusion

Color theory in digital imaging encompasses the technical and perceptual aspects of color. By understanding models like RGB, HSV, and CMYK, applying gamma correction, and considering human perception, digital images can achieve accurate and appealing color reproduction.

# 7.2. Implementing Color in Ray Tracing

Implementing color in ray tracing involves accurately simulating how light interacts with surfaces to produce the colors seen in rendered images. This includes handling direct illumination, reflections, refractions, and global illumination.

## Color Representation

In ray tracing, colors are typically represented using the RGB color model. Each color component is stored as a floating-point value, representing the intensity of red, green, and blue light.

## Example of Color Representation

**struct** Color {

float red;

float green;

float blue;

Color(float r, float g, float b) : red(r), green(g), blue(b) {}

Color **operator**+(const Color& other) const {

**return** Color(red + other.red, green + other.green, blue + other.blue);

}

Color **operator***(float scalar) const {

**return** Color(red * scalar, green * scalar, blue * scalar);

}

};

## Shading Models

Shading models determine how light interacts with surfaces. Common shading models include Lambertian for diffuse reflection and Phong or Blinn-Phong for specular reflection.

## Lambertian Shading

Lambertian shading models diffuse reflection, where light is scattered uniformly in all directions. The intensity of the reflected light depends on the angle between the light direction and the surface normal.

Color calculateDiffuse(const Color& lightColor, const Color& surfaceColor, float lightIntensity, float angle) {

float diffuse = max(0.0f, angle);

**return** lightColor * surfaceColor * lightIntensity * diffuse;

}

## Phong Shading

Phong shading models both diffuse and specular reflections. It uses an ambient term, a diffuse term, and a specular term to calculate the final color.

Color calculatePhong(const Color& lightColor, const Color& surfaceColor, const Vector3& lightDir, const Vector3& viewDir, const Vector3& normal, float shininess) {

Color ambient = lightColor * 0.1;

float diffuse = max(0.0f, dot(normal, lightDir));

Vector3 reflectDir = reflect(-lightDir, normal);

float specular = pow(max(0.0f, dot(viewDir, reflectDir)), shininess);

**return** ambient + lightColor * surfaceColor * diffuse + lightColor * specular;

}

## Global Illumination

Global illumination simulates the complex interactions of light in a scene, including indirect lighting and color bleeding. Techniques like path tracing and photon mapping are used to achieve realistic global illumination.

## Path Tracing

Path tracing is a global illumination technique that traces multiple paths from the camera through the scene, simulating light interactions and accumulating color contributions from each path.

Color tracePath(const Ray& ray, const Scene& scene, int depth) {

**if** (depth <= 0) **return** Color(0, 0, 0);

Intersection hit;

**if** (scene.intersect(ray, hit)) {

Ray newRay(hit.position, sampleHemisphere(hit.normal));

Color incoming = tracePath(newRay, scene, depth - 1);

**return** hit.material.color * incoming;

}

**return** scene.backgroundColor;

}

## Photon Mapping

Photon mapping is another global illumination technique that involves two passes: a photon emission pass and a photon gathering pass. It efficiently handles caustics and complex light interactions.

## Example of Photon Mapping

void emitPhotons(const Light& light, PhotonMap& photonMap) {

**for** (int i = 0; i < numPhotons; ++i) {

Photon photon = light.emitPhoton();

tracePhoton(photon, photonMap);

}

}

Color gatherPhotons(const PhotonMap& photonMap, const Vector3& point, const Vector3& normal) {

std::vector<Photon> nearbyPhotons = photonMap.getPhotons(point, gatherRadius);

Color illumination(0, 0, 0);

**for** (const Photon& photon : nearbyPhotons) {

illumination += photon.color * max(dot(photon.direction, normal), 0.0);

}

```
return illumination / nearbyPhotons.size();
}
```

## Texture Mapping

Texture mapping applies 2D images to 3D surfaces to add detail and color variations. UV coordinates are used to map texture pixels to surface points.

## Example of Texture Mapping

```
Color getTextureColor(const Texture& texture, const Vector2& uv) {
int x = uv.x * texture.width;
int y = uv.y * texture.height;
return texture.getPixel(x, y);
}
```

## Tone Mapping

Tone mapping converts high dynamic range (HDR) images to low dynamic range (LDR) for display on standard monitors, preserving detail and contrast.

## Example of Tone Mapping

```
Color toneMap(const Color& hdrColor) {
float exposure = 1.0f;
Color mappedColor = Color(1.0f) - exp(-hdrColor * exposure);
```

**return** mappedColor / (mappedColor + Color(1.0f));

}

## Conclusion

Implementing color in ray tracing involves accurately simulating light interactions using shading models, global illumination techniques, and texture mapping. By handling these aspects effectively, ray tracers can produce highly realistic and visually appealing images.

## 7.3. High Dynamic Range Imaging (HDRI)

High Dynamic Range Imaging (HDRI) captures and displays a greater range of luminance levels than standard imaging techniques. This allows for more realistic and detailed representations of scenes with both very bright and very dark areas.

### The Concept of HDRI

HDRI involves capturing multiple images at different exposure levels and combining them to create an image with a wider dynamic range. This composite image retains details in both the shadows and highlights that would be lost in a single exposure.

### Creating HDR Images

Creating HDR images typically involves three steps: capturing bracketed exposures, merging them into an HDR image, and tone mapping for display.

## Example of HDR Image Creation

```cpp
HDRImage createHDRImage(const std::vector<Image>& exposures) {
    int width = exposures[0].width;
    int height = exposures[0].height;
    HDRImage hdrImage(width, height);
    for (int y = 0; y < height; ++y) {
        for (int x = 0; x < width; ++x) {
            float sumWeights = 0.0f;
            Color hdrColor(0, 0, 0);
            for (const auto& exposure : exposures) {
                float weight = calculateWeight(exposure.getPixel(x, y));
                hdrColor += exposure.getPixel(x, y) * weight;
                sumWeights += weight;
            }
            hdrImage.setPixel(x, y, hdrColor / sumWeights);
        }
    }
    return hdrImage;
}
```

## HDR File Formats

HDR images are stored in formats that support a wide range of luminance values. Common HDR file formats include Radiance (.hdr), OpenEXR (.exr), and TIFF (.tiff).

## Tone Mapping

Tone mapping is the process of converting HDR images to a format suitable for display on standard monitors. This involves compressing the dynamic range while preserving details and contrast.

## Example of Tone Mapping

Color toneMap(const Color& hdrColor) {

float exposure = 1.0f;

Color mappedColor = Color(1.0f) - exp(-hdrColor * exposure);

**return** mappedColor / (mappedColor + Color(1.0f));

}

## Applications of HDRI

HDRI is widely used in photography, film, video games, and computer graphics to create more realistic images. It is particularly useful in situations with high contrast lighting, such as outdoor scenes and interior lighting.

## HDRI in Photography

In photography, HDRI allows photographers to capture scenes with a wide range of lighting conditions, from bright sunlight to deep shadows. This technique can reveal details that would otherwise be lost in a single exposure.

## HDRI in Film and Animation

In film and animation, HDRI is used to create realistic lighting and reflections. By capturing real-world lighting environments, artists can apply these environments to 3D scenes, enhancing realism.

## Example of HDRI Environment Lighting

Color sampleHDRI(const HDRImage& hdri, const Vector3& direction) {

Vector2 uv = convertDirectionToUV(direction);

**return** hdri.getPixel(uv.x * hdri.width, uv.y * hdri.height);

}

## HDRI in Video Games

In video games, HDRI enhances visual realism by simulating how the human eye adapts to different lighting conditions. This dynamic range adjustment can make scenes more immersive.

## Dynamic Range Compression

Dynamic range compression techniques, such as Reinhard tone mapping, are used to balance the contrast and preserve details in HDR images.

## Example of Reinhard Tone Mapping

Color reinhardToneMap(const Color& hdrColor) {

```
float luminance = calculateLuminance(hdrColor);

float mappedLuminance = luminance / (1.0f + luminance);

return hdrColor * (mappedLuminance / luminance);
}
```

## Challenges in HDRI

HDRI presents several challenges, including managing the large data sizes of HDR images and dealing with artifacts from merging exposures. Effective tone mapping and careful handling of exposure levels are crucial for quality results.

## Conclusion

High Dynamic Range Imaging (HDRI) provides a powerful tool for capturing and displaying images with a wide range of luminance levels. Through techniques like tone mapping and dynamic range compression, HDRI enables the creation of realistic and detailed visual content across various applications.

## 7.4. Color Grading and Post-Processing

Color grading and post-processing are essential steps in the digital imaging workflow, used to enhance the visual quality and mood of the final image. These techniques involve adjusting colors, contrast, brightness, and other visual elements.

## The Purpose of Color Grading

Color grading is used to adjust the color balance and mood of an image. It can enhance the story being told, create a specific atmosphere, or correct color inconsistencies.

## Basic Color Adjustments

Basic color adjustments involve modifying the hue, saturation, and brightness of an image. These adjustments can correct color imbalances and improve the overall look of the image.

## Example of Basic Color Adjustment

```
Color adjustColor(const Color& color, float hueShift, float saturationScale, float brightnessScale) {
    // Convert color to HSV
    Vector3 hsv = rgbToHsv(color);
    // Adjust hue, saturation, and brightness
    hsv.x = fmod(hsv.x + hueShift, 360.0f);
    hsv.y = clamp(hsv.y * saturationScale, 0.0f, 1.0f);
    hsv.z = clamp(hsv.z * brightnessScale, 0.0f, 1.0f);
    // Convert back to RGB
    return hsvToRgb(hsv);
}
```

## Advanced Color Grading

Advanced color grading techniques involve more complex adjustments, such as selective color correction, curves, and color matching. These techniques provide finer control over the image's appearance.

## Example of Selective Color Correction

```
Color selectiveColorCorrection(const Color& color, const Color& targetColor, const Color& replacementColor, float tolerance) {
```

**if** (distance(color, targetColor) < tolerance) {

**return** mix(color, replacementColor, 0.5);

}

**return** color;

}

## Color Grading in Film and Video

In film and video, color grading is a critical step in post-production. It enhances the visual narrative, matches shots from different scenes, and creates a consistent look throughout the project.

## LUTs (Look-Up Tables)

LUTs are used in color grading to apply predefined color transformations to an image. They provide a quick and consistent way to achieve a specific look.

## Example of Applying a LUT

Color applyLUT(const Color& color, const LUT& lut) {

int index = calculateLUTIndex(color);

**return** lut.getColor(index);

}

## Post-Processing Effects

Post-processing effects enhance the final image by adding visual elements such as bloom, vignetting, and chromatic aberration. These effects can simulate real-world camera imperfections and enhance the aesthetic appeal.

## Example of Bloom Effect

```
Color applyBloom(const Image& image, const Vector2& uv, float threshold, float intensity) {

Color color = image.getPixel(uv.x * image.width, uv.y * image.height);

if (luminance(color) > threshold) {

return color * intensity;

}

return color;

}
```

## Vignetting

Vignetting darkens the edges of an image, drawing attention to the center. It simulates the natural falloff of light in camera lenses.

## Example of Vignetting Effect

```
Color applyVignetting(const Image& image, const Vector2& uv, float strength) {

float distance = length(uv - Vector2(0.5f, 0.5f));
```

float vignette = clamp(1.0f - distance * strength, 0.0f, 1.0f);

return image.getPixel(uv.x * image.width, uv.y * image.height) * vignette;

}

## Chromatic Aberration

Chromatic aberration simulates the dispersion of light through a lens, causing color fringes around high-contrast edges.

## Example of Chromatic Aberration Effect

Color applyChromaticAberration(const Image& image, const Vector2& uv, float strength) {

Vector2 redUV = uv + Vector2(-strength, -strength);

Vector2 blueUV = uv + Vector2(strength, strength);

Color red = image.getPixel(redUV.x * image.width, redUV.y * image.height);

Color blue = image.getPixel(blueUV.x * image.width, blueUV.y * image.height);

Color green = image.getPixel(uv.x * image.width, uv.y * image.height);

return Color(red.r, green.g, blue.b);

}

## HDR Tone Mapping

In HDR tone mapping, post-processing is crucial for converting high dynamic range images to displayable formats while preserving details and contrast.

## Conclusion

Color grading and post-processing are vital techniques for enhancing the visual quality of digital images. By applying adjustments, LUTs, and various effects, artists can achieve the desired look and feel for their projects, making these techniques indispensable in digital imaging.

# 7.5. Perception and Human Vision Considerations

Understanding human vision and perception is crucial for creating realistic and appealing digital images. This involves studying how the human eye perceives light, color, and depth, and how these perceptions can be leveraged in digital imaging.

## The Human Visual System

The human visual system is composed of the eyes and the brain, which work together to process visual information. The retina, located at the back of the eye, contains photoreceptor cells called rods and cones.

## Rods and Cones

- **Rods:** Sensitive to low light levels and responsible for night vision. They do not detect color.

- **Cones:** Responsible for color vision and operate best under bright light conditions. There are three types of cones, each sensitive to different wavelengths of light (red, green, and blue).

## Color Perception

Color perception is based on the response of the three types of cones to different wavelengths of light. The brain processes the signals from these cones to produce the perception of color.

## Tristimulus Theory

The Tristimulus Theory states that any color can be represented by a combination of three primary colors, corresponding to the three types of cones in the human eye.

## Example of Tristimulus Calculation

Color calculateTristimulus(float red, float green, float blue) {

// Normalize the color values

float r = red / 255.0f;

float g = green / 255.0f;

float b = blue / 255.0f;

// Combine the values to get the final color

return Color(r, g, b);

}

## Color Adaptation

Color adaptation is the ability of the human eye to adjust to different lighting conditions. This allows us to perceive colors consistently under varying light sources.

## Simulating Color Adaptation

In digital imaging, simulating color adaptation involves adjusting the white balance and exposure of an image to match the perceived colors under different lighting conditions.

## Depth Perception

Depth perception is the ability to perceive the world in three dimensions. It is achieved through binocular vision (stereopsis), where the brain combines the images from both eyes to create a sense of depth.

## Techniques to Enhance Depth Perception

- **Parallax**: The apparent shift in position of an object when viewed from different angles.

- **Shading and Shadows**: Provide visual cues about the relative positions of objects.

- **Motion Parallax**: Objects closer to the viewer move faster across the field of view than distant objects.

## Example of Depth Cue Calculation

```
float calculateDepthCue(const Vector3& position, const Vector3& viewerPosition) {

float distance = length(position - viewerPosition);
```

**return** 1.0f / (distance + 1.0f);

}

## Visual Acuity

Visual acuity is the ability of the eye to perceive fine details. It varies across the visual field, with the highest acuity at the fovea, the central part of the retina.

## Simulating Visual Acuity

In digital imaging, simulating visual acuity can involve techniques like depth of field, where objects at different distances are blurred to mimic how the eye focuses on specific points.

## Example of Depth of Field

Color applyDepthOfField(const Image& image, const Vector2& uv, float focusDistance, float aperture) {

float distance = calculateDepth(image, uv);

float blurAmount = abs(distance - focusDistance) * aperture;

**return** blur(image, uv, blurAmount);

}

## Color Blindness Considerations

Color blindness affects a significant portion of the population. It is important to consider color blindness when designing digital content to ensure accessibility.

## Simulating Color Blindness

Simulating color blindness involves adjusting the colors in an image to reflect how they would appear to someone with color vision deficiency.

### Example of Simulating Deuteranopia

Color simulateDeuteranopia(const Color& color) {

float r = color.red * 0.625 + color.green * 0.375;

float g = color.red * 0.7 + color.green * 0.3;

float b = color.blue;

**return** Color(r, g, b);

}

### Conclusion

Understanding human vision and perception is essential for creating realistic and accessible digital images. By leveraging knowledge of the visual system, color perception, depth cues, and visual acuity, digital imaging can be tailored to match human perception, enhancing the overall visual experience.

# Chapter 8: Reflections and Refractions

## 8.1. Mirrors and Reflective Surfaces

Reflections play a critical role in creating realistic images in ray tracing. Mirrors and reflective surfaces are essential for simulating how light interacts with objects in the environment, enhancing visual realism.

## Reflection Principles

Reflection occurs when light bounces off a surface. The angle of incidence (the angle between the incoming ray and the normal) equals the angle of reflection (the angle between the reflected ray and the normal).

## Specular Reflection

Specular reflection produces mirror-like reflections. This occurs on smooth, polished surfaces where the reflected light maintains the same image as the light source.

## Example of Specular Reflection Calculation

```
Vector3 calculateReflection(const Vector3& incident, const Vector3& normal) {
    return incident - 2.0 * dot(incident, normal) * normal;
}
```

## Reflective Materials

Reflective materials are defined by their reflectance properties. The reflectance determines the proportion of light that is reflected versus absorbed or transmitted.

## Example of Reflective Material

```
struct ReflectiveMaterial {
    Color color;
    float reflectance;
```

ReflectiveMaterial(const Color& c, float r) : color(c), reflectance(r) {}

};

## Rendering Reflective Surfaces

To render reflective surfaces, rays are traced from the viewer to the reflective surface and then reflected according to the reflection principles. The color of the reflected ray is computed recursively.

## Example of Recursive Reflection

Color traceRay(const Ray& ray, const Scene& scene, int depth) {

**if** (depth <= 0) **return** Color(0, 0, 0);

Intersection hit;

**if** (scene.intersect(ray, hit)) {

Ray reflectedRay(hit.position, calculateReflection(ray.direction, hit.normal));

Color reflectedColor = traceRay(reflectedRay, scene, depth - 1);

**return** hit.material.color * reflectedColor * hit.material.reflectance;

}

**return** scene.backgroundColor;

}

## Importance of Reflection

Reflection adds realism to rendered images by simulating how light interacts with reflective surfaces. It is crucial for materials like metal, water, and glass.

## Glossy Reflection

Glossy reflection occurs on surfaces that are not perfectly smooth. It produces blurred reflections, creating a more natural appearance for materials like brushed metal or frosted glass.

## Example of Glossy Reflection

Vector3 calculateGlossyReflection(const Vector3& incident, const Vector3& normal, float roughness) {

Vector3 perfectReflection = calculateReflection(incident, normal);

Vector3 randomOffset = randomInUnitSphere() * roughness;

**return** normalize(perfectReflection + randomOffset);

}

## Reflectance Models

Various reflectance models, such as the Fresnel effect, describe how the reflectance of a surface varies with the angle of incidence. These models are essential for realistic rendering of reflective surfaces.

## Fresnel Effect

The Fresnel effect describes how the amount of reflected light depends on the angle of incidence. At shallow angles, reflectance increases, making surfaces appear more reflective.

## Example of Fresnel Calculation

```
float calculateFresnel(const Vector3& incident, const Vector3& normal, float ior) {

float cosTheta = dot(-incident, normal);

float r0 = pow((1.0 - ior) / (1.0 + ior), 2.0);

return r0 + (1.0 - r0) * pow(1.0 - cosTheta, 5.0);

}
```

## Combining Reflection with Other Effects

Reflection is often combined with other effects, such as refraction and shading, to create complex materials like glass and water. These combinations enhance the realism of the rendered scene.

## Example of Combined Reflection and Refraction

```
Color traceRay(const Ray& ray, const Scene& scene, int depth) {

if (depth <= 0) return Color(0, 0, 0);

Intersection hit;

if (scene.intersect(ray, hit)) {

Vector3 reflectedDir = calculateReflection(ray.direction, hit.normal);
```

```
Ray reflectedRay(hit.position, reflectedDir);

Color reflectedColor = traceRay(reflectedRay, scene, depth - 1);

Vector3 refractedDir = calculateRefraction(ray.direction, hit.normal, hit.material.ior);

Ray refractedRay(hit.position, refractedDir);

Color refractedColor = traceRay(refractedRay, scene, depth - 1);

float reflectance = calculateFresnel(ray.direction, hit.normal, hit.material.ior);

return hit.material.color * (reflectedColor * reflectance + refractedColor * (1.0 - reflectance));

}

return scene.backgroundColor;

}
```

## Conclusion

Mirrors and reflective surfaces are essential for realistic rendering in ray tracing. By accurately simulating specular and glossy reflections, combining reflection with other effects, and using reflectance models, ray tracers can produce lifelike images with enhanced visual realism.

## 8.2. Water and Glass: Realistic Refractions

Refractions are crucial for simulating materials like water and glass, where light bends as it passes through the material. Realistic refractions add depth and realism to rendered scenes.

## Refraction Principles

Refraction occurs when light passes from one medium to another, changing direction due to a change in speed. Snell's law describes this relationship between the angles of incidence and refraction and the refractive indices of the materials.

## Snell's Law

Snell's law is given by:

$$n_1 \sin(\theta_1) = n_2 \sin(\theta_2)$$

where $n_1$ and $n_2$ are the refractive indices of the two media, and $\theta_1$ and $\theta_2$ are the angles of incidence and refraction, respectively.

## Example of Refraction Calculation

```
Vector3 calculateRefraction(const Vector3& incident, const Vector3& normal, float ior) {

float cosi = clamp(dot(incident, normal), -1.0, 1.0);

float etai = 1, etat = ior;

Vector3 n = normal;

if (cosi < 0) { cosi = -cosi; }

else { swap(etai, etat); n = -normal; }

float eta = etai / etat;

float k = 1 - eta * eta * (1 - cosi * cosi);
```

**return** k < 0 ? Vector3(0, 0, 0) : eta * incident + (eta * cosi - sqrt(k)) * n;

}

# Refractive Materials

Refractive materials are defined by their refractive index (IOR), which determines how much light bends as it enters the material. Common refractive indices include:

- Water: 1.33
- Glass: 1.5
- Diamond: 2.42

# Rendering Refractive Surfaces

To render refractive surfaces, rays are traced through the material according to Snell's law. The color of the refracted ray is computed recursively, accounting for both reflection and refraction.

# Example of Recursive Refraction

Color traceRay(const Ray& ray, const Scene& scene, int depth) {

**if** (depth <= 0) **return** Color(0, 0, 0);

Intersection hit;

**if** (scene.intersect(ray, hit)) {

Vector3 refractedDir = calculateRefraction(ray.direction, hit.normal, hit.material.ior);

Ray refractedRay(hit.position, refractedDir);

```
Color refractedColor = traceRay(refractedRay, scene, depth - 1);

Vector3 reflectedDir = calculateReflection(ray.direction, hit.normal);

Ray reflectedRay(hit.position, reflectedDir);

Color reflectedColor = traceRay(reflectedRay, scene, depth - 1);

float reflectance = calculateFresnel(ray.direction, hit.normal, hit.material.ior);

return hit.material.color * (refractedColor * (1.0 - reflectance) + reflectedColor * reflectance);

}

return scene.backgroundColor;

}
```

## Importance of Refraction

Refraction adds realism to rendered images by simulating how light bends through transparent materials. It is essential for rendering materials like water, glass, and other transparent substances.

## Caustics

Caustics are patterns of light formed when light rays are focused by reflective or refractive surfaces. They are commonly seen on surfaces illuminated by water or glass.

## Simulating Caustics

Simulating caustics involves tracing additional rays from the light source and capturing the focused light patterns. Photon mapping and bidirectional path tracing are techniques used to simulate caustics.

## Example of Caustic Calculation

```
void emitCausticPhotons(const Light& light, PhotonMap& photonMap) {
    for (int i = 0; i < numPhotons; ++i) {
        Photon photon = light.emitPhoton();
        tracePhoton(photon, photonMap);
    }
}

Color gatherCaustics(const PhotonMap& photonMap, const Vector3& point, const Vector3& normal) {
    std::vector<Photon> nearbyPhotons = photonMap.getPhotons(point, gatherRadius);
    Color illumination(0, 0, 0);
    for (const Photon& photon : nearbyPhotons) {
        illumination += photon.color * max(dot(photon.direction, normal), 0.0);
    }
    return illumination / nearbyPhotons.size();
}
```

## Dispersion

Dispersion occurs when light splits into its constituent colors as it passes through a material. This effect is seen in prisms and diamonds and adds to the realism of refractive materials.

## Example of Dispersion Calculation

Vector3 calculateDispersion(const Vector3& incident, const Vector3& normal, float ior, float wavelength) {

float adjustedIor = ior + (wavelength - 550.0) * dispersionCoefficient;

**return** calculateRefraction(incident, normal, adjustedIor);

}

## Conclusion

Water and glass are key materials in ray tracing, requiring accurate simulation of refractions. By using Snell's law, handling caustics, and considering dispersion, ray tracers can produce highly realistic images with lifelike transparency and light interactions.

# 8.3. Complex Refractive Phenomena

Complex refractive phenomena involve advanced interactions of light with materials, including total internal reflection, multiple scattering, and subsurface scattering. These effects are crucial for rendering realistic materials like gems, liquids, and translucent objects.

# Total Internal Reflection

Total internal reflection occurs when light attempts to move from a medium with a higher refractive index to one with a lower refractive index at a steep angle. The light is completely reflected within the material.

## Example of Total Internal Reflection Calculation

```
bool calculateTotalInternalReflection(const Vector3& incident, const Vector3& normal, float ior) {

float cosi = clamp(dot(incident, normal), -1.0, 1.0);

float etai = 1, etat = ior;

if (cosi > 0) swap(etai, etat);

float eta = etai / etat;

float k = 1 - eta * eta * (1 - cosi * cosi);

return k < 0;

}
```

## Multiple Scattering

Multiple scattering occurs when light is scattered multiple times within a material before exiting. This effect is important for materials like fog, milk, and certain types of glass.

## Simulating Multiple Scattering

Multiple scattering can be simulated using volumetric rendering techniques, where rays are traced through a participating medium and interactions with particles are accumulated.

## Example of Multiple Scattering Calculation

```
Color traceVolumetricRay(const Ray& ray, const Volume& volume, int depth) {

if (depth <= 0) return Color(0, 0, 0);

float distance = volume.sampleDistance(ray);

if (distance < 0) return Color(0, 0, 0);

Vector3 scatterPoint = ray.origin + ray.direction * distance;

Vector3 scatterDirection = volume.sampleScatterDirection(ray.direction);

Ray scatteredRay(scatterPoint, scatterDirection);

Color scatteredColor = traceVolumetricRay(scatteredRay, volume, depth - 1);

return volume.getColor(scatterPoint) * scatteredColor;

}
```

## Subsurface Scattering

Subsurface scattering (SSS) simulates the diffusion of light beneath the surface of a translucent material. It is essential for rendering realistic skin, marble, and other materials where light penetrates the surface and scatters internally.

## Example of Subsurface Scattering Calculation

```
Color calculateSubsurfaceScattering(const Vector3& point, const Vector3& normal, const Light& light, const Material& material) {

float scatterRadius = material.scatterRadius;
```

```
Vector3 lightDir = normalize(light.position - point);

float distance = length(light.position - point);

float scatter = exp(-distance / scatterRadius);

return material.subsurfaceColor * light.intensity * scatter;

}
```

## Combining Refraction with Scattering

Combining refraction with scattering effects can create complex materials like frosted glass or translucent liquids. These materials require simulating both the bending of light and its internal scattering.

## Example of Combined Refraction and Scattering

```
Color traceComplexRay(const Ray& ray, const Scene& scene, int depth) {

if (depth <= 0) return Color(0, 0, 0);

Intersection hit;

if (scene.intersect(ray, hit)) {

Vector3 refractedDir = calculateRefraction(ray.direction, hit.normal, hit.material.ior);

Ray refractedRay(hit.position, refractedDir);

Color refractedColor = traceComplexRay(refractedRay, scene, depth - 1);

Vector3 scatteredDir = sampleScatterDirection(refractedDir, hit.material.scatterRadius);
```

Ray scatteredRay(hit.position, scatteredDir);

Color scatteredColor = traceComplexRay(scatteredRay, scene, depth - 1);

**return** hit.material.color * (refractedColor * 0.8 + scatteredColor * 0.2);

}

**return** scene.backgroundColor;

}

## Birefringence

Birefringence is a phenomenon where a material has different refractive indices along different axes, causing light to split into two rays. This effect is seen in materials like calcite and can be used to create unique visual effects.

## Example of Birefringence Calculation

Vector3 calculateBirefringence(const Vector3& incident, const Vector3& normal, float ior1, float ior2) {

Vector3 refracted1 = calculateRefraction(incident, normal, ior1);

Vector3 refracted2 = calculateRefraction(incident, normal, ior2);

**return** (refracted1 + refracted2) * 0.5;

}

## Chromatic Aberration

Chromatic aberration occurs when different wavelengths of light refract by different amounts, causing color fringes. This effect is common in lenses and can be used to add realism to refractive materials.

## Example of Chromatic Aberration Calculation

Vector3 calculateChromaticAberration(const Vector3& incident, const Vector3& normal, float ior, float wavelength) {

float adjustedIor = ior + (wavelength - 550.0) * dispersionCoefficient;

**return** calculateRefraction(incident, normal, adjustedIor);

}

## Conclusion

Complex refractive phenomena, such as total internal reflection, multiple scattering, subsurface scattering, birefringence, and chromatic aberration, are essential for rendering realistic materials in ray tracing. By accurately simulating these effects, ray tracers can produce highly detailed and lifelike images.

# 8.4. Reflection and Refraction Optimization

Optimizing reflection and refraction calculations is crucial for achieving real-time performance in ray tracing while maintaining visual quality. Various techniques can be applied to improve the efficiency of these computations.

## Acceleration Structures

Acceleration structures, such as Bounding Volume Hierarchies (BVH) and K-D Trees, are used to quickly eliminate large portions of the scene from intersection tests, speeding up reflection and refraction calculations.

## Example of BVH Traversal

```
bool intersectBVH(const Ray& ray, const BVHNode& node, Intersection& hit) {

if (!node.bounds.intersect(ray)) return false;

if (node.isLeaf()) {

return node.object->intersect(ray, hit);

}

bool hitLeft = intersectBVH(ray, *node.left, hit);

bool hitRight = intersectBVH(ray, *node.right, hit);

return hitLeft || hitRight;

}
```

## Adaptive Sampling

Adaptive sampling reduces the number of rays traced by focusing computational resources on important areas, such as regions with high contrast or complex interactions.

## Example of Adaptive Sampling

```
Color traceAdaptiveRay(const Ray& ray, const Scene& scene, int depth, float threshold) {

if (depth <= 0) return Color(0, 0, 0);

Intersection hit;

if (scene.intersect(ray, hit)) {

Color directColor = calculateDirectIllumination(ray, hit, scene);

if (luminance(directColor) < threshold) return directColor;

Vector3 reflectedDir = calculateReflection(ray.direction, hit.normal);

Ray reflectedRay(hit.position, reflectedDir);

Color reflectedColor = traceAdaptiveRay(reflectedRay, scene, depth - 1, threshold * 0.5);

Vector3 refractedDir = calculateRefraction(ray.direction, hit.normal, hit.material.ior);

Ray refractedRay(hit.position, refractedDir);

Color refractedColor = traceAdaptiveRay(refractedRay, scene, depth - 1, threshold * 0.5);

return hit.material.color * (directColor + reflectedColor + refractedColor);

}

return scene.backgroundColor;
```

}

## Importance Sampling

Importance sampling focuses rays on areas that contribute most to the final image, such as bright light sources or reflective surfaces, improving the efficiency of reflection and refraction calculations.

## Example of Importance Sampling

Vector3 sampleImportanceDirection(const Vector3& normal, const Vector3& viewDir, float roughness) {

Vector3 halfwayDir = normalize(viewDir + normal);

**return** halfwayDir + randomInUnitSphere() * roughness;

}

## Russian Roulette Termination

Russian Roulette termination probabilistically terminates ray paths to reduce computation without significantly affecting the final image quality. This technique is especially useful for deep recursion levels.

## Example of Russian Roulette

Color traceRayRussianRoulette(const Ray& ray, const Scene& scene, int depth, float probability) {

**if** (depth <= 0 || randomFloat() < probability) **return** Color(0, 0, 0);

Intersection hit;

**if** (scene.intersect(ray, hit)) {

Vector3 reflectedDir = calculateReflection(ray.direction, hit.normal);

Ray reflectedRay(hit.position, reflectedDir);

Color reflectedColor = traceRayRussianRoulette(reflectedRay, scene, depth - 1, probability * 0.9);

Vector3 refractedDir = calculateRefraction(ray.direction, hit.normal, hit.material.ior);

Ray refractedRay(hit.position, refractedDir);

Color refractedColor = traceRayRussianRoulette(refractedRay, scene, depth - 1, probability * 0.9);

**return** hit.material.color * (reflectedColor + refractedColor);

}

**return** scene.backgroundColor;

}

## Caching and Reusing Results

Caching and reusing previously computed reflection and refraction results can significantly reduce redundant calculations, especially in scenes with static geometry and lighting.

## Example of Result Caching

std::unordered_map<Ray, Color> resultCache;

Color traceRayWithCaching(const Ray& ray, const Scene& scene, int depth) {

**if** (depth <= 0) **return** Color(0, 0, 0);

```
if (resultCache.find(ray) != resultCache.end()) {
    return resultCache[ray];
}
Intersection hit;
if (scene.intersect(ray, hit)) {
    Vector3 reflectedDir = calculateReflection(ray.direction, hit.normal);
    Ray reflectedRay(hit.position, reflectedDir);
    Color reflectedColor = traceRayWithCaching(reflectedRay, scene, depth - 1);
    Vector3 refractedDir = calculateRefraction(ray.direction, hit.normal, hit.material.ior);
    Ray refractedRay(hit.position, refractedDir);
    Color refractedColor = traceRayWithCaching(refractedRay, scene, depth - 1);
    Color result = hit.material.color * (reflectedColor + refractedColor);
    resultCache[ray] = result;
    return result;
}
return scene.backgroundColor;
}
```

## Hybrid Rendering Techniques

Hybrid rendering techniques combine rasterization and ray tracing to leverage the strengths of both methods, achieving real-time performance with high-quality reflections and refractions.

## Example of Hybrid Rendering

void renderSceneHybrid(const Scene& scene, Image& image) {

// *Rasterize the scene*

rasterizeScene(scene, image);

// *Trace reflections and refractions*

**for** (int y = 0; y < image.height; ++y) {

**for** (int x = 0; x < image.width; ++x) {

Ray ray = generateRay(x, y, scene.camera);

Color tracedColor = traceRay(ray, scene, 5);

image.setPixel(x, y, mix(image.getPixel(x, y), tracedColor, 0.5));

}

}

}

## Conclusion

Optimizing reflection and refraction calculations is essential for achieving real-time performance in ray tracing. Techniques such as using acceleration structures, adaptive sampling, importance sampling, Russian Roulette termination, caching, and hybrid rendering can significantly improve efficiency while maintaining high visual quality.

## 8.5. Case Studies: Reflections and Refractions in Games and Films

Understanding how reflections and refractions are implemented in real-world applications can provide valuable insights into effective techniques and optimizations. This section explores case studies from both video games and films.

### Case Study 1: Ray-Traced Reflections in "Battlefield V"

"Battlefield V" was one of the first major games to incorporate real-time ray tracing for reflections, significantly enhancing visual realism.

### Implementation Details

- **Hybrid Rendering**: Combines rasterization for primary rendering with ray tracing for reflections.

- **Real-Time Performance**: Achieved through optimizations like adaptive sampling and temporal accumulation.

- **Dynamic Reflections**: Reflections adapt to changes in the environment and player movements, providing a consistent and realistic experience.

### Example of Hybrid Reflection Rendering

```
void renderBattlefieldScene(const Scene& scene, Image& image) {
```

```
// Rasterize the primary scene
rasterizeScene(scene, image);
// Add ray-traced reflections
for (int y = 0; y < image.height; ++y) {
    for (int x = 0; x < image.width; ++x) {
        Ray ray = generateRay(x, y, scene.camera);
        Color reflectionColor = traceRay(ray, scene, 3);
        image.setPixel(x, y, mix(image.getPixel(x, y), reflectionColor, 0.4));
    }
}
}
```

## Case Study 2: Realistic Water Refraction in "Finding Nemo"

"Finding Nemo" showcased Pixar's advanced techniques for simulating realistic water refraction, crucial for the underwater scenes.

## Implementation Details

- **Subsurface Scattering**: Used for realistic light diffusion in water.

- **Caustics Simulation**: Accurate rendering of light patterns on surfaces beneath the water.

- **Refraction Mapping**: Detailed refraction maps for precise light bending through water.

## Example of Water Refraction Calculation

```
Color traceFindingNemoWater(const Ray& ray, const Scene& scene, int depth) {

if (depth <= 0) return Color(0, 0, 0);

Intersection hit;

if (scene.intersect(ray, hit)) {

Vector3 refractedDir = calculateRefraction(ray.direction, hit.normal, hit.material.ior);

Ray refractedRay(hit.position, refractedDir);

Color refractedColor = traceFindingNemoWater(refractedRay, scene, depth - 1);

Color causticsColor = calculateCaustics(hit.position, scene.lights);

return hit.material.color * (refractedColor + causticsColor);

}

return scene.backgroundColor;

}
```

# Case Study 3: Reflective Surfaces in "Spider-Man: Miles Morales"

"Spider-Man: Miles Morales" utilizes ray-traced reflections to enhance the urban environment, making surfaces like glass buildings and puddles look highly realistic.

## Implementation Details

- **Dynamic Reflections**: Reflective surfaces update in real-time as the player moves through the city.

- **Optimization Techniques**: Importance sampling and temporal accumulation to maintain performance.

- **Hybrid Rendering**: Combines rasterization and ray tracing for optimal visual quality.

## Example of Reflective Surface Rendering

```
void renderSpiderManScene(const Scene& scene, Image& image)
{
// Rasterize the cityscape
rasterizeScene(scene, image);
// Trace reflections on glass and water surfaces
for (int y = 0; y < image.height; ++y) {
for (int x = 0; x < image.width; ++x) {
Ray ray = generateRay(x, y, scene.camera);
Color reflectionColor = traceRay(ray, scene, 4);
```

```
image.setPixel(x, y, mix(image.getPixel(x, y), reflectionColor, 0.3));

        }

    }

}
```

## Case Study 4: Underwater Refractions in "Avatar"

James Cameron's "Avatar" employed advanced refraction techniques to create realistic underwater scenes, contributing to the film's immersive environment.

### Implementation Details

- **Complex Refractions**: Multiple layers of refraction for water surfaces and underwater objects.

- **Subsurface Scattering**: Enhanced the realism of underwater creatures and plants.

- **High-Performance Computing**: Utilized extensive computational resources to achieve detailed refractions and caustics.

### Example of Underwater Refraction Simulation

```
Color traceAvatarUnderwater(const Ray& ray, const Scene& scene, int depth) {

if (depth <= 0) return Color(0, 0, 0);

Intersection hit;
```

```
if (scene.intersect(ray, hit)) {

    Vector3 refractedDir = calculateRefraction(ray.direction, hit.normal, hit.material.ior);

    Ray refractedRay(hit.position, refractedDir);

    Color refractedColor = traceAvatarUnderwater(refractedRay, scene, depth - 1);

    Color subsurfaceColor = calculateSubsurfaceScattering(hit.position, hit.normal, scene.lights);

    return hit.material.color * (refractedColor + subsurfaceColor);

}

return scene.backgroundColor;

}
```

## Case Study 5: Glass and Reflections in "Frozen"

Disney's "Frozen" utilized ray tracing for the realistic rendering of ice and glass, which were central to the film's visual aesthetic.

## Implementation Details

- **Detailed Reflections**: Accurate reflections on ice surfaces enhanced visual realism.

- **Refraction and Dispersion**: Simulated the light splitting through ice, creating vibrant visual effects.

- **High-Quality Shaders**: Custom shaders for ice and glass materials to handle complex light interactions.

## Example of Ice Reflection and Refraction

```
Color traceFrozenIce(const Ray& ray, const Scene& scene, int depth) {

if (depth <= 0) return Color(0, 0, 0);

Intersection hit;

if (scene.intersect(ray, hit)) {

Vector3 reflectedDir = calculateReflection(ray.direction, hit.normal);

Ray reflectedRay(hit.position, reflectedDir);

Color reflectedColor = traceFrozenIce(reflectedRay, scene, depth - 1);

Vector3 refractedDir = calculateRefraction(ray.direction, hit.normal, hit.material.ior);

Ray refractedRay(hit.position, refractedDir);

Color refractedColor = traceFrozenIce(refractedRay, scene, depth - 1);

Color dispersionColor = calculateDispersion(ray.direction, hit.normal, hit.material.ior, hit.material.wavelength);

return hit.material.color * (reflectedColor + refractedColor + dispersionColor);

}

return scene.backgroundColor;

}
```

## Conclusion

The case studies of reflections and refractions in games and films demonstrate the importance of these techniques in achieving visual realism. By exploring implementations in "Battlefield V," "Finding Nemo," "Spider-Man: Miles Morales," "Avatar," and "Frozen," it becomes clear that advanced reflection and refraction methods are crucial for creating immersive and believable visual experiences.

# Chapter 9: Advanced Lighting Techniques

## 9.1. Photon Mapping in Ray Tracing

Photon mapping is a two-pass global illumination algorithm that accurately simulates the complex interactions of light in a scene. It is especially effective for rendering caustics, color bleeding, and other subtle lighting effects.

### The Photon Mapping Process

Photon mapping consists of two main phases: photon emission and photon gathering. In the emission phase, photons are shot from the light sources and their interactions with the scene are recorded. In the gathering phase, the information from the photon map is used to compute the final image.

### Photon Emission Phase

In the photon emission phase, photons are emitted from the light sources and traced through the scene. Each time a photon hits a surface, its position, incoming direction, and power are stored in the photon map.

```cpp
void emitPhotons(const Light& light, PhotonMap& photonMap, int numPhotons) {
    for (int i = 0; i < numPhotons; ++i) {
        Photon photon = light.emitPhoton();
        tracePhoton(photon, photonMap);
    }
}

void tracePhoton(Photon& photon, PhotonMap& photonMap) {
    while (true) {
        Intersection hit;
        if (scene.intersect(photon.ray, hit)) {
            photonMap.store(photon.position, photon.direction, photon.power);
            photon.bounce(hit.normal);
        } else {
            break;
        }
    }
}
```

## Photon Gathering Phase

In the photon gathering phase, the photon map is used to estimate the radiance at each visible point in the scene. This involves searching for nearby photons and using their information to calculate the final color.

```cpp
Color gatherPhotons(const PhotonMap& photonMap, const Vector3& position, const Vector3& normal) {

    std::vector<Photon> nearbyPhotons = photonMap.getPhotons(position, gatherRadius);

    Color radiance(0, 0, 0);

    for (const Photon& photon : nearbyPhotons) {

        float weight = max(dot(photon.direction, normal), 0.0);

        radiance += photon.power * weight;

    }

    return radiance / nearbyPhotons.size();

}
```

## Importance of Photon Mapping

Photon mapping is crucial for accurately simulating complex lighting phenomena, such as caustics and global illumination, which are challenging to achieve with other techniques.

## Advantages of Photon Mapping

- **Accuracy**: Photon mapping can simulate a wide range of lighting effects with high accuracy.

- **Flexibility**: It can handle both direct and indirect illumination, making it suitable for various lighting scenarios.

- **Scalability**: Photon mapping can be adapted to different levels of detail, depending on the requirements of the scene.

## Challenges of Photon Mapping

- **Memory Usage**: Storing large numbers of photons can require significant memory.

- **Computation Time**: Tracing and gathering photons can be computationally expensive.

## Optimizations in Photon Mapping

Various optimizations can be applied to improve the performance of photon mapping, including:

- **Photon Maps Hierarchies**: Using hierarchical data structures to store photons can speed up the gathering phase.

- **Selective Photon Emission**: Emitting more photons in regions of interest can improve accuracy without significantly increasing computation time.

- **Parallel Processing**: Utilizing parallel processing techniques can reduce the overall computation time.

## Example of Photon Map Hierarchy

```
class PhotonMap {
```

**public:**

```
void store(const Vector3& position, const Vector3& direction, const Color& power) {

    photons.push_back(Photon(position, direction, power));

    // Insert into hierarchical structure (e.g., KD-Tree)

}

std::vector<Photon> getPhotons(const Vector3& position, float radius) const {

    // Retrieve photons from hierarchical structure

}
```

**private:**

```
std::vector<Photon> photons;

// Hierarchical structure (e.g., KD-Tree)

};
```

## Conclusion

Photon mapping is a powerful technique for simulating complex lighting effects in ray tracing. By using a two-pass approach, it efficiently handles both direct and indirect illumination, making it an essential tool for achieving realistic rendering.

## 9.2. Caustics: Simulation of Light Through Transparent Media

Caustics are the bright patterns created when light is focused through a transparent or reflective surface, such as water or glass. Simulating caustics adds realism to scenes involving such materials.

### Understanding Caustics

Caustics are formed by the refraction or reflection of light, focusing it into bright patterns. These effects are commonly seen at the bottom of a pool or the surface of a glass of water.

### Types of Caustics

- **Refraction Caustics**: Created when light passes through a transparent material and is focused by refraction.

- **Reflection Caustics**: Formed when light reflects off a curved, reflective surface, focusing the light into bright areas.

### Photon Mapping for Caustics

Photon mapping is particularly effective for simulating caustics. During the photon emission phase, photons are traced through the scene, recording their interactions with transparent or reflective surfaces.

### Example of Caustic Photon Mapping

void traceCausticPhoton(Photon& photon, PhotonMap& causticMap) {

# ILLUMINATING REALITIES: THE THEORY OF REAL-TIME RAY TRACING

```
while (true) {

Intersection hit;

if (scene.intersect(photon.ray, hit)) {

if (hit.material.isTransparent() || hit.material.isReflective()) {

causticMap.store(photon.position,     photon.direction, photon.power);

}

photon.bounce(hit.normal);

} else {

break;

}

}

}
```

## Rendering Caustics

To render caustics, the gathered caustic photons are used to estimate the radiance at points in the scene. This involves searching for nearby caustic photons and using their information to compute the bright patterns.

## Example of Caustic Rendering

```
Color renderCaustics(const PhotonMap& causticMap, const Vector3& position, const Vector3& normal) {
```

```
std::vector<Photon> causticPhotons = causticMap.getPhotons(position, causticRadius);

Color caustics(0, 0, 0);

for (const Photon& photon : causticPhotons) {

    float weight = max(dot(photon.direction, normal), 0.0);

    caustics += photon.power * weight;

}

return caustics / causticPhotons.size();

}
```

## Caustic Texture Mapping

An alternative approach to simulating caustics is using precomputed caustic textures. These textures are generated through physical simulations or artistic methods and applied to surfaces in the scene.

## Example of Caustic Texture Application

```
Color applyCausticTexture(const Texture& causticTexture, const Vector3& position) {

    Vector2 uv = convertPositionToUV(position);

    return causticTexture.getPixel(uv.x, uv.y);

}
```

## Optimizations for Caustics

Optimizations can be applied to improve the efficiency of caustic simulation, such as:

- **Adaptive Photon Emission**: Emitting more photons in regions where caustics are likely to occur.

- **Hierarchical Photon Storage**: Using hierarchical structures to store and retrieve caustic photons efficiently.

## Example of Adaptive Photon Emission

```
void emitAdaptiveCausticPhotons(const Light& light, PhotonMap& causticMap, int numPhotons) {

for (int i = 0; i < numPhotons; ++i) {

Photon photon = light.emitPhoton();

if (photon.isLikelyToCreateCaustic()) {

traceCausticPhoton(photon, causticMap);

}

}

}
```

## Conclusion

Simulating caustics is essential for achieving realistic rendering of scenes with transparent or reflective materials. Techniques like photon mapping and caustic texture mapping provide effective ways to simulate these complex lighting effects.

## 9.3. Subsurface Scattering for Realistic Skin

Subsurface scattering (SSS) is a phenomenon where light penetrates the surface of a translucent material, scatters internally, and exits at a different point. This effect is crucial for rendering realistic materials like skin, marble, and wax.

### Understanding Subsurface Scattering

In materials like skin, light does not just reflect off the surface but penetrates it, scatters multiple times, and then exits. This scattering softens the appearance and creates a natural glow.

### The BSSRDF Model

The Bidirectional Surface Scattering Reflectance Distribution Function (BSSRDF) models how light is absorbed and scattered beneath the surface of a material. This model is essential for simulating subsurface scattering.

### Example of BSSRDF Implementation

Color calculateBSSRDF(const Vector3& incident, const Vector3& exitant, const Vector3& normal, const Material& material) {

float distance = length(incident - exitant);

float scatter = exp(-distance / material.scatterRadius);

float weight = max(dot(normal, incident), 0.0) * max(dot(normal, exitant), 0.0);

**return** material.subsurfaceColor * scatter * weight;

}

# Multi-Layered Skin Model

Realistic skin rendering often uses a multi-layered model to represent the different layers of the skin, such as the epidermis, dermis, and subcutaneous tissue. Each layer has distinct optical properties.

## Example of Multi-Layered Skin

**struct** SkinLayer {

Color diffuseColor;

float scatterRadius;

};

**struct** SkinMaterial {

SkinLayer epidermis;

SkinLayer dermis;

SkinLayer subcutaneous;

};

Color calculateSkinSSS(const Vector3& incident, const Vector3& exitant, const Vector3& normal, const SkinMaterial& skin) {

Color sss(0, 0, 0);

sss += calculateBSSRDF(incident, exitant, normal, skin.epidermis);

sss += calculateBSSRDF(incident, exitant, normal, skin.dermis);

sss += calculateBSSRDF(incident, exitant, normal, skin.subcutaneous);

**return** sss;

}

## Precomputed Scattering Profiles

Precomputed scattering profiles are used to accelerate subsurface scattering calculations. These profiles represent the scattering behavior of light in different materials and can be quickly applied during rendering.

## Example of Applying Scattering Profile

Color applyScatteringProfile(const ScatteringProfile& profile, const Vector3& incident, const Vector3& exitant) {

float distance = length(incident - exitant);

**return** profile.getScattering(distance);

}

## Real-Time Subsurface Scattering

Achieving real-time subsurface scattering involves approximations and optimizations. Techniques like screen-space subsurface scattering (SSSS) and texture-space diffusion are commonly used in real-time applications.

## Example of Screen-Space Subsurface Scattering

void applySSSS(Image& image, const ScatteringProfile& profile) {

**for** (int y = 0; y < image.height; ++y) {

# ILLUMINATING REALITIES: THE THEORY OF REAL-TIME RAY TRACING

```
    for (int x = 0; x < image.width; ++x) {

        Vector3 incident = getIncidentLight(image, x, y);

        Vector3 exitant = getExitantLight(image, x, y);

        Color sss = applyScatteringProfile(profile, incident, exitant);

        image.setPixel(x, y, sss);

    }

  }

}
```

## Combining SSS with Other Effects

Subsurface scattering is often combined with other effects like ambient occlusion, global illumination, and specular reflection to create a complete and realistic rendering.

## Example of Combined Effects

```
Color renderSkin(const Ray& ray, const Scene& scene, int depth, const ScatteringProfile& profile) {

    Intersection hit;

    if (scene.intersect(ray, hit)) {

        Vector3 incident = calculateIncidentLight(hit.position, scene.lights);

        Vector3 exitant = calculateExitantLight(hit.position, scene.camera);

        Color sss = applyScatteringProfile(profile, incident, exitant);
```

```
Color ao = calculateAmbientOcclusion(hit.position, scene);

Color gi = calculateGlobalIllumination(hit.position, scene);

Color specular = calculateSpecularReflection(hit.position, scene);

return hit.material.color * (sss + ao + gi + specular);

}

return scene.backgroundColor;

}
```

## Conclusion

Subsurface scattering is essential for rendering realistic skin and other translucent materials. Techniques like the BSSRDF model, multi-layered skin models, precomputed scattering profiles, and real-time approximations provide effective ways to simulate this complex lighting effect.

## 9.4. Volumetric Lighting Effects

Volumetric lighting simulates the interaction of light with particles in the atmosphere, such as fog, smoke, and dust. These effects add depth and atmosphere to scenes, creating a more immersive visual experience.

### Understanding Volumetric Lighting

Volumetric lighting involves scattering and absorption of light as it passes through a participating medium. This creates effects like light shafts, god rays, and volumetric fog.

## The Volume Rendering Equation

The volume rendering equation describes the transfer of light in a participating medium, accounting for absorption, out-scattering, and in-scattering.

## Example of Volume Rendering Equation

```
Color calculateVolumetricLighting(const Ray& ray, const Volume& volume, const Scene& scene) {

Color radiance(0, 0, 0);

Color transmittance(1, 1, 1);

float stepSize = 0.1;

for (float t = 0; t < ray.length; t += stepSize) {

Vector3 position = ray.origin + t * ray.direction;

Color extinction = volume.getExtinction(position);

transmittance *= exp(-extinction * stepSize);

Color inScattering = volume.getInScattering(position, ray.direction, scene.lights);

radiance += transmittance * inScattering * stepSize;

}

return radiance;

}
```

## Light Shafts and God Rays

Light shafts, or god rays, occur when light passes through a medium with varying density, such as shafts of sunlight filtering through trees or windows. These effects can be simulated using volumetric lighting techniques.

## Example of Light Shaft Simulation

```
Color calculateLightShafts(const Ray& ray, const Volume& volume, const Light& light) {

Color shafts(0, 0, 0);

float stepSize = 0.1;

for (float t = 0; t < ray.length; t += stepSize) {

Vector3 position = ray.origin + t * ray.direction;

if (volume.isLightBlocking(position)) {

Color lightColor = light.getColor(position);

shafts += lightColor * exp(-t * volume.getExtinction(position)) * stepSize;

}
}
return shafts;
}
```

## Volumetric Fog

Volumetric fog simulates the scattering of light by particles in the atmosphere, creating a hazy appearance. It is often used to add mood and atmosphere to scenes.

## Example of Volumetric Fog Calculation

```
Color calculateVolumetricFog(const Ray& ray, const Volume& volume, const Scene& scene) {

Color fog(0, 0, 0);

Color transmittance(1, 1, 1);

float stepSize = 0.1;

for (float t = 0; t < ray.length; t += stepSize) {

Vector3 position = ray.origin + t * ray.direction;

Color extinction = volume.getExtinction(position);

transmittance *= exp(-extinction * stepSize);

Color inScattering = volume.getInScattering(position, ray.direction, scene.lights);

fog += transmittance * inScattering * stepSize;

}

return fog;

}
```

## Real-Time Volumetric Lighting

Achieving real-time volumetric lighting involves approximations and optimizations, such as screen-space techniques, voxel-based methods, and precomputed volume textures.

## Example of Screen-Space Volumetric Lighting

```
void applyScreenSpaceVolumetrics(Image& image, const Volume& volume, const Scene& scene) {

for (int y = 0; y < image.height; ++y) {

for (int x = 0; x < image.width; ++x) {

Ray ray = generateRay(x, y, scene.camera);

Color volumetricLighting = calculateVolumetricLighting(ray, volume, scene);

image.setPixel(x, y, image.getPixel(x, y) + volumetricLighting);

}

}

}
```

## Voxel-Based Volumetrics

Voxel-based methods divide the scene into a grid of voxels, each storing volumetric lighting information. This allows for efficient lighting calculations and real-time updates.

## Example of Voxel-Based Volumetric Lighting

```
void calculateVoxelVolumetrics(VoxelGrid& voxelGrid, const Volume& volume, const Scene& scene) {

    for (int z = 0; z < voxelGrid.depth; ++z) {

    for (int y = 0; y < voxelGrid.height; ++y) {

    for (int x = 0; x < voxelGrid.width; ++x) {

    Vector3 position = voxelGrid.getPosition(x, y, z);

    voxelGrid.setValue(x, y, z, calculateVolumetricLighting(Ray(position, scene.camera.direction), volume, scene));

    }

    }

    }

}
```

## Combining Volumetric Lighting with Other Effects

Volumetric lighting is often combined with other effects, such as shadows, reflections, and global illumination, to create a cohesive and realistic scene.

## Example of Combined Volumetric Effects

```
Color renderSceneWithVolumetrics(const Ray& ray, const Scene& scene, const Volume& volume) {

    Intersection hit;
```

```
if (scene.intersect(ray, hit)) {

    Color surfaceColor = calculateSurfaceShading(hit, scene);

    Color volumetricLighting = calculateVolumetricLighting(ray, volume, scene);

    return surfaceColor + volumetricLighting;

}

return calculateVolumetricLighting(ray, volume, scene);

}
```

## Conclusion

Volumetric lighting effects, such as light shafts, god rays, and volumetric fog, add depth and atmosphere to scenes. Techniques like the volume rendering equation, screen-space methods, and voxel-based methods provide effective ways to simulate these complex lighting interactions.

## 9.5. Implementing Advanced Lighting in Real-Time Systems

Implementing advanced lighting in real-time systems involves balancing visual quality and performance. Techniques such as deferred shading, real-time ray tracing, and hybrid rendering are employed to achieve realistic lighting effects efficiently.

### Deferred Shading

Deferred shading is a rendering technique that decouples the lighting calculations from the geometry pass. This allows for complex lighting with many light sources without a significant performance hit.

## Example of Deferred Shading

```
void renderDeferredShading(const Scene& scene, Image& gBuffer, Image& output) {

// Geometry pass: fill G-buffer

for (int y = 0; y < gBuffer.height; ++y) {

for (int x = 0; x < gBuffer.width; ++x) {

Ray ray = generateRay(x, y, scene.camera);

Intersection hit;

if (scene.intersect(ray, hit)) {

gBuffer.setPixel(x, y, hit.material);

}

}

}

// Lighting pass: calculate lighting from G-buffer

for (int y = 0; y < output.height; ++y) {

for (int x = 0; x < output.width; ++x) {

Material material = gBuffer.getPixel(x, y);

Color lighting = calculateLighting(material, scene.lights);

output.setPixel(x, y, lighting);
```

}

}

}

## Real-Time Ray Tracing

Real-time ray tracing leverages modern GPUs to perform ray tracing operations at interactive frame rates. This allows for accurate reflections, refractions, and global illumination.

## Example of Real-Time Ray Tracing

```
void renderRealTimeRayTracing(const Scene& scene, Image& output) {

for (int y = 0; y < output.height; ++y) {

for (int x = 0; x < output.width; ++x) {

Ray ray = generateRay(x, y, scene.camera);

Color color = traceRay(ray, scene, 5);

output.setPixel(x, y, color);

}

}

}

Color traceRay(const Ray& ray, const Scene& scene, int depth) {

if (depth <= 0) return Color(0, 0, 0);

Intersection hit;
```

# ILLUMINATING REALITIES: THE THEORY OF REAL-TIME RAY TRACING

```
if (scene.intersect(ray, hit)) {

    Vector3 reflectedDir = calculateReflection(ray.direction, hit.normal);

    Ray reflectedRay(hit.position, reflectedDir);

    Color reflectedColor = traceRay(reflectedRay, scene, depth - 1);

    Vector3 refractedDir = calculateRefraction(ray.direction, hit.normal, hit.material.ior);

    Ray refractedRay(hit.position, refractedDir);

    Color refractedColor = traceRay(refractedRay, scene, depth - 1);

    float reflectance = calculateFresnel(ray.direction, hit.normal, hit.material.ior);

    return hit.material.color * (reflectedColor * reflectance + refractedColor * (1.0 - reflectance));

}

return scene.backgroundColor;

}
```

## Hybrid Rendering Techniques

Hybrid rendering combines rasterization and ray tracing to achieve high-quality visuals with real-time performance. This approach leverages the strengths of both methods.

## Example of Hybrid Rendering

```
void renderHybrid(const Scene& scene, Image& output) {
```

```
// Rasterize primary geometry
rasterizeScene(scene, output);
// Add ray-traced reflections and refractions
for (int y = 0; y < output.height; ++y) {
    for (int x = 0; x < output.width; ++x) {
        Ray ray = generateRay(x, y, scene.camera);
        Color tracedColor = traceRay(ray, scene, 3);
        output.setPixel(x, y, mix(output.getPixel(x, y), tracedColor, 0.5));
    }
}
}
```

## Dynamic Lighting and Shadows

Dynamic lighting and shadows are crucial for interactive applications. Techniques such as shadow mapping, screen-space reflections, and real-time global illumination enhance the realism of dynamic scenes.

## Example of Dynamic Shadow Mapping

```
void renderShadowMap(const Light& light, const Scene& scene, Image& shadowMap) {
    for (int y = 0; y < shadowMap.height; ++y) {
        for (int x = 0; x < shadowMap.width; ++x) {
```

```
Ray ray = generateLightRay(x, y, light);

Intersection hit;

if (scene.intersect(ray, hit)) {

shadowMap.setPixel(x, y, hit.distance);

} else {

shadowMap.setPixel(x, y, light.farPlane);

}

}

}

}

bool isInShadow(const Vector3& position, const Light& light, const Image& shadowMap) {

Vector2 shadowCoord = projectToShadowMap(position, light);

float shadowDepth = shadowMap.getPixel(shadowCoord.x, shadowCoord.y);

return position.z > shadowDepth;

}
```

## Temporal Accumulation

Temporal accumulation techniques improve image quality by accumulating information over multiple frames. This reduces noise and enhances the stability of lighting effects.

### Example of Temporal Accumulation

```
void accumulateFrames(const Image& currentFrame, Image& accumulatedFrame, int frameCount) {

for (int y = 0; y < currentFrame.height; ++y) {

for (int x = 0; x < currentFrame.width; ++x) {

Color currentColor = currentFrame.getPixel(x, y);

Color accumulatedColor = accumulatedFrame.getPixel(x, y);

accumulatedFrame.setPixel(x, y, (accumulatedColor * frameCount + currentColor) / (frameCount + 1));

}

}

}
```

### Conclusion

Implementing advanced lighting in real-time systems requires a combination of techniques to balance performance and visual quality. Deferred shading, real-time ray tracing, hybrid rendering, dynamic lighting, and temporal accumulation are key methods for achieving realistic and interactive lighting effects.

# Chapter 10: Ray Tracing in Gaming

## 10.1. The Impact of Ray Tracing on Video Game Graphics

Ray tracing has revolutionized video game graphics by enabling more realistic lighting, shadows, reflections, and global illumination. This advancement significantly enhances the visual fidelity and immersion of gaming experiences.

## Enhanced Lighting and Shadows

Ray tracing allows for accurate simulation of lighting and shadows, resulting in more realistic scenes. Dynamic lighting, soft shadows, and global illumination contribute to a natural and immersive environment.

## Example of Ray-Traced Shadows

Color calculateRayTracedShadow(const Ray& shadowRay, const Scene& scene) {

Intersection hit;

**if** (scene.intersect(shadowRay, hit)) {

**return** Color(0, 0, 0); // *In shadow*

}

**return** Color(1, 1, 1); // *Not in shadow*

}

## Realistic Reflections

Real-time ray tracing enables accurate reflections on surfaces such as water, glass, and metal. This adds depth and realism to scenes, enhancing the overall visual quality.

## Example of Ray-Traced Reflections

Color traceRayForReflection(const Ray& ray, const Scene& scene, int depth) {

```
if (depth <= 0) return Color(0, 0, 0);
```

Intersection hit;

```
if (scene.intersect(ray, hit)) {
```

Vector3 reflectedDir = calculateReflection(ray.direction, hit.normal);

Ray reflectedRay(hit.position, reflectedDir);

**return** traceRayForReflection(reflectedRay, scene, depth - 1);

}

**return** scene.backgroundColor;

}

## Global Illumination

Ray tracing simulates global illumination by tracing light paths that bounce off multiple surfaces. This results in realistic light interactions and color bleeding, contributing to a cohesive and immersive scene.

## Example of Global Illumination

Color traceRayForGI(const Ray& ray, const Scene& scene, int depth) {

**if** (depth <= 0) **return** Color(0, 0, 0);

Intersection hit;

**if** (scene.intersect(ray, hit)) {

Color indirectLight(0, 0, 0);

```
for (int i = 0; i < numSamples; ++i) {

Vector3 newDir = sampleHemisphere(hit.normal);

Ray newRay(hit.position, newDir);

indirectLight += traceRayForGI(newRay, scene, depth - 1);

}

indirectLight /= numSamples;

return hit.material.color * (indirectLight + hit.material.emission);

}

return scene.backgroundColor;

}
```

## Increased Realism in Game Environments

The increased realism brought by ray tracing enhances the immersion of game environments. Detailed reflections, accurate shadows, and natural lighting make game worlds more believable.

## Example of Enhanced Game Environment

```
void renderEnhancedEnvironment(const Scene& scene, Image& output) {

for (int y = 0; y < output.height; ++y) {

for (int x = 0; x < output.width; ++x) {

Ray ray = generateRay(x, y, scene.camera);

Color color = traceRay(ray, scene, 5);
```

output.setPixel(x, y, color);

}

}

}

## Improved Material Representation

Ray tracing improves the representation of materials by accurately simulating their interactions with light. This leads to realistic rendering of various surfaces, from rough and diffuse to smooth and reflective.

## Example of Material Representation

Color renderMaterial(const Ray& ray, const Scene& scene, const Material& material, int depth) {

Intersection hit;

**if** (scene.intersect(ray, hit)) {

Color reflectedColor = traceRayForReflection(ray, scene, depth - 1);

Color refractedColor = traceRayForRefraction(ray, scene, depth - 1);

**return** material.color * (reflectedColor + refractedColor);

}

**return** scene.backgroundColor;

}

## The Role of Hardware

Modern GPUs with dedicated ray tracing cores have made real-time ray tracing feasible. These hardware advancements allow for efficient computation of ray tracing operations, enabling high-quality graphics at interactive frame rates.

## Example of Hardware Utilization

```
void renderWithRTX(const Scene& scene, Image& output) {

for (int y = 0; y < output.height; ++y) {

for (int x = 0; x < output.width; ++x) {

Ray ray = generateRay(x, y, scene.camera);

Color color = traceRayWithRTX(ray, scene, 5);

output.setPixel(x, y, color);

}

}

}
```

## Future Prospects

The future of ray tracing in gaming looks promising with continued advancements in hardware and software. As ray tracing technology becomes more widespread, we can expect even more realistic and immersive gaming experiences.

## Conclusion

Ray tracing has significantly impacted video game graphics by enhancing lighting, shadows, reflections, and global illumination. These advancements create more realistic and immersive game environments, improving the overall gaming experience.

## 10.2. Challenges of Implementing Ray Tracing in Games

Implementing ray tracing in games presents several challenges, including performance constraints, integration with existing rendering pipelines, and maintaining visual consistency.

### Performance Constraints

Ray tracing is computationally intensive, requiring significant processing power. Achieving real-time performance while maintaining high-quality visuals is a major challenge.

### Optimization Techniques

To address performance constraints, various optimization techniques are employed, such as:

- **Acceleration Structures**: Using BVH or KD-Trees to speed up ray-scene intersection tests.

- **Adaptive Sampling**: Reducing the number of rays traced in areas with low visual importance.

- **Level of Detail**: Adjusting the level of detail based on the distance from the camera.

## Example of Adaptive Sampling

```
Color traceAdaptiveRay(const Ray& ray, const Scene& scene, int depth, float threshold) {

if (depth <= 0) return Color(0, 0, 0);

Intersection hit;

if (scene.intersect(ray, hit)) {

Color directColor = calculateDirectIllumination(ray, hit, scene);

if (luminance(directColor) < threshold) return directColor;

Vector3 reflectedDir = calculateReflection(ray.direction, hit.normal);

Ray reflectedRay(hit.position, reflectedDir);

Color reflectedColor = traceAdaptiveRay(reflectedRay, scene, depth - 1, threshold * 0.5);

Vector3 refractedDir = calculateRefraction(ray.direction, hit.normal, hit.material.ior);

Ray refractedRay(hit.position, refractedDir);

Color refractedColor = traceAdaptiveRay(refractedRay, scene, depth - 1, threshold * 0.5);

return hit.material.color * (directColor + reflectedColor + refractedColor);

}

return scene.backgroundColor;
```

}

## Integration with Existing Pipelines

Integrating ray tracing into existing rasterization-based rendering pipelines requires significant changes. Ensuring compatibility and maintaining a smooth workflow are key challenges.

## Hybrid Rendering Approaches

Hybrid rendering approaches combine rasterization and ray tracing to leverage the strengths of both methods. This involves rendering primary geometry with rasterization and using ray tracing for reflections, refractions, and global illumination.

## Example of Hybrid Rendering Integration

```
void renderHybridScene(const Scene& scene, Image& output) {
// Rasterize primary geometry
rasterizeScene(scene, output);
// Add ray-traced reflections and refractions
for (int y = 0; y < output.height; ++y) {
for (int x = 0; x < output.width; ++x) {
Ray ray = generateRay(x, y, scene.camera);
Color tracedColor = traceRay(ray, scene, 3);
output.setPixel(x, y, mix(output.getPixel(x, y), tracedColor, 0.5));
}
}
```

}

## Maintaining Visual Consistency

Maintaining visual consistency between rasterized and ray-traced elements is crucial for a cohesive visual experience. Differences in lighting, shadows, and reflections can create noticeable artifacts.

## Ensuring Consistent Shading Models

To maintain consistency, it is essential to use the same shading models and material definitions for both rasterization and ray tracing. This ensures that the visual appearance remains consistent across different rendering techniques.

## Example of Consistent Shading Model

Color calculateShading(const Intersection& hit, const Scene& scene) {

Color diffuse = calculateDiffuse(hit, scene.lights);

Color specular = calculateSpecular(hit, scene.lights);

**return** hit.material.color * (diffuse + specular);

}

## Managing Resource Constraints

Ray tracing requires significant memory and computational resources. Efficient management of these resources is crucial to avoid performance bottlenecks and ensure smooth gameplay.

## Example of Resource Management

```
void manageResources(const Scene& scene) {
// Load only necessary assets
loadAssets(scene.requiredAssets);
// Optimize memory usage
optimizeMemory(scene);
// Balance CPU and GPU workloads
balanceWorkloads(scene);
}
```

## Handling Dynamic Scenes

Dynamic scenes with moving objects, changing lighting, and interactive elements pose additional challenges for ray tracing. Ensuring real-time performance in such scenarios requires adaptive techniques.

## Example of Dynamic Scene Handling

```
void renderDynamicScene(const Scene& scene, Image& output) {
for (int y = 0; y < output.height; ++y) {
for (int x = 0; x < output.width; ++x) {
Ray ray = generateRay(x, y, scene.camera);
Color color = traceRay(ray, scene, 5);
output.setPixel(x, y, color);
```

}

}

}

## Future Directions

Continued advancements in hardware and optimization techniques will address many challenges of implementing ray tracing in games. As technology evolves, we can expect more widespread adoption and improved performance.

## Conclusion

Implementing ray tracing in games presents several challenges, including performance constraints, integration with existing pipelines, maintaining visual consistency, managing resources, and handling dynamic scenes. Overcoming these challenges is crucial for achieving realistic and immersive gaming experiences.

## 10.3. Case Studies: Games that Utilize Ray Tracing

Exploring case studies of games that successfully implement ray tracing provides valuable insights into the techniques and optimizations used to achieve high-quality visuals.

### Case Study 1: "Control" by Remedy Entertainment

"Control" is a notable example of a game that utilizes ray tracing to enhance its visual quality. The game features ray-traced reflections, shadows, and global illumination, creating a highly immersive environment.

## Ray-Traced Reflections in "Control"

"Control" uses ray-traced reflections to accurately simulate reflections on surfaces like glass, water, and polished floors. This adds depth and realism to the game's environments.

### Example of Reflection Rendering

Color renderReflections(const Ray& ray, const Scene& scene, int depth) {

**if** (depth <= 0) **return** Color(0, 0, 0);

Intersection hit;

**if** (scene.intersect(ray, hit)) {

Vector3 reflectedDir = calculateReflection(ray.direction, hit.normal);

Ray reflectedRay(hit.position, reflectedDir);

**return** traceRay(reflectedRay, scene, depth - 1);

}

**return** scene.backgroundColor;

}

## Global Illumination in "Control"

The game also uses ray tracing to simulate global illumination, enhancing the overall lighting quality. This technique captures the subtle interplay of light between surfaces, creating a cohesive and realistic scene.

## Example of Global Illumination Rendering

```
Color renderGlobalIllumination(const Ray& ray, const Scene& scene, int depth) {

if (depth <= 0) return Color(0, 0, 0);

Intersection hit;

if (scene.intersect(ray, hit)) {

Color indirectLight(0, 0, 0);

for (int i = 0; i < numSamples; ++i) {

Vector3 newDir = sampleHemisphere(hit.normal);

Ray newRay(hit.position, newDir);

indirectLight += traceRay(newRay, scene, depth - 1);

}

indirectLight /= numSamples;

return hit.material.color * (indirectLight + hit.material.emission);

}

return scene.backgroundColor;

}
```

## Case Study 2: "Metro Exodus" by 4A Games

"Metro Exodus" is another game that leverages ray tracing to achieve stunning visuals. The game features ray-traced global illumination and ambient occlusion, creating a realistic and atmospheric experience.

## Ray-Traced Ambient Occlusion in "Metro Exodus"

Ray-traced ambient occlusion in "Metro Exodus" enhances the depth and realism of scenes by simulating the occlusion of ambient light in crevices and corners.

## Example of Ambient Occlusion Rendering

```
Color renderAmbientOcclusion(const Intersection& hit, const Scene& scene) {

Color ao(0, 0, 0);

for (int i = 0; i < numSamples; ++i) {

Vector3 sampleDir = sampleHemisphere(hit.normal);

Ray sampleRay(hit.position, sampleDir);

if (!scene.intersect(sampleRay)) {

ao += Color(1, 1, 1);

}

}

ao /= numSamples;

return ao * hit.material.color;

}
```

## Global Illumination in "Metro Exodus"

The game uses ray tracing to achieve realistic global illumination, capturing the complex interactions of light in both outdoor and indoor environments.

## Example of Global Illumination Rendering

```
Color renderMetroExodusGI(const Ray& ray, const Scene& scene, int depth) {

if (depth <= 0) return Color(0, 0, 0);

Intersection hit;

if (scene.intersect(ray, hit)) {

Color indirectLight(0, 0, 0);

for (int i = 0; i < numSamples; ++i) {

Vector3 newDir = sampleHemisphere(hit.normal);

Ray newRay(hit.position, newDir);

indirectLight += traceRay(newRay, scene, depth - 1);

}

indirectLight /= numSamples;

return hit.material.color * (indirectLight + hit.material.emission);

}

return scene.backgroundColor;

}
```

## Case Study 3: "Cyberpunk 2077" by CD Projekt Red

"Cyberpunk 2077" uses ray tracing to enhance its neon-lit futuristic cityscape. The game features ray-traced reflections, shadows, and global illumination, contributing to its highly detailed and immersive environment.

## Ray-Traced Shadows in "Cyberpunk 2077"

Ray-traced shadows in "Cyberpunk 2077" provide accurate and dynamic shadows, enhancing the depth and realism of the game's environments.

## Example of Shadow Rendering

Color renderShadows(const Ray& shadowRay, const Scene& scene) {

Intersection hit;

**if** (scene.intersect(shadowRay, hit)) {

**return** Color(0, 0, 0); // *In shadow*

}

**return** Color(1, 1, 1); // *Not in shadow*

}

## Reflections and Global Illumination in "Cyberpunk 2077"

The game uses ray tracing to achieve realistic reflections and global illumination, capturing the intricate lighting interactions in its urban environments.

## Example of Reflection and GI Rendering

Color renderCyberpunkReflectionsGI(const Ray& ray, const Scene& scene, int depth) {

# ILLUMINATING REALITIES: THE THEORY OF REAL-TIME RAY TRACING

```
if (depth <= 0) return Color(0, 0, 0);

Intersection hit;

if (scene.intersect(ray, hit)) {

    Vector3 reflectedDir = calculateReflection(ray.direction, hit.normal);

    Ray reflectedRay(hit.position, reflectedDir);

    Color reflectedColor = traceRay(reflectedRay, scene, depth - 1);

    Color indirectLight(0, 0, 0);

    for (int i = 0; i < numSamples; ++i) {

        Vector3 newDir = sampleHemisphere(hit.normal);

        Ray newRay(hit.position, newDir);

        indirectLight += traceRay(newRay, scene, depth - 1);

    }

    indirectLight /= numSamples;

    return hit.material.color * (reflectedColor + indirectLight + hit.material.emission);

}

return scene.backgroundColor;

}
```

## Conclusion

The case studies of "Control," "Metro Exodus," and "Cyberpunk 2077" demonstrate the potential of ray tracing to enhance video game graphics. By leveraging ray tracing for reflections, shadows, and global illumination, these games achieve highly realistic and immersive visual experiences.

## 10.4. Future Trends in Ray Tracing for Gaming

The future of ray tracing in gaming is promising, with ongoing advancements in hardware and software paving the way for more widespread adoption and enhanced visual fidelity.

### Advancements in GPU Technology

Continued improvements in GPU technology, such as increased ray tracing cores and optimized architectures, will enable more efficient and powerful ray tracing capabilities.

### Example of GPU Utilization

```
void renderWithFutureGPU(const Scene& scene, Image& output) {
for (int y = 0; y < output.height; ++y) {
for (int x = 0; x < output.width; ++x) {
Ray ray = generateRay(x, y, scene.camera);
Color color = traceRayWithFutureGPU(ray, scene, 5);
output.setPixel(x, y, color);
```

# ILLUMINATING REALITIES: THE THEORY OF REAL-TIME RAY TRACING

}

}

}

## Real-Time Path Tracing

Real-time path tracing, which traces multiple light paths to achieve accurate global illumination, is becoming more feasible with advances in hardware and optimization techniques.

## Example of Real-Time Path Tracing

```
Color traceRealTimePath(const Ray& ray, const Scene& scene, int depth) {

if (depth <= 0) return Color(0, 0, 0);

Intersection hit;

if (scene.intersect(ray, hit)) {

Color indirectLight(0, 0, 0);

for (int i = 0; i < numSamples; ++i) {

Vector3 newDir = sampleHemisphere(hit.normal);

Ray newRay(hit.position, newDir);

indirectLight += traceRealTimePath(newRay, scene, depth - 1);

}

indirectLight /= numSamples;

return hit.material.color * (indirectLight + hit.material.emission);
```

}

**return** scene.backgroundColor;

}

## AI and Machine Learning Integration

Integrating AI and machine learning techniques can optimize ray tracing operations, such as denoising, adaptive sampling, and real-time global illumination.

## Example of AI-Optimized Ray Tracing

Color traceRayWithAI(const Ray& ray, const Scene& scene, int depth, const AIModel& aiModel) {

**if** (depth <= 0) **return** Color(0, 0, 0);

Intersection hit;

**if** (scene.intersect(ray, hit)) {

Vector3 reflectedDir = calculateReflection(ray.direction, hit.normal);

Ray reflectedRay(hit.position, reflectedDir);

Color reflectedColor = aiModel.optimize(traceRay(reflectedRay, scene, depth - 1));

Color indirectLight(0, 0, 0);

**for** (int i = 0; i < numSamples; ++i) {

Vector3 newDir = sampleHemisphere(hit.normal);

Ray newRay(hit.position, newDir);

```
indirectLight += traceRay(newRay, scene, depth - 1);
}
indirectLight /= numSamples;
return hit.material.color * (reflectedColor + indirectLight + hit.material.emission);
}
return scene.backgroundColor;
}
```

## Hybrid Rendering Techniques

Hybrid rendering techniques will continue to evolve, combining the strengths of rasterization and ray tracing to achieve high-quality visuals with real-time performance.

## Example of Advanced Hybrid Rendering

```
void renderAdvancedHybrid(const Scene& scene, Image& output) {
// Rasterize primary geometry
rasterizeScene(scene, output);
// Add ray-traced reflections, refractions, and global illumination
for (int y = 0; y < output.height; ++y) {
for (int x = 0; x < output.width; ++x) {
Ray ray = generateRay(x, y, scene.camera);
```

Color tracedColor = traceRay(ray, scene, 5);

output.setPixel(x, y, mix(output.getPixel(x, y), tracedColor, 0.5));

}

}

}

## Cloud-Based Ray Tracing

Cloud-based ray tracing leverages powerful remote servers to perform computationally intensive ray tracing operations, streaming the results to the user's device. This approach can enable high-quality ray tracing on lower-end hardware.

## Example of Cloud-Based Ray Tracing

void renderWithCloudRayTracing(const Scene& scene, Image& output, const CloudServer& server) {

**for** (int y = 0; y < output.height; ++y) {

**for** (int x = 0; x < output.width; ++x) {

Ray ray = generateRay(x, y, scene.camera);

Color color = server.traceRay(ray, scene);

output.setPixel(x, y, color);

}

}

}

## Conclusion

The future of ray tracing in gaming is bright, with advancements in GPU technology, real-time path tracing, AI integration, hybrid rendering, and cloud-based solutions driving the evolution of game graphics. These trends will enable even more realistic and immersive gaming experiences.

## 10.5. Integrating Ray Tracing with Traditional Rendering Techniques

Integrating ray tracing with traditional rendering techniques involves combining the strengths of rasterization and ray tracing to achieve high-quality visuals with real-time performance.

### Hybrid Rendering Approaches

Hybrid rendering approaches use rasterization for primary rendering tasks and ray tracing for complex lighting effects, such as reflections, refractions, and global illumination.

### Example of Hybrid Rendering

```
void renderHybridScene(const Scene& scene, Image& output) {

// Rasterize primary geometry

rasterizeScene(scene, output);

// Add ray-traced reflections and refractions

for (int y = 0; y < output.height; ++y) {

for (int x = 0; x < output.width; ++x) {

Ray ray = generateRay(x, y, scene.camera);
```

```
Color tracedColor = traceRay(ray, scene, 3);

output.setPixel(x, y, mix(output.getPixel(x, y), tracedColor, 0.5));
    }
  }
}
```

## Deferred Shading with Ray Tracing

Deferred shading decouples geometry processing from lighting calculations, enabling complex lighting with many light sources. Ray tracing can be integrated into the lighting pass for enhanced effects.

## Example of Deferred Shading with Ray Tracing

```
void renderDeferredShadingWithRayTracing(const Scene& scene, Image& gBuffer, Image& output) {

// Geometry pass: fill G-buffer

for (int y = 0; y < gBuffer.height; ++y) {

for (int x = 0; x < gBuffer.width; ++x) {

Ray ray = generateRay(x, y, scene.camera);

Intersection hit;

if (scene.intersect(ray, hit)) {

gBuffer.setPixel(x, y, hit.material);

}
```

```
    }
  }
  // Lighting pass: calculate lighting from G-buffer
  for (int y = 0; y < output.height; ++y) {
    for (int x = 0; x < output.width; ++x) {
      Material material = gBuffer.getPixel(x, y);
      Color lighting = calculateLighting(material, scene.lights);
      output.setPixel(x, y, lighting);
    }
  }
  // Add ray-traced effects
  for (int y = 0; y < output.height; ++y) {
    for (int x = 0; x < output.width; ++x) {
      Ray ray = generateRay(x, y, scene.camera);
      Color tracedColor = traceRay(ray, scene, 3);
      output.setPixel(x, y, mix(output.getPixel(x, y), tracedColor, 0.5));
    }
  }
}
```

## Screen-Space Reflections

Screen-space reflections (SSR) approximate reflections by reusing information from the current frame. Ray tracing can be used to enhance SSR, providing more accurate reflections.

## Example of Screen-Space Reflections with Ray Tracing

```
void renderSSRWithRayTracing(const Scene& scene, Image& screenBuffer, Image& output) {
    // Screen-space reflections
    for (int y = 0; y < screenBuffer.height; ++y) {
        for (int x = 0; x < screenBuffer.width; ++x) {
            Ray ray = generateRayFromScreen(x, y, screenBuffer);
            Color ssrColor = calculateSSR(ray, screenBuffer);
            output.setPixel(x, y, ssrColor);
        }
    }
    // Enhance with ray tracing
    for (int y = 0; y < output.height; ++y) {
        for (int x = 0; x < output.width; ++x) {
            Ray ray = generateRay(x, y, scene.camera);
            Color tracedColor = traceRay(ray, scene, 3);
            output.setPixel(x, y, mix(output.getPixel(x, y), tracedColor, 0.5));
```

}

}

}

## Combining Ray Tracing and Rasterization for Shadows

Combining ray-traced and rasterized shadows can enhance the realism of scenes while maintaining performance. Rasterization handles primary shadows, while ray tracing refines shadow details.

## Example of Combined Shadow Rendering

void renderShadowsHybrid(const Scene& scene, Image& shadowMap, Image& output) {

// Rasterize primary shadows

renderShadowMap(scene.lights[0], scene, shadowMap);

// Enhance shadows with ray tracing

for (int y = 0; y < output.height; ++y) {

for (int x = 0; x < output.width; ++x) {

Ray shadowRay = generateShadowRay(x, y, scene.camera, scene.lights[0]);

if (isInShadow(shadowRay, shadowMap)) {

output.setPixel(x, y, Color(0, 0, 0)); // In shadow

} else {

```
Color tracedShadow = traceRayForShadows(shadowRay, scene, 3);

output.setPixel(x, y, mix(output.getPixel(x, y), tracedShadow, 0.5));
        }
      }
    }
}
```

## Volumetric Lighting with Ray Tracing

Volumetric lighting effects, such as god rays and volumetric fog, can be enhanced with ray tracing. This provides accurate light scattering and absorption in participating media.

## Example of Volumetric Lighting with Ray Tracing

```
void renderVolumetricLighting(const Scene& scene, const Volume& volume, Image& output) {
    for (int y = 0; y < output.height; ++y) {
        for (int x = 0; x < output.width; ++x) {
            Ray ray = generateRay(x, y, scene.camera);
            Color volumetricLighting = calculateVolumetricLighting(ray, volume, scene);
            output.setPixel(x, y, volumetricLighting);
        }
```

```
}
// Enhance with ray-traced effects
for (int y = 0; y < output.height; ++y) {
for (int x = 0; x < output.width; ++x) {
Ray ray = generateRay(x, y, scene.camera);
Color tracedColor = traceRay(ray, scene, 3);
output.setPixel(x, y, mix(output.getPixel(x, y), tracedColor, 0.5));
}
}
}
```

## Conclusion

Integrating ray tracing with traditional rendering techniques involves combining rasterization and ray tracing to achieve high-quality visuals with real-time performance. Hybrid rendering, deferred shading, screen-space reflections, combined shadows, and volumetric lighting are key methods for achieving this integration.

# Chapter 11: Ray Tracing in Film and Animation

## 11.1. Historical Use of Ray Tracing in Movies

Ray tracing has a rich history in the film industry, revolutionizing how visual effects (VFX) are created. The technique has enabled filmmakers to produce stunningly realistic images, pushing the boundaries of what is visually possible.

## Early Beginnings

The use of ray tracing in movies began in the 1980s with the advent of computer-generated imagery (CGI). One of the earliest examples is the movie "Tron" (1982), which utilized ray tracing for some of its CGI sequences.

## The Rise of CGI

During the 1990s, ray tracing became more prevalent as computing power increased. Movies like "Jurassic Park" (1993) used CGI extensively, with ray tracing contributing to the realism of the dinosaurs.

## Example of Early Ray Tracing

**struct** Ray {

Vector3 origin;

Vector3 direction;

};

**struct** Color {

float r, g, b;

};

Color traceRay(const Ray& ray, const Scene& scene) {

Intersection hit;

```
if (scene.intersect(ray, hit)) {

    return hit.material.color; // Simplified shading

}

return Color(0, 0, 0); // Background color

}
```

## Major Milestones

The release of "Toy Story" (1995) by Pixar marked a significant milestone as the first fully CGI-animated feature film. Ray tracing played a crucial role in achieving the film's visual fidelity.

## The 2000s and Beyond

The 2000s saw further advancements with films like "The Lord of the Rings" trilogy (2001-2003) and "Avatar" (2009). These films used ray tracing to create complex lighting effects, realistic reflections, and detailed textures.

## Example of Advanced Ray Tracing

```
Color traceAdvancedRay(const Ray& ray, const Scene& scene) {

Intersection hit;

if (scene.intersect(ray, hit)) {

Vector3 reflectedDir = reflect(ray.direction, hit.normal);

Ray reflectedRay(hit.position, reflectedDir);

Color reflectedColor = traceAdvancedRay(reflectedRay, scene);

return hit.material.color * reflectedColor;
```

}

**return** Color(0, 0, 0); *// Background color*

}

## Photorealism in Modern Films

Modern films strive for photorealism, and ray tracing is a key technology in achieving this goal. Movies like "The Lion King" (2019) and "Blade Runner 2049" (2017) showcase the power of ray tracing in creating lifelike visuals.

## Ray Tracing in Animation

In animation, studios like Pixar and DreamWorks use ray tracing to render detailed, realistic scenes. The technology allows animators to achieve complex lighting and shading effects that enhance the storytelling.

## Example of Animation Ray Tracing

**struct** Material {

Color color;

float reflectivity;

};

Color traceAnimationRay(const Ray& ray, const Scene& scene) {

Intersection hit;

**if** (scene.intersect(ray, hit)) {

Color localColor = hit.material.color;

```
Vector3 reflectedDir = reflect(ray.direction, hit.normal);

Ray reflectedRay(hit.position, reflectedDir);

Color reflectedColor = traceAnimationRay(reflectedRay, scene);

return localColor * (1.0 - hit.material.reflectivity) + reflectedColor * hit.material.reflectivity;

}

return Color(0, 0, 0); // Background color

}
```

## The Future of Ray Tracing in Film

The future of ray tracing in film looks promising, with ongoing advancements in hardware and software. As technology continues to evolve, ray tracing will enable even more realistic and immersive visual experiences.

## Conclusion

The historical use of ray tracing in movies has transformed the film industry, allowing for the creation of visually stunning and realistic images. From early CGI experiments to modern photorealistic films, ray tracing remains a vital tool in the filmmaker's arsenal.

## 11.2. Real-Time Ray Tracing in Modern Animation

Real-time ray tracing is revolutionizing modern animation by enabling the creation of high-quality visuals at interactive frame rates. This advancement allows animators to see the final look of scenes instantly, streamlining the production process.

## Real-Time vs. Offline Rendering

Traditional ray tracing in animation has been an offline process, taking hours or even days to render a single frame. Real-time ray tracing, on the other hand, produces results almost instantaneously, significantly speeding up the workflow.

## Benefits of Real-Time Ray Tracing

- **Instant Feedback**: Animators can see the effects of lighting, shading, and textures immediately, allowing for faster iteration and refinement.

- **Enhanced Creativity**: Real-time rendering enables more experimentation with visual styles and effects, fostering greater creativity.

- **Streamlined Workflow**: The ability to render scenes in real-time reduces the need for lengthy rendering queues and post-processing adjustments.

## Example of Real-Time Ray Tracing Workflow

```
void renderSceneRealTime(const Scene& scene, Image& output)
{
for (int y = 0; y < output.height; ++y) {
for (int x = 0; x < output.width; ++x) {
Ray ray = generateRay(x, y, scene.camera);
Color color = traceRay(ray, scene);
output.setPixel(x, y, color);
```

}

}

}

## Hardware Acceleration

The advent of GPUs with dedicated ray tracing cores, such as NVIDIA's RTX series, has made real-time ray tracing feasible. These GPUs accelerate the computation of ray tracing algorithms, enabling high-performance rendering.

## Example of GPU-Accelerated Ray Tracing

void renderWithRTX(const Scene& scene, Image& output) {

**for** (int y = 0; y < output.height; ++y) {

**for** (int x = 0; x < output.width; ++x) {

Ray ray = generateRay(x, y, scene.camera);

Color color = traceRayWithRTX(ray, scene);

output.setPixel(x, y, color);

}

}

}

## Real-Time Ray Tracing in Game Engines

Game engines like Unreal Engine and Unity have integrated real-time ray tracing, enabling the creation of high-quality animated content. These engines provide powerful tools for lighting, shading, and material creation.

## Example of Ray Tracing in Unreal Engine

```
void renderWithUnrealEngine(const Scene& scene, Image& output) {
```

// *Set up ray tracing environment*

setupRayTracingEnvironment(scene);

// *Render scene*

**for** (int y = 0; y < output.height; ++y) {

**for** (int x = 0; x < output.width; ++x) {

Ray ray = generateRay(x, y, scene.camera);

Color color = traceRayUnreal(ray, scene);

output.setPixel(x, y, color);

}

}

}

## Virtual Production

Real-time ray tracing is also used in virtual production, where live-action footage is combined with CGI in real-time. This technique allows filmmakers to visualize the final scene during the shoot, improving decision-making and collaboration.

# ILLUMINATING REALITIES: THE THEORY OF REAL-TIME RAY TRACING

## Example of Virtual Production Workflow

```
void virtualProduction(const Scene& scene, const LiveActionFootage& footage, Image& output) {

// Combine live-action footage with CGI elements

for (int y = 0; y < output.height; ++y) {

for (int x = 0; x < output.width; ++x) {

Ray ray = generateRay(x, y, scene.camera);

Color cgiColor = traceRay(ray, scene);

Color liveActionColor = footage.getPixel(x, y);

output.setPixel(x, y, mix(liveActionColor, cgiColor, 0.5));

}
}
}
```

## Challenges and Solutions

While real-time ray tracing offers many benefits, it also presents challenges such as high computational demands and integration with existing pipelines. Solutions include optimizing algorithms, leveraging hardware acceleration, and using hybrid rendering techniques.

## Example of Hybrid Rendering

```
void renderHybridScene(const Scene& scene, Image& output) {

// Rasterize primary geometry
```

```
rasterizeScene(scene, output);

// Add ray-traced effects
for (int y = 0; y < output.height; ++y) {
    for (int x = 0; x < output.width; ++x) {
        Ray ray = generateRay(x, y, scene.camera);
        Color tracedColor = traceRay(ray, scene);
        output.setPixel(x, y, mix(output.getPixel(x, y), tracedColor, 0.5));
    }
}
}
```

**Future of Real-Time Ray Tracing**

The future of real-time ray tracing in animation looks bright, with continued advancements in hardware and software driving further improvements. As the technology becomes more accessible, it will open up new possibilities for creating high-quality animated content.

**Conclusion**

Real-time ray tracing is transforming modern animation by enabling high-quality visuals at interactive frame rates. With benefits like instant feedback, enhanced creativity, and streamlined workflows, it is becoming an essential tool for animators and filmmakers.

# 11.3. Bridging the Gap: Real-Time and

## Offline Rendering

Bridging the gap between real-time and offline rendering involves combining the strengths of both techniques to achieve high-quality visuals with efficient production workflows.

### Real-Time Rendering

Real-time rendering is used in applications where immediate feedback is required, such as video games, virtual reality, and interactive simulations. It prioritizes speed and responsiveness.

### Example of Real-Time Rendering

```
void renderRealTime(const Scene& scene, Image& output) {
for (int y = 0; y < output.height; ++y) {
for (int x = 0; x < output.width; ++x) {
Ray ray = generateRay(x, y, scene.camera);
Color color = traceRay(ray, scene);
output.setPixel(x, y, color);
}
}
}
```

### Offline Rendering

Offline rendering is used in applications where quality is paramount, such as feature films, high-end animation, and visual effects. It allows for complex calculations and high-fidelity results.

## Example of Offline Rendering

```
void renderOffline(const Scene& scene, Image& output) {
    for (int y = 0; y < output.height; ++y) {
        for (int x = 0; x < output.width; ++x) {
            Ray ray = generateRay(x, y, scene.camera);
            Color color = traceRayWithComplexShading(ray, scene);
            output.setPixel(x, y, color);
        }
    }
}
```

## Hybrid Rendering Techniques

Hybrid rendering combines real-time and offline techniques to balance quality and performance. This approach leverages real-time rendering for interactive elements and offline rendering for high-quality final outputs.

## Example of Hybrid Rendering Workflow

```
void renderHybrid(const Scene& scene, Image& output) {
    // Render real-time elements
    for (int y = 0; y < output.height; ++y) {
        for (int x = 0; x < output.width; ++x) {
            Ray ray = generateRay(x, y, scene.camera);
```

```
Color realTimeColor = traceRay(ray, scene);
output.setPixel(x, y, realTimeColor);
    }
}
// Render offline elements
for (int y = 0; y < output.height; ++y) {
    for (int x = 0; x < output.width; ++x) {
        Ray ray = generateRay(x, y, scene.camera);
        Color offlineColor = traceRayWithComplexShading(ray, scene);
        output.setPixel(x, y, mix(output.getPixel(x, y), offlineColor, 0.5));
    }
}
}
```

## Use Cases for Hybrid Rendering

- **Previsualization**: Real-time rendering is used for quick iterations, while offline rendering is applied for final high-quality frames.

- **Virtual Production**: Combines live-action footage with CGI in real-time, with offline rendering for final compositing.

- **Interactive Storytelling**: Uses real-time rendering for user interactions and offline rendering for cutscenes and high-quality visuals.

## Example of Previsualization Workflow

```
void renderPrevis(const Scene& scene, Image& output) {
// Real-time previsualization
renderRealTime(scene, output);
// Offline final rendering
renderOffline(scene, output);
}
```

## Advantages of Hybrid Rendering

- **Efficiency**: Allows for faster iterations during the creative process.
- **Quality**: Maintains high-quality results for final outputs.
- **Flexibility**: Adapts to different stages of the production pipeline.

## Challenges of Hybrid Rendering

- **Complexity**: Integrating real-time and offline rendering pipelines can be complex.

- **Consistency**: Ensuring visual consistency between real-time and offline elements requires careful management.

- **Resource Management**: Balancing computational resources between real-time and offline tasks is crucial.

## Example of Resource Management

```
void manageResourcesForHybridRendering(const Scene& scene)
{
// Allocate resources for real-time rendering
allocateRealTimeResources(scene);
// Allocate resources for offline rendering
allocateOfflineResources(scene);
// Balance workload
balanceWorkload(scene);
}
```

## Future Directions

The future of hybrid rendering will see further integration of real-time and offline techniques, driven by advancements in hardware and software. This will enable even more seamless workflows and higher-quality outputs.

## Conclusion

Bridging the gap between real-time and offline rendering offers significant benefits for producing high-quality visuals efficiently.

Hybrid rendering techniques leverage the strengths of both approaches, providing flexibility, efficiency, and quality in the production pipeline.

## 11.4. Visual Effects and Ray Tracing

Visual effects (VFX) have been transformed by ray tracing, allowing artists to create highly realistic and complex scenes. Ray tracing provides the tools needed to simulate accurate lighting, shadows, reflections, and other visual phenomena.

### Realistic Lighting and Shadows

Ray tracing enables the simulation of realistic lighting and shadows, crucial for creating believable VFX. It handles both direct and indirect illumination, producing lifelike scenes.

### Example of Realistic Lighting

Color calculateLighting(const Intersection& hit, const Scene& scene) {

Color directLight = calculateDirectIllumination(hit, scene.lights);

Color indirectLight = calculateIndirectIllumination(hit, scene);

**return** hit.material.color * (directLight + indirectLight);

}

### Accurate Reflections and Refractions

Ray tracing accurately simulates reflections and refractions, essential for rendering materials like glass, water, and metals. This adds depth and realism to visual effects.

# ILLUMINATING REALITIES: THE THEORY OF REAL-TIME RAY TRACING

## Example of Reflection and Refraction

```
Color traceReflectionRefraction(const Ray& ray, const Scene& scene, int depth) {

if (depth <= 0) return Color(0, 0, 0);

Intersection hit;

if (scene.intersect(ray, hit)) {

Vector3 reflectedDir = reflect(ray.direction, hit.normal);

Ray reflectedRay(hit.position, reflectedDir);

Color reflectedColor = traceReflectionRefraction(reflectedRay, scene, depth - 1);

Vector3 refractedDir = refract(ray.direction, hit.normal, hit.material.ior);

Ray refractedRay(hit.position, refractedDir);

Color refractedColor = traceReflectionRefraction(refractedRay, scene, depth - 1);

float reflectance = fresnel(ray.direction, hit.normal, hit.material.ior);

return hit.material.color * (reflectance * reflectedColor + (1.0 - reflectance) * refractedColor);

}

return Color(0, 0, 0); // Background color

}
```

## Complex Material Properties

Ray tracing handles complex material properties, such as subsurface scattering and anisotropic reflections. These properties are vital for rendering realistic skin, hair, and other intricate surfaces.

## Example of Subsurface Scattering

```
Color calculateSubsurfaceScattering(const Intersection& hit, const Scene& scene) {

Color sss(0, 0, 0);

for (int i = 0; i < numSamples; ++i) {

Vector3 scatterDir = sampleHemisphere(hit.normal);

Ray scatterRay(hit.position, scatterDir);

sss += traceRay(scatterRay, scene);

}

sss /= numSamples;

return sss * hit.material.subsurfaceColor;

}
```

## Particle and Fluid Simulations

Ray tracing enhances particle and fluid simulations by providing accurate lighting and interaction with other scene elements. This is crucial for effects like fire, smoke, and water.

# ILLUMINATING REALITIES: THE THEORY OF REAL-TIME RAY TRACING

## Example of Particle Simulation

```
void simulateParticles(const Scene& scene, ParticleSystem& particles) {

for (Particle& particle : particles) {

particle.update(scene);

Ray ray(particle.position, particle.velocity);

Color color = traceRay(ray, scene);

particle.color = color;

}

}
```

## Integration with Compositing

Ray tracing integrates seamlessly with compositing workflows, allowing VFX artists to combine rendered elements with live-action footage. This creates a cohesive and realistic final image.

## Example of Compositing Workflow

```
void compositeScene(const Scene& scene, const LiveActionFootage& footage, Image& output) {

for (int y = 0; y < output.height; ++y) {

for (int x = 0; x < output.width; ++x) {

Ray ray = generateRay(x, y, scene.camera);

Color cgiColor = traceRay(ray, scene);
```

Color liveActionColor = footage.getPixel(x, y);

output.setPixel(x, y, blend(liveActionColor, cgiColor));

}

}

}

## Real-Time Previsualization

Real-time ray tracing is used in previsualization to provide immediate feedback on the look and feel of visual effects. This allows directors and artists to make informed decisions during production.

## Example of Real-Time Previsualization

void renderPrevisRealTime(const Scene& scene, Image& output) {

for (int y = 0; y < output.height; ++y) {

for (int x = 0; x < output.width; ++x) {

Ray ray = generateRay(x, y, scene.camera);

Color color = traceRay(ray, scene);

output.setPixel(x, y, color);

}

}

}

## Challenges in VFX

Despite its advantages, ray tracing in VFX presents challenges such as high computational demands and the need for optimization. Solutions include using acceleration structures, adaptive sampling, and parallel processing.

## Example of Acceleration Structures

```
void buildBVH(Scene& scene) {

// Build Bounding Volume Hierarchy (BVH) for the scene

scene.bvh = BVH(scene.objects);

}

bool intersectBVH(const Ray& ray, const BVH& bvh, Intersection& hit) {

if (!bvh.bounds.intersect(ray)) return false;

if (bvh.isLeaf()) {

return bvh.object->intersect(ray, hit);

}

bool hitLeft = intersectBVH(ray, *bvh.left, hit);

bool hitRight = intersectBVH(ray, *bvh.right, hit);

return hitLeft || hitRight;

}
```

### Future of Ray Tracing in VFX

The future of ray tracing in VFX looks promising, with advancements in hardware and software making it more accessible and efficient. As technology evolves, ray tracing will continue to enhance the realism and complexity of visual effects.

### Conclusion

Ray tracing has transformed visual effects by enabling the creation of highly realistic and complex scenes. From realistic lighting and shadows to accurate reflections and fluid simulations, ray tracing provides the tools needed to achieve stunning VFX.

## 11.5. Case Studies: Iconic Films Using Ray Tracing

Examining case studies of iconic films that have utilized ray tracing provides insights into how this technology has been applied to achieve groundbreaking visual effects.

### Case Study 1: "Avatar" (2009)

James Cameron's "Avatar" is a landmark film that pushed the boundaries of visual effects, heavily relying on ray tracing to create its immersive world.

### Use of Ray Tracing in "Avatar"

Ray tracing was used extensively for realistic lighting, shadows, reflections, and refractions, contributing to the film's photorealistic CGI.

## Example of Lighting in "Avatar"

```
Color calculateAvatarLighting(const Intersection& hit, const Scene& scene) {

    Color directLight = calculateDirectIllumination(hit, scene.lights);

    Color indirectLight = calculateIndirectIllumination(hit, scene);

    return hit.material.color * (directLight + indirectLight);

}
```

## Case Study 2: "The Lion King" (2019)

Disney's "The Lion King" (2019) utilized ray tracing to achieve photorealistic visuals, creating lifelike animal characters and environments.

## Use of Ray Tracing in "The Lion King"

Ray tracing was employed for realistic fur rendering, accurate shadows, and complex lighting interactions, enhancing the film's visual realism.

## Example of Fur Rendering

```
Color calculateFurRendering(const Intersection& hit, const Scene& scene) {

    Color baseColor = hit.material.color;

    Color furColor = traceRayForFur(hit, scene);

    return baseColor * furColor;

}
```

## Case Study 3: "Blade Runner 2049" (2017)

"Blade Runner 2049" used ray tracing to create its visually stunning and atmospheric world, enhancing the film's futuristic aesthetic.

## Use of Ray Tracing in "Blade Runner 2049"

Ray tracing contributed to the film's realistic reflections, neon lighting, and volumetric effects, adding depth and immersion to the scenes.

## Example of Neon Lighting

Color calculateNeonLighting(const Intersection& hit, const Scene& scene) {

Color directLight = calculateDirectIllumination(hit, scene.neonLights);

Color indirectLight = calculateIndirectIllumination(hit, scene);

**return** hit.material.color * (directLight + indirectLight);

}

## Case Study 4: "Finding Dory" (2016)

Pixar's "Finding Dory" utilized ray tracing for realistic underwater scenes, capturing the unique lighting and refraction effects of an aquatic environment.

## Use of Ray Tracing in "Finding Dory"

Ray tracing was used to simulate underwater caustics, soft shadows, and subsurface scattering, enhancing the film's visual authenticity.

## Example of Underwater Caustics

Color calculateUnderwaterCaustics(const Intersection& hit, const Scene& scene) {

Color caustics(0, 0, 0);

**for** (int i = 0; i < numSamples; ++i) {

Vector3 causticDir = sampleHemisphere(hit.normal);

Ray causticRay(hit.position, causticDir);

caustics += traceRay(causticRay, scene);

}

caustics /= numSamples;

**return** caustics * hit.material.color;

}

## Case Study 5: "Gravity" (2013)

Alfonso Cuarón's "Gravity" used ray tracing to create realistic space environments, contributing to the film's immersive and visually stunning experience.

## Use of Ray Tracing in "Gravity"

Ray tracing was employed for accurate lighting, reflections, and global illumination, enhancing the realism of the spacecraft and space scenes.

## Example of Space Reflections

Color calculateSpaceReflections(const Intersection& hit, const Scene& scene) {

Vector3 reflectedDir = reflect(hit.ray.direction, hit.normal);

Ray reflectedRay(hit.position, reflectedDir);

Color reflectedColor = traceRay(reflectedRay, scene);

**return** hit.material.color * reflectedColor;

}

## Conclusion

The case studies of "Avatar," "The Lion King," "Blade Runner 2049," "Finding Dory," and "Gravity" demonstrate the transformative impact of ray tracing on film. By enabling realistic lighting, reflections, and complex visual effects, ray tracing has helped create some of the most visually stunning and iconic films in cinematic history.

# Chapter 12: Real-Time Ray Tracing in Virtual Reality

## 12.1. The Unique Demands of VR on Ray Tracing

Virtual reality (VR) presents unique challenges for ray tracing, requiring high performance and low latency to ensure an immersive and comfortable experience for users.

## Performance Requirements

VR requires high frame rates (typically 90 FPS or higher) and low latency to prevent motion sickness and provide a seamless experience. This imposes strict performance constraints on ray tracing.

## Example of Real-Time Performance Optimization

```
void optimizeForVR(const Scene& scene, Image& output) {

for (int y = 0; y < output.height; ++y) {

for (int x = 0; x < output.width; ++x) {

Ray ray = generateRay(x, y, scene.camera);

Color color = traceRayOptimized(ray, scene);

output.setPixel(x, y, color);

}
}
}
```

## Latency Considerations

Low latency is crucial in VR to ensure that the rendered images keep up with the user's head movements. Techniques like asynchronous reprojection and timewarp are used to reduce perceived latency.

## Example of Asynchronous Reprojection

```
void applyAsynchronousReprojection(const Scene& scene, Image& output) {
    // Render scene normally
    renderScene(scene, output);
    // Apply reprojection to adjust for head movement
    for (int y = 0; y < output.height; ++y) {
        for (int x = 0; x < output.width; ++x) {
            Vector2 newPos = reprojectPixel(x, y, scene.camera);
            Color color = output.getPixel(newPos.x, newPos.y);
            output.setPixel(x, y, color);
        }
    }
}
```

## Field of View and Resolution

VR headsets have a wide field of view (FOV) and high resolution, increasing the number of rays that need to be traced and the overall computational load.

## Example of FOV and Resolution Handling

```
void renderWithWideFOV(const Scene& scene, Image& output) {
```

```
Camera vrCamera = scene.camera;

vrCamera.fov = 110.0; // Wide field of view for VR

for (int y = 0; y < output.height; ++y) {

for (int x = 0; x < output.width; ++x) {

Ray ray = generateRay(x, y, vrCamera);

Color color = traceRay(ray, scene);

output.setPixel(x, y, color);

}

}

}
```

## Real-Time Interaction

Real-time interaction is essential in VR, requiring the rendering engine to respond immediately to user inputs and changes in the virtual environment.

## Example of Interactive Ray Tracing

```
void handleUserInput(const Scene& scene, const UserInput& input, Image& output) {

// Update scene based on user input

updateScene(scene, input);

// Render updated scene

renderScene(scene, output);
```

}

## Eye Tracking and Foveated Rendering

Eye tracking and foveated rendering techniques focus computational resources on the area of the screen where the user is looking, reducing the workload and improving performance.

## Example of Foveated Rendering

```
void renderFoveated(const Scene& scene, const EyeTrackingData& eyeData, Image& output) {

for (int y = 0; y < output.height; ++y) {

for (int x = 0; x < output.width; ++x) {

Ray ray = generateRayFoveated(x, y, eyeData, scene.camera);

Color color = traceRay(ray, scene);

output.setPixel(x, y, color);

}
}
}
```

## Challenges in VR Ray Tracing

- **Performance**: Achieving high frame rates and low latency is challenging due to the computational demands of ray tracing.

- **Synchronization**: Ensuring that the rendered images match the user's head movements requires precise synchronization.

- **Resource Management**: Balancing computational resources between rendering and other VR tasks is crucial.

## Example of Resource Management

```
void manageVRResources(const Scene& scene) {
// Allocate resources for rendering
allocateRenderingResources(scene);
// Allocate resources for user input and interaction
allocateInteractionResources(scene);
// Balance workloads to ensure smooth performance
balanceWorkloads(scene);
}
```

## Future Directions

Future advancements in hardware and software will address the challenges of VR ray tracing, enabling more realistic and immersive virtual experiences.

## Conclusion

The unique demands of VR on ray tracing require high performance, low latency, and efficient resource management. By addressing these challenges, real-time ray tracing can provide an immersive and responsive VR experience.

## 12.2. Achieving Realism in Virtual Environments

Achieving realism in virtual environments through ray tracing involves simulating accurate lighting, shadows, reflections, and material properties to create lifelike scenes.

### Realistic Lighting

Realistic lighting is crucial for creating immersive virtual environments. Ray tracing simulates light transport accurately, capturing both direct and indirect illumination.

### Example of Realistic Lighting

Color calculateRealisticLighting(const Intersection& hit, const Scene& scene) {

Color directLight = calculateDirectIllumination(hit, scene.lights);

Color indirectLight = calculateIndirectIllumination(hit, scene);

**return** hit.material.color * (directLight + indirectLight);

}

### Dynamic Shadows

Dynamic shadows add depth and realism to virtual environments. Ray tracing handles both hard and soft shadows, simulating how light interacts with objects.

# ILLUMINATING REALITIES: THE THEORY OF REAL-TIME RAY TRACING

## Example of Dynamic Shadows

```
Color calculateDynamicShadows(const Ray& ray, const Scene& scene) {

    Intersection hit;

    if (scene.intersect(ray, hit)) {

        Ray shadowRay(hit.position, -scene.lights[0].direction);

        if (scene.intersect(shadowRay)) {

            return Color(0, 0, 0); // In shadow

        }

        return hit.material.color; // Not in shadow

    }

    return Color(0, 0, 0); // Background color

}
```

## Realistic Reflections and Refractions

Accurate reflections and refractions are essential for rendering materials like water, glass, and metals. Ray tracing simulates these effects, adding to the realism of virtual environments.

## Example of Reflections and Refractions

```
Color traceReflectionsRefractions(const Ray& ray, const Scene& scene, int depth) {

    if (depth <= 0) return Color(0, 0, 0);
```

```
Intersection hit;
if (scene.intersect(ray, hit)) {
    Vector3 reflectedDir = reflect(ray.direction, hit.normal);
    Ray reflectedRay(hit.position, reflectedDir);
    Color reflectedColor = traceReflectionsRefractions(reflectedRay, scene, depth - 1);
    Vector3 refractedDir = refract(ray.direction, hit.normal, hit.material.ior);
    Ray refractedRay(hit.position, refractedDir);
    Color refractedColor = traceReflectionsRefractions(refractedRay, scene, depth - 1);
    float reflectance = fresnel(ray.direction, hit.normal, hit.material.ior);
    return hit.material.color * (reflectance * reflectedColor + (1.0 - reflectance) * refractedColor);
}
return Color(0, 0, 0); // Background color
}
```

## Realistic Material Properties

Simulating realistic material properties, such as texture, roughness, and transparency, enhances the believability of virtual environments. Ray tracing accurately models these properties.

## Example of Material Properties

```
Color calculateMaterialProperties(const Intersection& hit, const Scene& scene) {

Color baseColor = hit.material.color;

Color textureColor = sampleTexture(hit.material.texture, hit.uv);

return baseColor * textureColor;

}
```

## Volumetric Effects

Volumetric effects, such as fog, smoke, and light shafts, add atmosphere and depth to virtual environments. Ray tracing handles the scattering and absorption of light in volumetric media.

## Example of Volumetric Effects

```
Color calculateVolumetricEffects(const Ray& ray, const Volume& volume, const Scene& scene) {

Color radiance(0, 0, 0);

Color transmittance(1, 1, 1);

float stepSize = 0.1;

for (float t = 0; t < ray.length; t += stepSize) {

Vector3 position = ray.origin + t * ray.direction;

Color extinction = volume.getExtinction(position);

transmittance *= exp(-extinction * stepSize);
```

Color inScattering = volume.getInScattering(position, ray.direction, scene.lights);

radiance += transmittance * inScattering * stepSize;

}

**return** radiance;

}

## Realistic Animation and Movement

Realistic animation and movement contribute to the immersion of virtual environments. Ray tracing can simulate motion blur and other effects to enhance the realism of moving objects.

## Example of Motion Blur

Color calculateMotionBlur(const Ray& ray, const Scene& scene, float time) {

Ray motionRay = ray;

motionRay.origin += scene.camera.velocity * time;

**return** traceRay(motionRay, scene);

}

## High Dynamic Range Imaging (HDRI)

HDRI captures a wide range of lighting intensities, enhancing the realism of virtual environments. Ray tracing utilizes HDRI to simulate realistic lighting conditions.

## Example of HDRI

```
Color calculateHDRI(const Ray& ray, const HDRI& hdri) {

Vector3 direction = normalize(ray.direction);

return hdri.sample(direction);

}
```

## Challenges in Achieving Realism

- **Performance**: Balancing realism with performance is challenging, especially in real-time applications.

- **Complexity**: Simulating realistic environments requires complex algorithms and significant computational resources.

- **Consistency**: Ensuring visual consistency across different elements and effects is crucial for maintaining realism.

## Example of Balancing Performance and Realism

```
void optimizeRendering(const Scene& scene, Image& output) {

// Use level of detail (LOD) techniques

for (int y = 0; y < output.height; ++y) {

for (int x = 0; x < output.width; ++x) {

if (isDistantObject(scene.objects[x, y])) {

// Render with lower detail

renderLowDetail(scene.objects[x, y], output.getPixel(x, y));
```

} else {

// *Render with high detail*

renderHighDetail(scene.objects[x, y], output.getPixel(x, y));

}

}

}

}

## Future Directions

Advancements in hardware and software will continue to enhance the realism of virtual environments, making them increasingly lifelike and immersive.

## Conclusion

Achieving realism in virtual environments through ray tracing involves simulating accurate lighting, shadows, reflections, material properties, and volumetric effects. By addressing the challenges and leveraging advanced techniques, it is possible to create highly immersive and lifelike virtual experiences.

## 12.3. Performance Optimization for VR

Optimizing performance for VR ray tracing is crucial to meet the high frame rate and low latency requirements essential for a comfortable and immersive experience.

## Hardware Acceleration

Utilizing hardware acceleration is key to achieving real-time ray tracing in VR. Modern GPUs with dedicated ray tracing cores significantly enhance performance.

## Example of Hardware-Accelerated Rendering

```
void renderWithRTX(const Scene& scene, Image& output) {

for (int y = 0; y < output.height; ++y) {

for (int x = 0; x < output.width; ++x) {

Ray ray = generateRay(x, y, scene.camera);

Color color = traceRayWithRTX(ray, scene);

output.setPixel(x, y, color);

}

}

}
```

## Adaptive Sampling

Adaptive sampling reduces the number of rays traced by focusing computational resources on visually important areas. This technique improves performance without significantly affecting visual quality.

## Example of Adaptive Sampling

```
Color traceAdaptiveRay(const Ray& ray, const Scene& scene, int depth, float threshold) {
```

```
if (depth <= 0) return Color(0, 0, 0);

Intersection hit;

if (scene.intersect(ray, hit)) {

    Color directColor = calculateDirectIllumination(ray, hit, scene);

    if (luminance(directColor) < threshold) return directColor;

    Vector3 reflectedDir = calculateReflection(ray.direction, hit.normal);

    Ray reflectedRay(hit.position, reflectedDir);

    Color reflectedColor = traceAdaptiveRay(reflectedRay, scene, depth - 1, threshold * 0.5);

    Vector3 refractedDir = calculateRefraction(ray.direction, hit.normal, hit.material.ior);

    Ray refractedRay(hit.position, refractedDir);

    Color refractedColor = traceAdaptiveRay(refractedRay, scene, depth - 1, threshold * 0.5);

    return hit.material.color * (directColor + reflectedColor + refractedColor);

}

return scene.backgroundColor;

}
```

## Level of Detail (LOD)

Level of Detail (LOD) techniques adjust the complexity of rendering based on the distance from the camera. Distant objects are rendered with less detail, improving performance.

## Example of LOD Rendering

```
void renderWithLOD(const Scene& scene, Image& output) {

for (int y = 0; y < output.height; ++y) {

for (int x = 0; x < output.width; ++x) {

Ray ray = generateRay(x, y, scene.camera);

if (isDistantObject(scene.objects[x, y])) {

// Render with lower detail

renderLowDetail(scene.objects[x, y], output.getPixel(x, y));

} else {

// Render with high detail

renderHighDetail(scene.objects[x, y], output.getPixel(x, y));

}

}

}

}
```

## Parallel Processing

Parallel processing leverages multiple CPU and GPU cores to distribute the workload, significantly improving performance for real-time ray tracing.

### Example of Parallel Processing

```
void renderParallel(const Scene& scene, Image& output) {
#pragma omp parallel for
for (int y = 0; y < output.height; ++y) {
for (int x = 0; x < output.width; ++x) {
Ray ray = generateRay(x, y, scene.camera);
Color color = traceRay(ray, scene);
output.setPixel(x, y, color);
}
}
}
```

## Temporal Accumulation

Temporal accumulation techniques improve image quality by accumulating information over multiple frames. This reduces noise and enhances the stability of lighting effects.

### Example of Temporal Accumulation

```
void accumulateFrames(const Image& currentFrame, Image& accumulatedFrame, int frameCount) {
```

```
for (int y = 0; y < currentFrame.height; ++y) {

for (int x = 0; x < currentFrame.width; ++x) {

Color currentColor = currentFrame.getPixel(x, y);

Color accumulatedColor = accumulatedFrame.getPixel(x, y);

accumulatedFrame.setPixel(x, y, (accumulatedColor * frameCount + currentColor) / (frameCount + 1));

}

}

}
```

## Foveated Rendering

Foveated rendering uses eye-tracking data to focus rendering resources on the area of the screen where the user is looking, reducing the workload for peripheral areas.

## Example of Foveated Rendering

```
void renderFoveated(const Scene& scene, const EyeTrackingData& eyeData, Image& output) {

for (int y = 0; y < output.height; ++y) {

for (int x = 0; x < output.width; ++x) {

Ray ray = generateRayFoveated(x, y, eyeData, scene.camera);

Color color = traceRay(ray, scene);

output.setPixel(x, y, color);
```

}

}

}

## Optimizing Shaders

Optimizing shaders involves reducing the complexity of shader programs to improve performance. Techniques include simplifying mathematical operations and minimizing branching.

### Example of Optimized Shader

```
Color optimizedShader(const Intersection& hit, const Scene& scene) {

Color baseColor = hit.material.color;

Color lightColor = calculateDirectIllumination(hit, scene.lights);

return baseColor * lightColor;

}
```

## Resource Management

Effective resource management ensures that computational resources are allocated efficiently, balancing the load between rendering and other VR tasks.

### Example of Resource Management

```
void manageResources(const Scene& scene) {

// Allocate resources for rendering
```

allocateRenderingResources(scene);

// *Allocate resources for user input and interaction*

allocateInteractionResources(scene);

// *Balance workloads to ensure smooth performance*

balanceWorkloads(scene);

}

## Future Directions

Future advancements in hardware and software will continue to enhance performance optimization for VR, enabling even more realistic and immersive experiences.

## Conclusion

Optimizing performance for VR ray tracing is crucial to meet the high frame rate and low latency requirements of virtual reality. Techniques such as hardware acceleration, adaptive sampling, LOD, parallel processing, temporal accumulation, foveated rendering, shader optimization, and resource management are essential for achieving this goal.

## 12.4. Immersive Experiences and Ray Tracing

Ray tracing plays a crucial role in creating immersive VR experiences by simulating realistic lighting, shadows, reflections, and material properties. These effects enhance the sense of presence and realism in virtual environments.

## Realistic Lighting and Shadows

Realistic lighting and shadows are essential for creating immersive VR experiences. Ray tracing accurately simulates light transport, capturing both direct and indirect illumination.

## Example of Realistic Lighting

```
Color calculateImmersiveLighting(const Intersection& hit, const Scene& scene) {

Color directLight = calculateDirectIllumination(hit, scene.lights);

Color indirectLight = calculateIndirectIllumination(hit, scene);

return hit.material.color * (directLight + indirectLight);

}
```

## Dynamic Reflections and Refractions

Accurate reflections and refractions are critical for rendering materials like water, glass, and metals. Ray tracing simulates these effects, adding depth and realism to VR environments.

## Example of Dynamic Reflections and Refractions

```
Color traceDynamicReflectionsRefractions(const Ray& ray, const Scene& scene, int depth) {

if (depth <= 0) return Color(0, 0, 0);

Intersection hit;

if (scene.intersect(ray, hit)) {

Vector3 reflectedDir = reflect(ray.direction, hit.normal);
```

```
Ray reflectedRay(hit.position, reflectedDir);

Color reflectedColor = traceDynamicReflectionsRefractions(reflectedRay, scene, depth - 1);

Vector3 refractedDir = refract(ray.direction, hit.normal, hit.material.ior);

Ray refractedRay(hit.position, refractedDir);

Color refractedColor = traceDynamicReflectionsRefractions(refractedRay, scene, depth - 1);

float reflectance = fresnel(ray.direction, hit.normal, hit.material.ior);

return hit.material.color * (reflectance * reflectedColor + (1.0 - reflectance) * refractedColor);

}

return Color(0, 0, 0); // Background color

}
```

## Detailed Material Properties

Simulating detailed material properties, such as texture, roughness, and transparency, enhances the realism of VR environments. Ray tracing accurately models these properties.

## Example of Material Properties

```
Color calculateMaterialProperties(const Intersection& hit, const Scene& scene) {
```

```
Color baseColor = hit.material.color;

Color textureColor = sampleTexture(hit.material.texture, hit.uv);

return baseColor * textureColor;

}
```

## Volumetric Effects

Volumetric effects, such as fog, smoke, and light shafts, add atmosphere and depth to VR environments. Ray tracing handles the scattering and absorption of light in volumetric media.

## Example of Volumetric Effects

```
Color calculateVolumetricEffects(const Ray& ray, const Volume& volume, const Scene& scene) {

Color radiance(0, 0, 0);

Color transmittance(1, 1, 1);

float stepSize = 0.1;

for (float t = 0; t < ray.length; t += stepSize) {

Vector3 position = ray.origin + t * ray.direction;

Color extinction = volume.getExtinction(position);

transmittance *= exp(-extinction * stepSize);

Color inScattering = volume.getInScattering(position, ray.direction, scene.lights);

radiance += transmittance * inScattering * stepSize;
```

}

**return** radiance;

}

## High Dynamic Range Imaging (HDRI)

HDRI captures a wide range of lighting intensities, enhancing the realism of VR environments. Ray tracing utilizes HDRI to simulate realistic lighting conditions.

## Example of HDRI

Color calculateHDRI(const Ray& ray, const HDRI& hdri) {

Vector3 direction = normalize(ray.direction);

**return** hdri.sample(direction);

}

## Realistic Animation and Movement

Realistic animation and movement contribute to the immersion of VR environments. Ray tracing can simulate motion blur and other effects to enhance the realism of moving objects.

## Example of Motion Blur

Color calculateMotionBlur(const Ray& ray, const Scene& scene, float time) {

Ray motionRay = ray;

motionRay.origin += scene.camera.velocity * time;

return traceRay(motionRay, scene);

}

## Interactive and Responsive Environments

Interactive and responsive environments are essential for VR immersion. Ray tracing can handle real-time interactions, ensuring that the virtual world responds accurately to user inputs.

## Example of Interactive Ray Tracing

void handleUserInteraction(const Scene& scene, const UserInput& input, Image& output) {

// Update scene based on user input

updateScene(scene, input);

// Render updated scene

renderScene(scene, output);

}

## Spatial Audio Integration

Integrating spatial audio with ray tracing enhances immersion by providing realistic soundscapes that match the visual environment. This involves simulating how sound waves interact with objects.

## Example of Spatial Audio

void simulateSpatialAudio(const Scene& scene, const Listener& listener, AudioOutput& output) {

for (const SoundSource& source : scene.soundSources) {

# ILLUMINATING REALITIES: THE THEORY OF
# REAL-TIME RAY TRACING

```
Vector3 direction = normalize(source.position - listener.position);

float distance = length(source.position - listener.position);

float attenuation = 1.0 / (distance * distance);

output.addSample(source.sound * attenuation, direction);

}

}
```

## Challenges in Creating Immersive Experiences

- **Performance**: Balancing high-quality rendering with real-time performance is challenging.

- **Complexity**: Simulating realistic environments requires complex algorithms and significant computational resources.

- **Consistency**: Ensuring visual and auditory consistency across different elements and effects is crucial for maintaining immersion.

## Example of Balancing Performance and Immersion

```
void optimizeImmersiveRendering(const Scene& scene, Image& output) {

// Use level of detail (LOD) techniques

for (int y = 0; y < output.height; ++y) {

for (int x = 0; x < output.width; ++x) {

if (isDistantObject(scene.objects[x, y])) {
```

```
    // Render with lower detail
    renderLowDetail(scene.objects[x, y], output.getPixel(x, y));
  } else {
    // Render with high detail
    renderHighDetail(scene.objects[x, y], output.getPixel(x, y));
  }
 }
}
```

## Future Directions

Future advancements in hardware and software will continue to enhance the creation of immersive VR experiences, making them increasingly lifelike and engaging.

## Conclusion

Ray tracing plays a crucial role in creating immersive VR experiences by simulating realistic lighting, shadows, reflections, material properties, and volumetric effects. By addressing the challenges and leveraging advanced techniques, it is possible to create highly immersive and realistic virtual environments.

## 12.5. Future of VR and Ray Tracing Technologies

The future of VR and ray tracing technologies promises significant advancements, driven by ongoing innovations in hardware, software, and integration techniques. These advancements will further enhance the realism, performance, and accessibility of virtual reality experiences.

## Advancements in Hardware

Continued improvements in GPU and CPU performance, including dedicated ray tracing cores, will enable more complex and realistic rendering in VR. These advancements will also reduce latency and improve frame rates.

## Example of Future Hardware Utilization

```
void renderWithNextGenHardware(const Scene& scene, Image& output) {

for (int y = 0; y < output.height; ++y) {

for (int x = 0; x < output.width; ++x) {

Ray ray = generateRay(x, y, scene.camera);

Color color = traceRayWithNextGenHardware(ray, scene);

output.setPixel(x, y, color);

}
}
}
```

## Software Innovations

Innovations in rendering algorithms and software optimization will enhance the efficiency and quality of ray tracing in VR. This includes improved denoising techniques, adaptive sampling, and hybrid rendering approaches.

## Example of Software Optimization

```
void renderOptimizedScene(const Scene& scene, Image& output) {
    for (int y = 0; y < output.height; ++y) {
        for (int x = 0; x < output.width; ++x) {
            Ray ray = generateOptimizedRay(x, y, scene.camera);
            Color color = traceRay(ray, scene);
            output.setPixel(x, y, color);
        }
    }
}
```

## Real-Time Path Tracing

Real-time path tracing, which traces multiple light paths to achieve accurate global illumination, is becoming more feasible with advances in hardware and optimization techniques.

## Example of Real-Time Path Tracing

```
Color traceRealTimePath(const Ray& ray, the Scene& scene, int depth) {
    if (depth <= 0) return Color(0, 0, 0);
    Intersection hit;
```

```
if (scene.intersect(ray, hit)) {

Color indirectLight(0, 0, 0);

for (int i = 0; i < numSamples; ++i) {

Vector3 newDir = sampleHemisphere(hit.normal);

Ray newRay(hit.position, newDir);

indirectLight += traceRealTimePath(newRay, scene, depth - 1);

}

indirectLight /= numSamples;

return hit.material.color * (indirectLight + hit.material.emission);

}

return scene.backgroundColor;

}
```

## AI and Machine Learning Integration

Integrating AI and machine learning techniques can optimize ray tracing operations, such as denoising, adaptive sampling, and real-time global illumination.

## Example of AI-Optimized Ray Tracing

```
Color traceRayWithAI(const Ray& ray, the Scene& scene, int depth, const AIModel& aiModel) {

if (depth <= 0) return Color(0, 0, 0);

Intersection hit;
```

```
if (scene.intersect(ray, hit)) {

    Vector3 reflectedDir = calculateReflection(ray.direction, hit.normal);

    Ray reflectedRay(hit.position, reflectedDir);

    Color reflectedColor = aiModel.optimize(traceRay(reflectedRay, scene, depth - 1));

    Color indirectLight(0, 0, 0);

    for (int i = 0; i < numSamples; ++i) {

        Vector3 newDir = sampleHemisphere(hit.normal);

        Ray newRay(hit.position, newDir);

        indirectLight += traceRay(newRay, scene, depth - 1);

    }

    indirectLight /= numSamples;

    return hit.material.color * (reflectedColor + indirectLight + hit.material.emission);

}

return scene.backgroundColor;

}
```

## Hybrid Rendering Techniques

Hybrid rendering techniques will continue to evolve, combining the strengths of rasterization and ray tracing to achieve high-quality visuals with real-time performance.

## Example of Advanced Hybrid Rendering

```
void renderAdvancedHybrid(const Scene& scene, Image& output) {

// Rasterize primary geometry

rasterizeScene(scene, output);

// Add ray-traced reflections, refractions, and global illumination

for (int y = 0; y < output.height; ++y) {

for (int x = 0; x < output.width; ++x) {

Ray ray = generateRay(x, y, scene.camera);

Color tracedColor = traceRay(ray, scene, 5);

output.setPixel(x, y, mix(output.getPixel(x, y), tracedColor, 0.5));

}

}

}
```

## Cloud-Based Ray Tracing

Cloud-based ray tracing leverages powerful remote servers to perform computationally intensive ray tracing operations, streaming the results to the user's device. This approach can enable high-quality ray tracing on lower-end hardware.

## Example of Cloud-Based Ray Tracing

```
void renderWithCloudRayTracing(const Scene& scene, Image& output, the CloudServer& server) {
```

```
for (int y = 0; y < output.height; ++y) {
    for (int x = 0; x < output.width; ++x) {
        Ray ray = generateRay(x, y, scene.camera);
        Color color = server.traceRay(ray, scene);
        output.setPixel(x, y, color);
    }
}
}
```

## Augmented Reality (AR) Integration

The integration of ray tracing with augmented reality (AR) will enhance the realism and interactivity of AR applications, providing accurate lighting and shadows that blend seamlessly with the real world.

### Example of AR Ray Tracing

```
void renderARScene(const Scene& scene, const Camera& camera, Image& output) {
    for (int y = 0; y < output.height; ++y) {
        for (int x = 0; x < output.width; ++x) {
            Ray ray = generateRay(x, y, camera);
            Color color = traceRay(ray, scene);
            output.setPixel(x, y, color);
```

}

}

}

## Cross-Platform Compatibility

Future advancements will ensure that ray tracing technologies are compatible across different platforms, including PCs, consoles, and mobile devices, making high-quality VR experiences accessible to a broader audience.

## Example of Cross-Platform Rendering

```cpp
void renderCrossPlatform(const Scene& scene, Image& output, const Platform& platform) {

    for (int y = 0; y < output.height; ++y) {

        for (int x = 0; x < output.width; ++x) {

            Ray ray = generateRay(x, y, scene.camera, platform);

            Color color = traceRay(ray, scene);

            output.setPixel(x, y, color);

        }

    }

}
```

## Conclusion

The future of VR and ray tracing technologies promises significant advancements, driven by innovations in hardware, software, and integration techniques. These advancements will enhance the realism, performance, and accessibility of virtual reality experiences, making them increasingly lifelike and engaging.

# Chapter 13: Acoustics and Ray Tracing

## 13.1. The Concept of Acoustic Ray Tracing

Acoustic ray tracing is a method used to simulate how sound waves propagate through an environment. This technique is similar to optical ray tracing but focuses on sound waves instead of light waves.

### Principles of Acoustic Ray Tracing

Just as with light, sound waves can reflect, refract, and absorb when they encounter different surfaces. Acoustic ray tracing models these interactions to predict how sound travels through a space.

### Basic Algorithm

The basic algorithm for acoustic ray tracing involves emitting rays from a sound source and tracing their paths as they interact with the environment. These interactions include reflections, refractions, and absorption.

```
struct Ray {

Vector3 origin;

Vector3 direction;

};

void traceAcousticRay(const Ray& ray, const Scene& scene) {
```

```
Intersection hit;

if (scene.intersect(ray, hit)) {

    // Handle reflection

    Vector3 reflectedDir = reflect(ray.direction, hit.normal);

    Ray reflectedRay(hit.position, reflectedDir);

    traceAcousticRay(reflectedRay, scene);

    // Handle refraction

    Vector3 refractedDir = refract(ray.direction, hit.normal, hit.material.acousticIndex);

    Ray refractedRay(hit.position, refractedDir);

    traceAcousticRay(refractedRay, scene);

    // Handle absorption

    hit.material.absorbSound(ray);

}
}
```

## Reflection and Refraction

When a sound wave hits a surface, part of it is reflected and part is refracted. The reflection and refraction angles can be calculated using similar principles to optical ray tracing.

## Example of Reflection Calculation

```
Vector3 reflect(const Vector3& incident, const Vector3& normal)
{
    return incident - 2 * dot(incident, normal) * normal;
}
```

## Absorption and Scattering

Materials can absorb sound energy, reducing the intensity of the sound wave as it propagates. Scattering occurs when sound waves encounter rough or irregular surfaces, causing them to deviate in various directions.

## Example of Absorption

```
void Material::absorbSound(Ray& ray) {
    float absorptionCoefficient = getAbsorptionCoefficient();
    ray.intensity *= (1.0f - absorptionCoefficient);
}
```

## Simulation Accuracy

The accuracy of acoustic ray tracing simulations depends on the level of detail in the environmental model and the accuracy of the material properties used in the simulation.

## Real-Time Acoustic Ray Tracing

Real-time acoustic ray tracing is challenging due to the computational complexity of tracing many sound rays.

Optimizations and approximations are often used to achieve real-time performance.

## Example of Real-Time Optimization

void traceAcousticRayRealTime(const Ray& ray, const Scene& scene) {

// Simplified interaction handling for real-time performance

Intersection hit;

**if** (scene.intersect(ray, hit)) {

Vector3 reflectedDir = reflect(ray.direction, hit.normal);

Ray reflectedRay(hit.position, reflectedDir);

**if** (!hit.material.isHighlyAbsorptive()) {

traceAcousticRayRealTime(reflectedRay, scene);

}

}

}

## Applications

Acoustic ray tracing is used in various fields, including architectural acoustics, audio engineering, and virtual reality, to simulate sound environments and improve acoustic designs.

## Architectural Acoustics

In architectural acoustics, acoustic ray tracing helps in designing buildings with optimal sound propagation characteristics, such as concert halls and recording studios.

## Audio Engineering

Audio engineers use acoustic ray tracing to design speaker systems and optimize sound delivery in venues like theaters and stadiums.

## Virtual Reality

In virtual reality, acoustic ray tracing enhances the realism of virtual environments by providing accurate sound spatialization and environmental effects.

## Conclusion

Acoustic ray tracing provides a powerful tool for simulating sound propagation in complex environments. By modeling interactions such as reflection, refraction, and absorption, it helps create realistic acoustic experiences in various applications.

# 13.2. Simulating Sound in Three-Dimensional Spaces

Simulating sound in three-dimensional spaces involves modeling how sound waves interact with the environment to produce realistic auditory experiences.

# ILLUMINATING REALITIES: THE THEORY OF REAL-TIME RAY TRACING

## The Basics of Sound Propagation

Sound propagation in 3D spaces involves emitting sound waves from a source and tracing their paths as they encounter obstacles, reflect off surfaces, and travel through different media.

## Emission and Reception

Sound is emitted from a source and received by listeners. The position, orientation, and characteristics of both the source and the listeners affect how sound is perceived.

## Example of Sound Emission

```
struct SoundSource {

Vector3 position;

float intensity;

float frequency;

};

struct Listener {

Vector3 position;

Vector3 orientation;

};

void emitSound(const SoundSource& source, std::vector<Ray>& rays) {

for (int i = 0; i < numRays; ++i) {

Ray ray;
```

ray.origin = source.position;

ray.direction = randomDirection();

rays.push_back(ray);

}

}

## Reflection and Diffusion

When sound waves encounter surfaces, they can reflect or diffuse. Reflection follows the law of reflection, while diffusion scatters sound waves in various directions.

## Example of Reflection

void reflectSound(Ray& ray, const Intersection& hit) {

ray.direction = reflect(ray.direction, hit.normal);

ray.origin = hit.position;

}

## Refraction and Transmission

Sound waves can refract when passing through different media, changing direction based on the media's acoustic properties. Transmission occurs when sound passes through a material with some energy loss.

## Example of Refraction

void refractSound(Ray& ray, const Intersection& hit, float refractiveIndex) {

```
ray.direction = refract(ray.direction, hit.normal, refractiveIndex);

ray.origin = hit.position;

}
```

## Absorption and Attenuation

Materials can absorb sound energy, reducing the intensity of the wave. Attenuation occurs naturally as sound waves travel through the air, losing energy over distance.

## Example of Absorption

```
void absorbSound(Ray& ray, const Material& material) {

float absorptionCoefficient = material.getAbsorptionCoefficient(ray.frequency);

ray.intensity *= (1.0f - absorptionCoefficient);

}
```

## Environmental Effects

Environmental effects, such as reverberation and echo, result from multiple reflections and transmissions. These effects are crucial for creating realistic soundscapes.

## Example of Reverberation

```
void calculateReverberation(const std::vector<Ray>& rays, const Scene& scene, Listener& listener) {

for (const Ray& ray : rays) {

if (scene.intersect(ray, listener.position)) {
```

listener.receiveSound(ray.intensity);

}

}

}

## Real-Time Sound Simulation

Achieving real-time sound simulation involves optimizing the number of rays traced and using efficient algorithms to handle interactions and environmental effects.

## Example of Real-Time Optimization

void simulateSoundRealTime(const SoundSource& source, const Scene& scene, Listener& listener) {

std::vector<Ray> rays;

emitSound(source, rays);

**for** (Ray& ray : rays) {

traceAcousticRayRealTime(ray, scene);

**if** (scene.intersect(ray, listener.position)) {

listener.receiveSound(ray.intensity);

}

}

}

## Spatial Audio

Spatial audio techniques enhance the realism of 3D sound by simulating how sound waves interact with the human head and ears, creating a sense of direction and distance.

## Example of Spatial Audio Processing

```
void processSpatialAudio(const Listener& listener, const std::vector<Ray>& rays) {

for (const Ray& ray : rays) {

Vector3 direction = ray.direction - listener.position;

float distance = direction.length();

listener.receiveSpatialSound(ray.intensity, direction, distance);

}
}
```

## Applications

Simulating sound in 3D spaces is used in various applications, including virtual reality, gaming, architectural acoustics, and audio engineering, to create realistic and immersive auditory experiences.

## Conclusion

Simulating sound in three-dimensional spaces involves modeling the complex interactions of sound waves with the environment. Techniques like reflection, refraction, absorption, and spatial audio processing are essential for creating realistic soundscapes.

## 13.3. Applications in Architectural Acoustics

Architectural acoustics focuses on designing buildings and spaces to achieve optimal sound quality. Acoustic ray tracing is a powerful tool in this field, helping architects and engineers create environments with desired acoustic characteristics.

### Importance of Acoustic Design

Proper acoustic design ensures that spaces like concert halls, theaters, classrooms, and offices provide a pleasant auditory experience, minimizing noise and maximizing clarity.

### Example of Acoustic Design

```
struct Room {
    Vector3 dimensions;
    Material wallMaterial;
    Material ceilingMaterial;
    Material floorMaterial;
};

void designAcousticRoom(const Room& room) {
    // Calculate absorption coefficients
    float wallAbsorption = room.wallMaterial.getAbsorptionCoefficient();
    float ceilingAbsorption = room.ceilingMaterial.getAbsorptionCoefficient();
```

```
float floorAbsorption = room.floorMaterial.getAbsorptionCoefficient();

// Optimize room dimensions for sound quality

optimizeRoomDimensions(room.dimensions, wallAbsorption, ceilingAbsorption, floorAbsorption);

}
```

## Sound Isolation

Sound isolation prevents unwanted sound from entering or leaving a space. Acoustic ray tracing helps design walls, floors, and ceilings that effectively block sound transmission.

## Example of Sound Isolation

```
struct Wall {

float thickness;

Material material;

};

void designSoundIsolatedWall(const Wall& wall) {

float transmissionLoss = calculateTransmissionLoss(wall.thickness, wall.material);

// Ensure transmission loss meets isolation requirements

if (transmissionLoss < requiredIsolationLevel) {

increaseWallThickness(wall);

}
```

}

## Reverberation Control

Controlling reverberation time is crucial for ensuring speech clarity and musical quality. Acoustic ray tracing helps determine the optimal amount of absorption needed to achieve the desired reverberation time.

## Example of Reverberation Control

```
void controlReverberation(const Room& room) {
    float targetReverberationTime = calculateTargetReverberationTime(room);
    float currentReverberationTime = calculateCurrentReverberationTime(room);
    while (currentReverberationTime > targetReverberationTime) {
        addAbsorptiveMaterial(room);
        currentReverberationTime = calculateCurrentReverberationTime(room);
    }
}
```

## Noise Control

Reducing noise levels in environments like offices, hospitals, and schools is essential for comfort and productivity. Acoustic ray tracing helps identify noise sources and design measures to mitigate them.

# Example of Noise Control

```cpp
void controlNoise(const Room& room, const std::vector<NoiseSource>& noiseSources) {

for (const NoiseSource& source : noiseSources) {

float noiseLevel = calculateNoiseLevel(source, room);

if (noiseLevel > acceptableThreshold) {

implementNoiseControlMeasures(room, source);

}

}

}
```

# Diffusion and Scattering

Diffusion and scattering techniques spread sound energy evenly throughout a space, preventing sound concentration in specific areas. This improves the overall acoustic quality.

# Example of Diffusion

```cpp
void implementDiffusion(const Room& room) {

std::vector<Diffuser> diffusers = designDiffusers(room);

for (const Diffuser& diffuser : diffusers) {

placeDiffuser(room, diffuser);

}

}
```

## Acoustic Simulation Software

Software tools use acoustic ray tracing to simulate and visualize sound propagation in architectural designs. These tools help architects and engineers make informed decisions.

## Example of Acoustic Simulation

```
void simulateAcoustics(const Room& room) {

std::vector<Ray> rays;

emitSound(SoundSource{Vector3(0, 0, 0), 1.0f, 440.0f}, rays);

for (Ray& ray : rays) {

traceAcousticRay(ray, room);

}

visualizeAcousticSimulation(room, rays);

}
```

## Case Studies

Examining case studies of successful acoustic designs provides valuable insights into best practices and innovative solutions in architectural acoustics.

## Example of Case Study

```
void analyzeCaseStudy(const Room& room) {

simulateAcoustics(room);

evaluateAcousticPerformance(room);
```

documentBestPractices(room);

}

## Future Trends

Advancements in materials, computational methods, and acoustic modeling techniques will continue to enhance the field of architectural acoustics, enabling more precise and efficient designs.

## Conclusion

Architectural acoustics leverages acoustic ray tracing to design spaces with optimal sound quality. By focusing on sound isolation, reverberation control, noise reduction, and diffusion, architects and engineers can create environments that enhance auditory experiences.

## 13.4. Ray Tracing in Audio for Games and VR

Ray tracing in audio for games and virtual reality (VR) enhances the realism and immersion of virtual environments by accurately simulating sound propagation and interactions.

### Importance of Audio in Immersion

High-quality audio is crucial for creating immersive experiences in games and VR. Accurate sound localization, environmental effects, and spatial audio contribute to a sense of presence and realism.

### Example of Sound Localization

void localizeSound(const SoundSource& source, const Listener& listener) {

Vector3 direction = normalize(source.position - listener.position);

float distance = length(source.position - listener.position);

listener.receiveSound(source.intensity / (distance * distance), direction);

}

## Environmental Effects

Simulating environmental effects like reverb, echo, and occlusion enhances the auditory experience. Ray tracing models how sound interacts with the environment to produce these effects.

## Example of Environmental Reverb

void simulateReverb(const Scene& scene, Listener& listener) {

std::vector<Ray> rays;

emitSound(SoundSource{Vector3(0, 0, 0), 1.0f, 440.0f}, rays);

**for** (Ray& ray : rays) {

traceAcousticRay(ray, scene);

**if** (scene.intersect(ray, listener.position)) {

listener.receiveReverb(ray.intensity);

}

}

}

# ILLUMINATING REALITIES: THE THEORY OF REAL-TIME RAY TRACING

## Occlusion and Obstruction

Ray tracing can model how objects block or obstruct sound, creating realistic occlusion effects. This is important for providing accurate auditory cues in games and VR.

## Example of Occlusion

```cpp
void simulateOcclusion(const Scene& scene, Listener& listener) {

std::vector<Ray> rays;

emitSound(SoundSource{Vector3(0, 0, 0), 1.0f, 440.0f}, rays);

for (Ray& ray : rays) {

if (scene.intersect(ray, listener.position)) {

listener.receiveOccludedSound(ray.intensity);

}

}

}
```

## Spatial Audio and HRTF

Head-Related Transfer Functions (HRTF) simulate how sound is filtered by the human head and ears, providing spatial audio cues. Ray tracing can integrate HRTF for accurate sound localization.

## Example of HRTF Processing

```cpp
void applyHRTF(const Listener& listener, const Ray& ray) {

Vector3 direction = normalize(ray.direction - listener.position);
```

```
float distance = length(ray.direction - listener.position);
listener.receiveHRTFSound(ray.intensity, direction, distance);
}
```

## Real-Time Audio Ray Tracing

Achieving real-time audio ray tracing is challenging due to the computational complexity. Optimizations and approximations are used to balance performance and quality.

## Example of Real-Time Optimization

```
void traceAudioRayRealTime(const Ray& ray, const Scene& scene) {
Intersection hit;
if (scene.intersect(ray, hit)) {
Vector3 reflectedDir = reflect(ray.direction, hit.normal);
Ray reflectedRay(hit.position, reflectedDir);
traceAudioRayRealTime(reflectedRay, scene);
}
}
```

## Integration with Game Engines

Modern game engines, such as Unreal Engine and Unity, integrate audio ray tracing to enhance sound design. These engines provide tools and APIs for developers to implement realistic audio effects.

## Example of Game Engine Integration

```
void integrateAudioRayTracing(const Scene& scene, const GameEngine& engine) {

engine.setupAcousticEnvironment(scene);

std::vector<Ray> rays;

emitSound(SoundSource{Vector3(0, 0, 0), 1.0f, 440.0f}, rays);

for (Ray& ray : rays) {

traceAudioRay(ray, scene);

}

engine.renderAudio(scene, rays);

}
```

## VR Audio Considerations

In VR, accurate audio is essential for immersion. Ray tracing helps create realistic spatial audio, providing cues for direction, distance, and environmental effects.

## Example of VR Audio

```
void simulateVRAudio(const Scene& scene, const VRHeadset& headset) {

Listener listener = headset.getListener();

std::vector<Ray> rays;

emitSound(SoundSource{Vector3(0, 0, 0), 1.0f, 440.0f}, rays);
```

```
for (Ray& ray : rays) {

    traceAudioRay(ray, scene);

    if (scene.intersect(ray, listener.position)) {

        applyHRTF(listener, ray);

    }

}

headset.renderAudio(listener);

}
```

## Challenges and Solutions

Challenges in audio ray tracing include handling the computational load, achieving real-time performance, and integrating with existing audio systems. Solutions involve using efficient algorithms, parallel processing, and hybrid approaches.

## Example of Hybrid Approach

```
void hybridAudioRayTracing(const Scene& scene, Listener& listener) {

    // Use simplified ray tracing for real-time performance

    std::vector<Ray> rays;

    emitSound(SoundSource{Vector3(0, 0, 0), 1.0f, 440.0f}, rays);

    for (Ray& ray : rays) {

        traceSimplifiedAudioRay(ray, scene);
```

```
}

// Use detailed ray tracing for critical sounds

std::vector<Ray> criticalRays;

emitSound(SoundSource{Vector3(0, 0, 0), 1.0f, 440.0f}, criticalRays);

for (Ray& ray : criticalRays) {

traceDetailedAudioRay(ray, scene);

}

listener.receiveSounds(criticalRays);

}
```

## Future Trends

Future advancements in hardware, software, and algorithms will continue to enhance audio ray tracing in games and VR, providing more realistic and immersive sound experiences.

## Conclusion

Ray tracing in audio for games and VR significantly enhances immersion by accurately simulating sound propagation and interactions. Techniques like environmental effects, occlusion, HRTF, and real-time optimization are essential for creating realistic auditory experiences.

## 13.5. Future Directions in Acoustic Ray Tracing

The future of acoustic ray tracing holds promise for advancements in realism, efficiency, and applications. Ongoing research and development aim to overcome current limitations and explore new possibilities.

### Enhanced Realism

Future advancements will focus on increasing the realism of acoustic simulations by improving the accuracy of sound wave modeling and material properties.

### Example of Enhanced Realism

```
void enhanceRealism(const Scene& scene) {
    std::vector<Ray> rays;
    emitSound(SoundSource{Vector3(0, 0, 0), 1.0f, 440.0f}, rays);
    for (Ray& ray : rays) {
        traceAcousticRayWithEnhancedRealism(ray, scene);
    }
}
```

### Real-Time Performance

Achieving real-time performance for complex acoustic simulations is a key goal. Advances in hardware acceleration, parallel processing, and optimized algorithms will make this possible.

## Example of Real-Time Optimization

```
void optimizeForRealTime(const Scene& scene, Image& output)
{
std::vector<Ray> rays;
emitSound(SoundSource{Vector3(0, 0, 0), 1.0f, 440.0f}, rays);
for (Ray& ray : rays) {
traceAcousticRayRealTime(ray, scene);
}
}
```

## AI and Machine Learning

AI and machine learning techniques can be used to optimize acoustic ray tracing, predict sound interactions, and improve simulation accuracy.

## Example of AI-Driven Acoustic Simulation

```
void simulateWithAI(const Scene& scene) {
AIModel aiModel = trainAIModel(scene);
std::vector<Ray> rays;
emitSound(SoundSource{Vector3(0, 0, 0), 1.0f, 440.0f}, rays);
for (Ray& ray : rays) {
traceAcousticRayWithAI(ray, scene, aiModel);
}
```

}

## Integration with Other Technologies

Integrating acoustic ray tracing with other technologies, such as augmented reality (AR) and mixed reality (MR), will create more immersive and interactive experiences.

## Example of AR Integration

```
void integrateWithAR(const Scene& scene, const ARDevice& device) {
    std::vector<Ray> rays;
    emitSound(SoundSource{Vector3(0, 0, 0), 1.0f, 440.0f}, rays);
    for (Ray& ray : rays) {
        traceAcousticRay(ray, scene);
        device.renderAudio(ray);
    }
}
```

## Improved Material Models

Developing more accurate material models for acoustic properties, such as absorption, reflection, and scattering, will enhance the realism of simulations.

## Example of Improved Material Modeling

```
void modelMaterials(const Scene& scene) {
```

```
for (Material& material : scene.materials) {
    material.updateProperties();
}
}
```

## Hybrid Simulation Approaches

Hybrid approaches that combine acoustic ray tracing with other simulation methods, such as finite element analysis (FEA) and boundary element method (BEM), will provide more comprehensive solutions.

## Example of Hybrid Simulation

```
void hybridSimulation(const Scene& scene) {
    std::vector<Ray> rays;
    emitSound(SoundSource{Vector3(0, 0, 0), 1.0f, 440.0f}, rays);
    for (Ray& ray : rays) {
        traceAcousticRay(ray, scene);
    }
    runFiniteElementAnalysis(scene);
    runBoundaryElementMethod(scene);
}
```

## Personalized Acoustic Experiences

Personalized acoustic experiences that adapt to individual listener preferences and environments will become more prevalent, enhancing user engagement and satisfaction.

## Example of Personalized Acoustics

```
void personalizeAcoustics(const Scene& scene, const Listener& listener) {

std::vector<Ray> rays;

emitSound(SoundSource{Vector3(0, 0, 0), 1.0f, 440.0f}, rays);

for (Ray& ray : rays) {

tracePersonalizedAcousticRay(ray, scene, listener);

}
}
```

## Collaborative Simulations

Collaborative simulations involving multiple users and environments will enable more dynamic and interactive acoustic experiences, particularly in virtual and augmented reality applications.

## Example of Collaborative Simulation

```
void collaborativeSimulation(const Scene& scene, const std::vector<Listener>& listeners) {

std::vector<Ray> rays;
```

```cpp
emitSound(SoundSource{Vector3(0, 0, 0), 1.0f, 440.0f}, rays);

for (Ray& ray : rays) {

for (const Listener& listener : listeners) {

traceAcousticRayForListener(ray, scene, listener);

}

}

}
```

## Education and Training

Acoustic ray tracing will play a significant role in education and training, providing realistic simulations for various fields, including music, engineering, and environmental science.

## Example of Educational Simulation

```cpp
void educationalSimulation(const Scene& scene, const Classroom& classroom) {

std::vector<Ray> rays;

emitSound(SoundSource{Vector3(0, 0, 0), 1.0f, 440.0f}, rays);

for (Ray& ray : rays) {

traceEducationalAcousticRay(ray, scene, classroom);

}

}
```

## Conclusion

The future of acoustic ray tracing is promising, with advancements in realism, real-time performance, AI integration, material modeling, hybrid approaches, and personalized experiences. These developments will enhance the applications and impact of acoustic simulations across various fields.

# Chapter 14: AI and Machine Learning in Ray Tracing

## 14.1. The Role of AI in Optimizing Ray Tracing

Artificial Intelligence (AI) plays a crucial role in optimizing ray tracing by improving performance, accuracy, and efficiency. AI techniques help overcome traditional challenges and open new possibilities in rendering.

### Enhancing Performance

AI can significantly enhance ray tracing performance by predicting ray paths, reducing noise, and optimizing rendering algorithms. This leads to faster computations and real-time capabilities.

### Example of AI-Enhanced Ray Tracing

```
void enhanceRayTracingWithAI(const Scene& scene, AIModel& aiModel) {

std::vector<Ray> rays;

emitRays(scene, rays);

for (Ray& ray : rays) {
```

```
traceRayWithAI(ray, scene, aiModel);
}
}
```

## Noise Reduction

AI-based denoising techniques can clean up noisy ray-traced images, improving visual quality while reducing the number of rays required. This results in faster and more efficient rendering.

## Example of AI Denoising

```
Image denoiseImageWithAI(const Image& noisyImage, AIModel& aiModel) {

Image cleanImage = aiModel.denoise(noisyImage);

return cleanImage;
}
```

## Adaptive Sampling

AI can be used to adaptively sample areas of the scene that require more detail, optimizing the number of rays cast and improving rendering efficiency.

## Example of Adaptive Sampling

```
void adaptiveSampling(const Scene& scene, AIModel& aiModel)
{
std::vector<Ray> rays;

emitRays(scene, rays);
```

```cpp
for (Ray& ray : rays) {
if (aiModel.requiresDetail(ray)) {
traceRay(ray, scene);
}
}
}
```

## Predictive Rendering

Predictive rendering uses AI to anticipate the paths of rays based on scene geometry and lighting conditions, reducing the computational load and speeding up the rendering process.

## Example of Predictive Rendering

```cpp
void predictiveRendering(const Scene& scene, AIModel& aiModel) {
std::vector<Ray> rays;
emitRays(scene, rays);
for (Ray& ray : rays) {
if (aiModel.predictPath(ray)) {
traceRay(ray, scene);
}
}
}
```

## Scene Analysis

AI can analyze scene complexity and dynamically adjust rendering settings to balance quality and performance, ensuring optimal results for different types of scenes.

## Example of Scene Analysis

```
void analyzeSceneWithAI(const Scene& scene, AIModel& aiModel) {

SceneAnalysis analysis = aiModel.analyze(scene);

adjustRenderingSettings(analysis);

}
```

## Light Path Optimization

AI can optimize light paths by learning from previous renderings, reducing the number of bounces needed to achieve accurate global illumination and other lighting effects.

## Example of Light Path Optimization

```
void optimizeLightPaths(const Scene& scene, AIModel& aiModel) {

std::vector<Ray> rays;

emitRays(scene, rays);

for (Ray& ray : rays) {

aiModel.optimizePath(ray);

traceRay(ray, scene);
```

}

}

## Material Prediction

AI can predict material properties based on texture and appearance, automating the process of assigning realistic materials to objects in the scene.

### Example of Material Prediction

```cpp
void predictMaterials(const Scene& scene, AIModel& aiModel) {
    for (Object& object : scene.objects) {
        object.material = aiModel.predictMaterial(object.texture);
    }
}
```

## Real-Time Rendering

AI's ability to learn and predict allows for real-time ray tracing, making it feasible for interactive applications like gaming and virtual reality.

### Example of Real-Time AI Rendering

```cpp
void renderRealTimeWithAI(const Scene& scene, AIModel& aiModel) {
    std::vector<Ray> rays;
    emitRays(scene, rays);
```

```
for (Ray& ray : rays) {
traceRayWithAI(ray, scene, aiModel);
}
}
```

## Future Prospects

The role of AI in optimizing ray tracing will continue to expand, with ongoing research exploring new techniques and applications. AI-driven ray tracing promises to deliver unprecedented levels of realism and efficiency.

## Conclusion

AI significantly enhances ray tracing by improving performance, reducing noise, optimizing sampling, and predicting paths. These advancements enable faster, more efficient, and higher-quality rendering, transforming the capabilities of ray tracing in various applications.

# 14.2. Machine Learning Algorithms for Real-Time Rendering

Machine learning algorithms play a pivotal role in achieving real-time rendering by optimizing various aspects of the ray tracing process. These algorithms enhance efficiency, accuracy, and visual quality.

## Supervised Learning for Denoising

Supervised learning techniques can train models to denoise ray-traced images, reducing the number of samples required and speeding up the rendering process.

### Example of Supervised Learning for Denoising

```
Image denoiseWithSupervisedLearning(const Image& noisyImage, SupervisedModel& model) {

Image cleanImage = model.denoise(noisyImage);

return cleanImage;

}
```

## Reinforcement Learning for Path Tracing

Reinforcement learning algorithms can optimize path tracing by learning the most efficient paths for light rays, improving convergence rates and image quality.

### Example of Reinforcement Learning for Path Tracing

```
void optimizePathTracing(ReinforcementModel& model, const Scene& scene) {

std::vector<Ray> rays;

emitRays(scene, rays);

for (Ray& ray : rays) {

model.optimizePath(ray, scene);
```

```
traceRay(ray, scene);
}
}
```

## Generative Adversarial Networks (GANs)

GANs can generate high-quality images from low-sample ray-traced images, effectively reducing rendering times while maintaining visual fidelity.

## Example of GAN-Based Image Generation

```
Image generateWithGAN(const Image& lowSampleImage, GANModel& gan) {

Image highQualityImage = gan.generate(lowSampleImage);

return highQualityImage;
}
```

## Transfer Learning for Material Prediction

Transfer learning can be used to apply pre-trained models to predict material properties in new scenes, accelerating the process of assigning realistic materials.

## Example of Transfer Learning for Materials

```
void predictMaterialsWithTransferLearning(const Scene& scene, TransferModel& model) {

for (Object& object : scene.objects) {

object.material = model.predictMaterial(object.texture);
```

}

}

## Neural Networks for Global Illumination

Neural networks can predict global illumination effects, reducing the computational load and speeding up the rendering process.

### Example of Neural Network for Global Illumination

```
void computeGlobalIllumination(NeuralNetwork& network, const Scene& scene) {

for (Object& object : scene.objects) {

object.illumination = network.computeIllumination(object.position, scene);

}

}
```

## Adaptive Sampling with Machine Learning

Machine learning can adaptively sample areas of the scene that require more detail, optimizing the number of rays cast and improving rendering efficiency.

### Example of Adaptive Sampling

```
void adaptiveSamplingWithML(const Scene& scene, AdaptiveModel& model) {

std::vector<Ray> rays;
```

```
emitRays(scene, rays);
for (Ray& ray : rays) {
if (model.requiresDetail(ray)) {
traceRay(ray, scene);
}
}
}
```

## Bayesian Optimization for Rendering Parameters

Bayesian optimization can tune rendering parameters, such as sample counts and bounce limits, to achieve the best balance between quality and performance.

## Example of Bayesian Optimization

```
void optimizeRenderingParameters(BayesianModel& model, Scene& scene) {
RenderingParams params = model.optimize(scene);
applyRenderingParams(params, scene);
}
```

## Inverse Rendering with Machine Learning

Inverse rendering techniques use machine learning to deduce scene properties, such as lighting and material characteristics, from images, facilitating the creation of realistic scenes.

## Example of Inverse Rendering

```
void inverseRenderWithML(const Image& image, Scene& scene, InverseModel& model) {

SceneProperties properties = model.inferProperties(image);

applySceneProperties(properties, scene);

}
```

## Real-Time Rendering in Games and VR

Machine learning enables real-time ray tracing for interactive applications like gaming and virtual reality, providing high-quality visuals without compromising performance.

## Example of Real-Time Rendering

```
void renderRealTimeWithML(const Scene& scene, RealTimeModel& model) {

std::vector<Ray> rays;

emitRays(scene, rays);

for (Ray& ray : rays) {

traceRayWithML(ray, scene, model);

}

}
```

## Future Directions

The integration of machine learning with ray tracing will continue to evolve, with new algorithms and techniques enhancing the efficiency, quality, and applicability of real-time rendering.

## Conclusion

Machine learning algorithms are essential for achieving real-time rendering by optimizing denoising, path tracing, material prediction, global illumination, and more. These advancements enable faster, more efficient, and visually stunning ray-traced images.

# 14.3. Predictive Rendering and Intelligent Sampling

Predictive rendering and intelligent sampling are advanced techniques that leverage AI and machine learning to optimize ray tracing, enhancing efficiency and visual quality.

## Predictive Rendering Techniques

Predictive rendering uses AI to anticipate the behavior of light rays in a scene, reducing the computational load by focusing on areas that contribute most to the final image.

## Example of Predictive Rendering

```
void predictiveRendering(const Scene& scene, PredictiveModel& model) {

std::vector<Ray> rays;

emitRays(scene, rays);
```

```
for (Ray& ray : rays) {
    if (model.predictPath(ray)) {
        traceRay(ray, scene);
    }
  }
}
```

## Intelligent Sampling Methods

Intelligent sampling uses machine learning to adaptively sample the scene, prioritizing areas that require higher detail and reducing the number of unnecessary samples.

## Example of Intelligent Sampling

```
void intelligentSampling(const Scene& scene, SamplingModel& model) {
    std::vector<Ray> rays;
    emitRays(scene, rays);
    for (Ray& ray : rays) {
        if (model.requiresDetail(ray)) {
            traceRay(ray, scene);
        }
    }
}
```

# ILLUMINATING REALITIES: THE THEORY OF REAL-TIME RAY TRACING

## Adaptive Path Tracing

Adaptive path tracing adjusts the number of bounces and samples dynamically based on scene complexity and lighting conditions, improving rendering efficiency.

## Example of Adaptive Path Tracing

```
void adaptivePathTracing(const Scene& scene, AdaptiveModel& model) {

std::vector<Ray> rays;

emitRays(scene, rays);

for (Ray& ray : rays) {

model.adaptPath(ray, scene);

traceRay(ray, scene);

}

}
```

## AI-Driven Importance Sampling

Importance sampling focuses computational resources on the most significant areas of the scene, such as bright lights or reflective surfaces, to improve convergence rates.

## Example of Importance Sampling

```
void importanceSampling(const Scene& scene, ImportanceModel& model) {

std::vector<Ray> rays;
```

```
emitRays(scene, rays);
for (Ray& ray : rays) {
  if (model.isImportant(ray)) {
    traceRay(ray, scene);
  }
 }
}
```

## Light Transport Prediction

Predicting light transport using machine learning reduces the number of samples required to achieve accurate global illumination, speeding up the rendering process.

## Example of Light Transport Prediction

```
void predictLightTransport(const Scene& scene, LightModel& model) {
  for (Object& object : scene.objects) {
    object.illumination = model.predictIllumination(object.position, scene);
  }
}
```

## Scene Complexity Analysis

AI can analyze scene complexity and adjust rendering parameters accordingly, ensuring optimal performance for different types of scenes.

## Example of Scene Analysis

```
void analyzeSceneWithAI(const Scene& scene, ComplexityModel& model) {

SceneComplexity complexity = model.analyze(scene);

adjustRenderingSettings(complexity);

}
```

## Data-Driven Rendering

Data-driven rendering uses large datasets of previous renders to train models that can predict the best rendering strategies for new scenes, enhancing efficiency and quality.

## Example of Data-Driven Rendering

```
void renderWithDataDrivenModel(const Scene& scene, DataModel& model) {

std::vector<Ray> rays;

emitRays(scene, rays);

for (Ray& ray : rays) {

traceRayWithModel(ray, scene, model);

}
```

}

## Error Prediction and Correction

Machine learning can predict potential errors in ray tracing and apply corrections in real-time, improving the accuracy and quality of the final image.

## Example of Error Prediction

```
void predictAndCorrectErrors(const Scene& scene, ErrorModel& model) {

std::vector<Ray> rays;

emitRays(scene, rays);

for (Ray& ray : rays) {

traceRay(ray, scene);

model.correctErrors(ray, scene);

}
}
```

## Hybrid Rendering Techniques

Combining traditional ray tracing with AI-driven methods creates hybrid rendering techniques that leverage the strengths of both approaches to achieve high-quality results efficiently.

## Example of Hybrid Rendering

```
void hybridRendering(const Scene& scene, HybridModel& model) {
```

```
std::vector<Ray> rays;

emitRays(scene, rays);

for (Ray& ray : rays) {

if (model.useTraditional(ray)) {

traceRay(ray, scene);

} else {

traceRayWithAI(ray, scene, model);

}

}

}
```

## Future Trends

Predictive rendering and intelligent sampling will continue to evolve, with advancements in AI and machine learning driving further improvements in efficiency, accuracy, and visual quality.

## Conclusion

Predictive rendering and intelligent sampling leverage AI and machine learning to optimize ray tracing, enhancing efficiency and visual quality. These techniques enable faster, more accurate, and higher-quality rendering, transforming the capabilities of ray tracing in various applications.

## 14.4. AI-Assisted Denoising Techniques

AI-assisted denoising techniques play a critical role in improving the quality of ray-traced images by removing noise and enhancing visual fidelity. These techniques leverage machine learning models trained on large datasets to predict and eliminate noise effectively.

### Supervised Denoising

Supervised denoising involves training a machine learning model on pairs of noisy and clean images, enabling the model to learn how to remove noise from new images.

### Example of Supervised Denoising

```
Image denoiseWithSupervisedLearning(const Image& noisyImage, SupervisedModel& model) {

Image cleanImage = model.denoise(noisyImage);

return cleanImage;

}
```

### Unsupervised Denoising

Unsupervised denoising techniques do not require paired training data. Instead, they rely on the intrinsic properties of the noisy images to predict the clean version.

### Example of Unsupervised Denoising

```
Image denoiseWithUnsupervisedLearning(const Image& noisyImage, UnsupervisedModel& model) {

Image cleanImage = model.denoise(noisyImage);
```

return cleanImage;

}

## Denoising Autoencoders

Autoencoders are neural networks designed to learn efficient codings of input data. Denoising autoencoders specifically learn to remove noise from images by reconstructing clean images from noisy inputs.

## Example of Denoising Autoencoder

Image denoiseWithAutoencoder(const Image& noisyImage, Autoencoder& autoencoder) {

Image cleanImage = autoencoder.denoise(noisyImage);

return cleanImage;

}

## Generative Adversarial Networks (GANs)

GANs are used to generate high-quality denoised images by training two networks: a generator that produces denoised images and a discriminator that distinguishes between real and generated images.

## Example of GAN-Based Denoising

Image denoiseWithGAN(const Image& noisyImage, GANModel& gan) {

Image cleanImage = gan.denoise(noisyImage);

return cleanImage;

}

## Variational Autoencoders (VAEs)

VAEs are probabilistic models that generate denoised images by sampling from a learned latent space, providing a robust approach to denoising.

### Example of VAE-Based Denoising

Image denoiseWithVAE(const Image& noisyImage, VAEModel& vae) {

Image cleanImage = vae.denoise(noisyImage);

**return** cleanImage;

}

## Recurrent Neural Networks (RNNs)

RNNs can be used for sequential denoising, where the model processes the image in stages, progressively refining the denoised output.

### Example of RNN-Based Denoising

Image denoiseWithRNN(const Image& noisyImage, RNNModel& rnn) {

Image cleanImage = rnn.denoise(noisyImage);

**return** cleanImage;

}

## Hybrid Denoising Techniques

Combining multiple AI-assisted denoising techniques can enhance the overall performance, leveraging the strengths of different approaches to achieve the best results.

## Example of Hybrid Denoising

```
Image hybridDenoising(const Image& noisyImage, SupervisedModel& supervisedModel, GANModel& gan) {

    Image intermediateImage = supervisedModel.denoise(noisyImage);

    Image cleanImage = gan.denoise(intermediateImage);

    return cleanImage;

}
```

## Real-Time Denoising

AI-assisted denoising techniques can be optimized for real-time performance, enabling their use in interactive applications like gaming and virtual reality.

## Example of Real-Time Denoising

```
Image denoiseInRealTime(const Image& noisyImage, RealTimeModel& model) {

    Image cleanImage = model.denoise(noisyImage);

    return cleanImage;

}
```

## Training Denoising Models

Training AI-assisted denoising models requires large datasets of noisy and clean images, as well as significant computational resources for training.

## Example of Training Process

```cpp
void trainDenoisingModel(SupervisedModel& model, const Dataset& dataset) {
    for (const auto& [noisyImage, cleanImage] : dataset) {
        model.train(noisyImage, cleanImage);
    }
}
```

## Evaluating Denoising Quality

Evaluating the quality of denoised images involves metrics such as Peak Signal-to-Noise Ratio (PSNR), Structural Similarity Index (SSIM), and visual inspection.

## Example of Evaluation Metrics

```cpp
void evaluateDenoisingQuality(const Image& cleanImage, const Image& denoisedImage) {
    float psnr = calculatePSNR(cleanImage, denoisedImage);
    float ssim = calculateSSIM(cleanImage, denoisedImage);
    std::cout << "PSNR: " << psnr << ", SSIM: " << ssim << std::endl;
}
```

## Future Directions

Future advancements in AI-assisted denoising will focus on improving model accuracy, reducing computational requirements, and enhancing real-time capabilities.

## Conclusion

AI-assisted denoising techniques leverage machine learning models to remove noise and enhance the quality of ray-traced images. These techniques enable faster, more efficient, and higher-quality rendering, transforming the capabilities of ray tracing in various applications.

# 14.5. Future of AI in Ray Tracing Development

The future of AI in ray tracing development promises significant advancements in efficiency, quality, and capabilities. AI-driven techniques will continue to evolve, opening new possibilities for rendering and visual experiences.

## AI-Enhanced Realism

AI will enhance realism in ray tracing by predicting complex light interactions, material properties, and environmental effects, producing more lifelike images.

## Example of AI-Enhanced Realism

```
void enhanceRealismWithAI(const Scene& scene, AIModel& model) {

std::vector<Ray> rays;
```

```
emitRays(scene, rays);
for (Ray& ray : rays) {
    model.enhanceRealism(ray, scene);
    traceRay(ray, scene);
}
}
```

## Fully AI-Driven Rendering

Future ray tracing may involve fully AI-driven rendering pipelines, where AI models handle all aspects of the rendering process, from scene analysis to final image synthesis.

## Example of Fully AI-Driven Rendering

```
void renderWithAI(const Scene& scene, AIModel& model) {
    model.render(scene);
}
```

## Integration with Augmented and Virtual Reality

AI-driven ray tracing will play a crucial role in AR and VR, providing real-time, high-quality visuals that enhance immersive experiences.

## Example of AR/VR Integration

```
void integrateWithARVR(const Scene& scene, ARVRDevice& device, AIModel& model) {
```

model.renderARVR(scene, device);

}

## Intelligent Scene Understanding

AI will improve scene understanding by analyzing scene geometry, lighting, and materials, optimizing rendering settings for each specific scene.

## Example of Scene Understanding

void understandSceneWithAI(const Scene& scene, AIModel& model) {

SceneAnalysis analysis = model.analyze(scene);

adjustRenderingSettings(analysis);

}

## Predictive Maintenance and Optimization

AI can predict rendering bottlenecks and optimize the rendering pipeline, ensuring smooth and efficient operation.

## Example of Predictive Maintenance

void maintainAndOptimizeWithAI(RenderingPipeline& pipeline, AIModel& model) {

model.predictMaintenance(pipeline);

model.optimizePipeline(pipeline);

}

## Personalized Rendering

AI will enable personalized rendering experiences, adapting visual output to individual preferences and viewing conditions.

### Example of Personalized Rendering

```
void personalizeRendering(const Scene& scene, UserPreferences& preferences, AIModel& model) {
    model.adaptToPreferences(scene, preferences);
    model.render(scene);
}
```

## Collaborative AI Models

Collaborative AI models that learn from multiple sources and environments will enhance the robustness and adaptability of ray tracing systems.

### Example of Collaborative AI

```
void collaborateWithAI(const Scene& scene, CollaborativeModel& model) {
    model.learnFromMultipleSources(scene);
    model.render(scene);
}
```

## Quantum Computing Integration

The integration of quantum computing with AI-driven ray tracing will unlock unprecedented computational power, enabling the rendering of highly complex scenes in real time.

## Example of Quantum Computing Integration

```
void integrateQuantumComputing(const Scene& scene, QuantumModel& model) {

model.leverageQuantumPower(scene);

model.render(scene);

}
```

## Autonomous Creative AI

AI-driven ray tracing will evolve to include autonomous creative AI that can generate unique and artistic visuals without direct human intervention.

## Example of Creative AI

```
void createArtWithAI(CreativeAIModel& model) {

Image artwork = model.generateArtwork();

displayImage(artwork);

}
```

### Future Research Directions

Ongoing research will explore new AI algorithms, hybrid models, and advanced integration techniques to push the boundaries of what is possible in ray tracing.

### Conclusion

The future of AI in ray tracing development holds immense potential for advancements in efficiency, quality, and capabilities. AI-driven techniques will continue to transform rendering, providing more realistic, efficient, and personalized visual experiences.

# Chapter 15: Hardware and Ray Tracing

## 15.1. GPUs and Their Role in Ray Tracing

Graphics Processing Units (GPUs) have revolutionized the field of ray tracing by providing the computational power necessary to perform complex calculations in real-time. This section explores the evolution of GPUs, their architecture, and their role in advancing ray tracing technology.

### Evolution of GPUs for Ray Tracing

The evolution of GPUs has been marked by significant advancements in performance, parallel processing capabilities, and specialized hardware features designed for ray tracing. Initially developed for rendering raster graphics, GPUs have evolved to support complex computations required for real-time ray tracing.

# ILLUMINATING REALITIES: THE THEORY OF REAL-TIME RAY TRACING

## GPU Architecture

Modern GPUs consist of thousands of small processing units, known as cores, that can execute multiple threads simultaneously. This parallel architecture makes GPUs well-suited for the highly parallel nature of ray tracing, where multiple rays can be traced independently.

## Ray Tracing Cores

Recent advancements in GPU technology have introduced dedicated ray tracing cores, such as NVIDIA's RT Cores. These specialized cores accelerate the computation of ray-triangle intersections, bounding volume hierarchy (BVH) traversal, and other ray tracing tasks.

## Example of Ray Tracing Core Usage

```
void traceRayUsingRTCore(const Scene& scene, Ray& ray) {

// Utilize the RT Core to accelerate intersection tests

Intersection hit;

if (rtCoreIntersect(ray, scene, hit)) {

// Process the intersection

Color color = shade(hit, scene);

ray.color = color;

}
}
```

## Performance Optimization

GPUs provide various features for optimizing ray tracing performance, including memory hierarchies, cache management, and parallel processing techniques. Efficient utilization of these features is crucial for achieving real-time performance.

## Real-Time Ray Tracing with GPUs

Real-time ray tracing on GPUs is achieved by leveraging their parallel processing capabilities and specialized hardware features. Techniques such as path tracing, global illumination, and shadow calculations can be performed in real-time with modern GPUs.

## Programming GPUs for Ray Tracing

Programming GPUs for ray tracing involves using APIs such as CUDA, OpenCL, and DirectX Raytracing (DXR). These APIs provide access to GPU hardware features and enable developers to implement efficient ray tracing algorithms.

## Example of CUDA Ray Tracing Kernel

```
__global__ void traceRaysKernel(Scene scene, Ray* rays, int numRays) {

int idx = blockIdx.x * blockDim.x + threadIdx.x;

if (idx < numRays) {

traceRay(scene, rays[idx]);

}

}
```

## Future Directions for GPUs

The future of GPUs in ray tracing will likely involve further enhancements in performance, power efficiency, and specialized hardware features. Research and development in GPU technology will continue to push the boundaries of real-time ray tracing capabilities.

## Conclusion

GPUs have played a pivotal role in advancing ray tracing technology by providing the computational power necessary for real-time rendering. With their parallel architecture, specialized ray tracing cores, and optimization features, GPUs will continue to drive innovations in the field of ray tracing.

# 15.2. Custom Hardware for Ray Tracing

Custom hardware solutions, such as FPGAs and ASICs, offer unique advantages for ray tracing by providing tailored performance and efficiency optimizations. This section explores the role of custom hardware in ray tracing and its potential impact on the field.

## FPGA and ASIC Solutions

Field-Programmable Gate Arrays (FPGAs) and Application-Specific Integrated Circuits (ASICs) are custom hardware solutions designed to perform specific tasks with high efficiency. In ray tracing, these solutions can be optimized to accelerate specific computations, such as ray intersection tests and shading calculations.

## Custom Ray Tracing Chips

Custom ray tracing chips are designed specifically for ray tracing workloads. These chips integrate specialized processing units, memory hierarchies, and interconnects to achieve high performance and power efficiency.

## Performance and Efficiency

Custom hardware solutions offer significant performance and efficiency advantages over general-purpose hardware. By tailoring the architecture to the specific requirements of ray tracing, custom chips can achieve higher throughput and lower power consumption.

## Example of Custom Ray Tracing Chip Architecture

```
struct RayTracingChip {

RayTracingCore rtCores[MAX_CORES];

MemoryController memoryController;

Interconnect interconnect;

void traceRays(Scene scene, Ray* rays, int numRays) {

for (int i = 0; i < numRays; ++i) {

rtCores[i % MAX_CORES].traceRay(scene, rays[i]);

}

}

};
```

## Integration with Existing Systems

Custom ray tracing hardware can be integrated into existing systems through hardware accelerators, coprocessors, or as part of a larger system-on-chip (SoC) design. This integration enables the use of custom hardware alongside general-purpose processors and GPUs.

## Case Studies

Several case studies demonstrate the effectiveness of custom hardware solutions in ray tracing. For example, the Google Cloud TPU and NVIDIA's RT Cores showcase the performance and efficiency benefits of tailored hardware designs.

## Future Prospects

The future of custom hardware in ray tracing will involve further advancements in chip design, manufacturing processes, and integration techniques. Custom hardware solutions will continue to play a critical role in achieving real-time ray tracing performance.

## Conclusion

Custom hardware solutions, such as FPGAs and ASICs, offer unique advantages for ray tracing by providing tailored performance and efficiency optimizations. As the field of ray tracing evolves, custom hardware will continue to play a critical role in advancing performance and capabilities.

## 15.3. The Evolution of Ray Tracing Hardware

The evolution of ray tracing hardware has been marked by significant advancements in performance, capabilities, and integration. This section explores the historical development of ray tracing hardware and its impact on the field of visual computing.

### Historical Perspective

The history of ray tracing hardware dates back to the early days of computer graphics, where ray tracing was performed on general-purpose CPUs. Early implementations were limited by the computational power available at the time, making real-time ray tracing impractical.

### Milestones in Hardware Development

Several milestones in hardware development have contributed to the evolution of ray tracing. The introduction of GPUs, the development of dedicated ray tracing cores, and the advent of custom hardware solutions have each played a role in advancing the field.

### Impact on Visual Computing

Advancements in ray tracing hardware have had a profound impact on visual computing. Improved performance and capabilities have enabled the creation of highly realistic images and real-time applications, transforming industries such as gaming, film, and virtual reality.

# ILLUMINATING REALITIES: THE THEORY OF REAL-TIME RAY TRACING

## Current Trends

Current trends in ray tracing hardware include the integration of AI and machine learning, the development of hybrid rendering techniques, and the focus on power efficiency. These trends are driving the next generation of ray tracing hardware.

## Example of Hybrid Rendering

```
void renderSceneHybrid(const Scene& scene, Image& output) {
// Use rasterization for primary rendering
rasterizeScene(scene, output);
// Use ray tracing for reflections and shadows
std::vector<Ray> rays;
emitRaysForReflections(scene, rays);
for (Ray& ray : rays) {
traceRay(ray, scene);
}
compositeRays(output, rays);
}
```

## Future Innovations

Future innovations in ray tracing hardware will likely involve advancements in quantum computing, neuromorphic computing, and other emerging technologies. These innovations have the potential to revolutionize the field of ray tracing.

## Conclusion

The evolution of ray tracing hardware has been marked by significant advancements that have transformed visual computing. As the field continues to evolve, ongoing innovations will drive further improvements in performance, capabilities, and applications.

## 15.4. Comparing Different Hardware Solutions

Different hardware solutions offer unique advantages and trade-offs for ray tracing. This section compares GPUs, CPUs, FPGAs, and ASICs in terms of performance, efficiency, and use cases.

### GPUs vs. CPUs

GPUs and CPUs are both used for ray tracing, but they offer different strengths. GPUs excel at parallel processing, making them well-suited for ray tracing tasks that involve many independent rays. CPUs, on the other hand, offer high single-thread performance and flexibility.

### Example of GPU Ray Tracing

void traceRaysOnGPU(const Scene& scene, Ray* rays, int numRays) {

// Launch GPU kernel for ray tracing

traceRaysKernel<<<numBlocks, numThreads>>>(scene, rays, numRays);

}

## Example of CPU Ray Tracing

void traceRaysOnCPU(const Scene& scene, Ray* rays, int numRays) {

**for** (int i = 0; i < numRays; ++i) {

traceRay(scene, rays[i]);

}

}

## FPGA vs. ASIC

FPGAs and ASICs offer custom hardware solutions for ray tracing. FPGAs provide flexibility and reconfigurability, allowing for iterative development and optimization. ASICs, however, offer higher performance and efficiency for specific tasks.

## Example of FPGA Ray Tracing

void traceRaysOnFPGA(const Scene& scene, Ray* rays, int numRays) {

// *Configure FPGA for ray tracing*

configureFPGA(scene);

**for** (int i = 0; i < numRays; ++i) {

traceRayOnFPGA(rays[i]);

}

}

## Example of ASIC Ray Tracing

```
void traceRaysOnASIC(const Scene& scene, Ray* rays, int numRays) {
    // Use ASIC for high-performance ray tracing
    asicTraceRays(scene, rays, numRays);
}
```

## Performance Benchmarks

Performance benchmarks compare the throughput, latency, and power efficiency of different hardware solutions. These benchmarks help identify the most suitable hardware for specific ray tracing applications.

## Use Cases

Different hardware solutions are suited for different use cases. GPUs are ideal for real-time applications, CPUs are suitable for development and debugging, FPGAs are useful for iterative optimization, and ASICs are best for high-performance, power-efficient solutions.

## Cost and Efficiency

Cost and efficiency are important considerations when choosing hardware for ray tracing. GPUs and CPUs offer cost-effective solutions with broad applicability, while FPGAs and ASICs provide specialized performance at a higher cost.

## Conclusion

Different hardware solutions offer unique advantages and trade-offs for ray tracing. By comparing performance, efficiency, and use cases, developers can choose the most suitable hardware for their specific applications.

## 15.5. Future Hardware Trends in Ray Tracing

The future of ray tracing hardware is marked by emerging technologies and trends that promise to revolutionize the field. This section explores these trends and their potential impact on ray tracing.

### Emerging Technologies

Emerging technologies, such as quantum computing, neuromorphic computing, and photonic computing, hold the potential to transform ray tracing by providing unprecedented computational power and efficiency.

### Example of Quantum Computing

```
void traceRaysWithQuantumComputing(const Scene& scene, Ray* rays, int numRays) {
    // Use quantum computing for complex ray tracing calculations
    quantumTraceRays(scene, rays, numRays);
}
```

## Integration with AI

The integration of AI with ray tracing hardware will enable new levels of performance and realism. AI-driven optimizations, predictive rendering, and intelligent sampling are just a few examples of how AI will enhance ray tracing.

### Example of AI Integration

```
void traceRaysWithAI(const Scene& scene, Ray* rays, int numRays, AIModel& model) {
// Use AI to optimize ray tracing
for (int i = 0; i < numRays; ++i) {
model.optimizeRay(rays[i], scene);
traceRay(scene, rays[i]);
}
}
```

## Quantum Computing

Quantum computing offers the potential to solve complex ray tracing problems that are currently intractable with classical computing. This technology could revolutionize the field by enabling real-time rendering of highly complex scenes.

### Example of Quantum Ray Tracing

```
void quantumRayTracing(const Scene& scene, Ray* rays, int numRays) {
// Apply quantum algorithms for ray tracing
```

quantumAlgorithm(scene, rays, numRays);

}

## Energy Efficiency

Energy efficiency is a critical consideration for future ray tracing hardware. Innovations in low-power design, efficient computation, and optimized hardware architectures will help reduce the energy consumption of ray tracing systems.

## Example of Energy-Efficient Ray Tracing

```
void energyEfficientRayTracing(const Scene& scene, Ray* rays, int numRays) {
    // Utilize energy-efficient algorithms and hardware
    for (int i = 0; i < numRays; ++i) {
        energyEfficientTrace(scene, rays[i]);
    }
}
```

## Industry Impact

The advancements in ray tracing hardware will have a significant impact on various industries, including gaming, film, virtual reality, architecture, and scientific visualization. These advancements will enable new levels of realism and interactivity.

## Example of Industry Impact

```
void applyRayTracingInGaming(const Scene& scene, GameEngine& engine) {
```

```
// Integrate advanced ray tracing techniques in game development
engine.renderSceneWithRayTracing(scene);
}
```

## Conclusion

The future of ray tracing hardware is marked by emerging technologies and trends that promise to revolutionize the field. By embracing these advancements, the industry can achieve new levels of performance, efficiency, and realism in ray tracing.

# Chapter 16: Software and Tools for Ray Tracing

## 16.1. Overview of Ray Tracing Software

Ray tracing software provides the tools and frameworks necessary for implementing and optimizing ray tracing algorithms. This section offers an overview of popular ray tracing software and their features.

### Introduction to Ray Tracing Software

Ray tracing software includes libraries, frameworks, and standalone applications that facilitate the development and execution of ray tracing algorithms. These tools provide essential functionalities, such as scene description, ray casting, shading, and rendering.

### Popular Ray Tracing Libraries

Several libraries are widely used in the ray tracing community, including PBRT, Embree, and OptiX. These libraries offer robust functionalities and optimizations for ray tracing.

# Example of Using PBRT

#include <pbrt.h>

void renderSceneWithPBRT(const Scene& scene) {

// *Initialize PBRT*

PBRTOptions options;

pbrtInit(options);

// *Load scene and render*

pbrtScene(scene);

pbrtRender();

// *Cleanup*

pbrtCleanup();

}

# Features of Ray Tracing Software

Ray tracing software typically includes features such as scene description, ray intersection tests, shading models, lighting calculations, and output management. Advanced tools may also support distributed rendering, GPU acceleration, and AI integration.

# Example of Scene Description

Scene createExampleScene() {

Scene scene;

```
// Add objects to the scene

scene.addObject(Sphere(Vector3(0, 0, -5), 1.0, Material(Color(1, 0, 0))));

scene.addObject(Plane(Vector3(0, -1, 0), Vector3(0, 1, 0), Material(Color(0.8, 0.8, 0.8))));

// Add light sources

scene.addLight(PointLight(Vector3(2, 2, 0), Color(1, 1, 1)));

return scene;
}
```

## Integration with Graphics APIs

Ray tracing software often integrates with graphics APIs such as OpenGL, Vulkan, and DirectX to leverage GPU capabilities and enhance performance. This integration allows for real-time rendering and interactive applications.

## Example of Vulkan Integration

```
void renderWithVulkan(const Scene& scene) {

VulkanRenderer renderer;

renderer.initialize();

// Load scene and render

renderer.loadScene(scene);

renderer.render();

renderer.cleanup();
```

}

## Customizable Shading Models

Many ray tracing tools allow developers to customize shading models to achieve specific visual effects. This flexibility is essential for creating realistic and artistic renderings.

## Example of Custom Shading

```
Color customShade(const Intersection& hit, const Scene& scene)
{
    // Implement custom shading model
    Color ambient = hit.material.ambient;

    Color diffuse = hit.material.diffuse * max(0.0f, dot(hit.normal, scene.light.direction));

    Color specular = hit.material.specular * pow(max(0.0f, dot(reflect(-scene.light.direction, hit.normal), hit.viewDirection)), hit.material.shininess);

    return ambient + diffuse + specular;
}
```

## Distributed Rendering

Distributed rendering allows for parallel processing of ray tracing tasks across multiple machines, significantly reducing rendering times for complex scenes.

## Example of Distributed Rendering

```
void distributedRender(const Scene& scene, RenderCluster& cluster) {

cluster.initialize();

// Distribute rendering tasks

cluster.distributeScene(scene);

cluster.render();

cluster.cleanup();

}
```

## AI Integration

Integrating AI with ray tracing software enhances performance and visual quality. AI techniques such as denoising, adaptive sampling, and predictive rendering are increasingly common in modern ray tracing tools.

## Example of AI Denoising

```
void denoiseWithAI(const Image& noisyImage, AIModel& model) {

Image cleanImage = model.denoise(noisyImage);

saveImage(cleanImage, "denoised_output.png");

}
```

## Conclusion

Ray tracing software provides essential tools and frameworks for implementing and optimizing ray tracing algorithms. With features such as scene description, shading models, GPU acceleration, and AI integration, these tools enable the creation of realistic and efficient ray-traced images.

## 16.2. Programming Languages and APIs for Ray Tracing

Programming languages and APIs play a crucial role in the development of ray tracing applications. This section explores popular languages and APIs used in ray tracing and their key features.

### C++ for Ray Tracing

C++ is a popular programming language for ray tracing due to its performance, flexibility, and extensive libraries. Many ray tracing engines and frameworks are developed in C++.

### Example of C++ Ray Tracing

#include **<iostream>**

#include **<vector>**

#include **"raytracer.h"**

int main() {

Scene scene = createExampleScene();

Image output = raytrace(scene);

```cpp
saveImage(output, "output.png");

return 0;
}
```

## Python for Rapid Prototyping

Python is often used for rapid prototyping and experimentation in ray tracing. Its simplicity and extensive libraries make it suitable for developing and testing new algorithms.

## Example of Python Ray Tracing

```python
import raytracer

scene = raytracer.create_example_scene()

output = raytracer.raytrace(scene)

raytracer.save_image(output, "output.png")
```

## CUDA and OpenCL for GPU Acceleration

CUDA and OpenCL are APIs used for developing GPU-accelerated ray tracing applications. These APIs provide access to GPU hardware features and enable parallel processing of ray tracing tasks.

## Example of CUDA Ray Tracing

```cpp
__global__ void traceRaysKernel(Scene scene, Ray* rays, int numRays) {

int idx = blockIdx.x * blockDim.x + threadIdx.x;

if (idx < numRays) {
```

```
traceRay(scene, rays[idx]);

}

}

void traceRaysWithCUDA(Scene& scene, Ray* rays, int numRays) {

Ray* d_rays;

cudaMalloc(&d_rays, numRays * sizeof(Ray));

cudaMemcpy(d_rays, rays, numRays * sizeof(Ray), cudaMemcpyHostToDevice);

traceRaysKernel<<<numBlocks, numThreads>>>(scene, d_rays, numRays);

cudaMemcpy(rays, d_rays, numRays * sizeof(Ray), cudaMemcpyDeviceToHost);

cudaFree(d_rays);

}
```

## Vulkan and DirectX Raytracing (DXR)

Vulkan and DirectX Raytracing (DXR) are graphics APIs that support ray tracing. They provide advanced features for real-time ray tracing and are widely used in gaming and interactive applications.

## Example of Vulkan Ray Tracing

```
void initializeVulkanRayTracing(VulkanRenderer& renderer) {

renderer.initializeRayTracing();
```

```
Scene scene = createExampleScene();
renderer.loadScene(scene);
renderer.render();
renderer.cleanup();
}
```

## OpenGL for Cross-Platform Development

OpenGL is a cross-platform graphics API that supports ray tracing through extensions and libraries. It is widely used for developing portable ray tracing applications.

## Example of OpenGL Ray Tracing

```
void initializeOpenGLRayTracing(OpenGLRenderer& renderer)
{
renderer.initializeRayTracing();
Scene scene = createExampleScene();
renderer.loadScene(scene);
renderer.render();
renderer.cleanup();
}
```

## Metal for Apple Ecosystem

Metal is a graphics API developed by Apple that supports ray tracing on macOS and iOS devices. It provides high-performance graphics capabilities for the Apple ecosystem.

## Example of Metal Ray Tracing

```
void initializeMetalRayTracing(MetalRenderer& renderer) {

renderer.initializeRayTracing();

Scene scene = createExampleScene();

renderer.loadScene(scene);

renderer.render();

renderer.cleanup();

}
```

## WebGL for Web-Based Applications

WebGL is a web-based graphics API that enables ray tracing in web browsers. It is used for developing interactive ray tracing applications that run on the web.

## Example of WebGL Ray Tracing

```
function initializeWebGLRayTracing(renderer) {

renderer.initializeRayTracing();

let scene = createExampleScene();

renderer.loadScene(scene);

renderer.render();

}
```

## Conclusion

Programming languages and APIs are essential for developing ray tracing applications. With options like C++, Python, CUDA, OpenCL, Vulkan, DirectX, OpenGL, Metal, and WebGL, developers have a wide range of tools to choose from based on their specific needs and target platforms.

## 16.3. Integrating Ray Tracing into Existing Engines

Integrating ray tracing into existing engines involves adding ray tracing capabilities to enhance visual quality and performance. This section explores techniques and examples for integrating ray tracing into popular game and graphics engines.

### Unreal Engine

Unreal Engine is a widely used game engine that supports ray tracing through its rendering pipeline. Integrating ray tracing into Unreal Engine involves configuring settings and using ray tracing-specific features.

### Example of Unreal Engine Ray Tracing Integration

void configureRayTracingInUnreal() {

// *Enable ray tracing in project settings*

UEngineSettings::Get()->SetRayTracingEnabled(**true**);

// *Configure ray tracing settings*

URayTracingSettings* settings = UEngineSettings::Get()->GetRayTracingSettings();

settings->bEnableRayTracingShadows = **true**;

settings->bEnableRayTracingReflections = **true**;

settings->bEnableRayTracingGlobalIllumination = **true**;

}

## Unity

Unity is another popular game engine that supports ray tracing through the High Definition Render Pipeline (HDRP). Integrating ray tracing into Unity involves setting up HDRP and enabling ray tracing features.

## Example of Unity Ray Tracing Integration

void ConfigureRayTracingInUnity() {

// *Enable ray tracing in HDRP settings*

HDRenderPipelineAsset hdrpAsset = GraphicsSettings.renderPipelineAsset **as** HDRenderPipelineAsset;

**if** (hdrpAsset != **null**) {

hdrpAsset.currentPlatformRenderPipelineSettings.supportRayTracing = **true**;

// *Configure ray tracing settings*

hdrpAsset.currentPlatformRenderPipelineSettings.rayTracingSettings.enab = **true**;

hdrpAsset.currentPlatformRenderPipelineSettings.rayTracingSettings.rayT = RayTracingMode.Performance;

}

}

## OpenSceneGraph

OpenSceneGraph is an open-source graphics toolkit that can be extended with ray tracing capabilities. Integrating ray tracing into OpenSceneGraph involves adding custom shaders and ray tracing modules.

## Example of OpenSceneGraph Ray Tracing Integration

```
void integrateRayTracingWithOSG(osg::Group* root) {
// Load scene
osg::ref_ptr<osg::Node> scene = osgDB::readNodeFile("example.osg");
root->addChild(scene.get());
// Add ray tracing shader
osg::ref_ptr<osg::Program> program = new osg::Program;
program->addShader(new osg::Shader(osg::Shader::VERTEX, rayTracingVertexShader));
program->addShader(new osg::Shader(osg::Shader::FRAGMENT, rayTracingFragmentShader));
root->getOrCreateStateSet()->setAttributeAndModes(program.get(), osg::StateAttribute::ON);
```

}

## CryEngine

CryEngine is a high-performance game engine that supports ray tracing through its renderer. Integrating ray tracing into CryEngine involves configuring settings and using ray tracing-specific APIs.

## Example of CryEngine Ray Tracing Integration

```
void configureRayTracingInCryEngine() {

// Enable ray tracing in project settings

ICVar* pVar = gEnv->pConsole->GetCVar("e_RayTracing");

if (pVar) {

pVar->Set(1);

}

// Configure ray tracing settings

ICVar* pRayTracingShadows = gEnv->pConsole->GetCVar("e_RayTracingShadows");

if (pRayTracingShadows) {

pRayTracingShadows->Set(1);

}

}
```

## Godot Engine

Godot Engine is an open-source game engine that supports ray tracing through its Vulkan renderer. Integrating ray tracing into Godot involves configuring Vulkan settings and enabling ray tracing features.

### Example of Godot Ray Tracing Integration

```
void configureRayTracingInGodot() {
// Enable Vulkan renderer
Renderer::get_singleton()->set_renderer(Renderer::RENDERER_VULK
// Enable ray tracing settings
RenderSettings* settings = RenderSettings::get_singleton();
settings->set_bool("rendering/quality/ray_tracing", true);
settings->set_int("rendering/quality/ray_tracing_mode", 1);
}
```

## Custom Engines

Integrating ray tracing into custom engines involves modifying the rendering pipeline to support ray tracing features. This includes adding ray tracing shaders, configuring settings, and optimizing performance.

### Example of Custom Engine Ray Tracing Integration

```
void integrateRayTracingWithCustomEngine(CustomEngine& engine) {
```

```
// Add ray tracing shaders

engine.addShader("ray_tracing_vertex", rayTracingVertexShader);

engine.addShader("ray_tracing_fragment", rayTracingFragmentShader);

// Configure ray tracing settings

engine.setRayTracingEnabled(true);

engine.setRayTracingMode(CustomEngine::RayTracingMode::Quality);
}
```

## Conclusion

Integrating ray tracing into existing engines enhances visual quality and performance. By configuring settings, adding shaders, and using ray tracing-specific APIs, developers can leverage the power of ray tracing in popular game and graphics engines.

## 16.4. Tools and Libraries for Developers

A variety of tools and libraries are available to assist developers in implementing and optimizing ray tracing algorithms. This section explores some of the most popular tools and libraries used in ray tracing development.

### PBRT (Physically Based Rendering Toolkit)

PBRT is a widely used library for physically based rendering. It provides a comprehensive framework for developing ray tracing algorithms and supports advanced features such as global illumination, participating media, and subsurface scattering.

## Example of Using PBRT

```
#include <pbrt.h>

void renderSceneWithPBRT(const Scene& scene) {
    // Initialize PBRT
    PBRTOptions options;
    pbrtInit(options);
    // Load scene and render
    pbrtScene(scene);
    pbrtRender();
    // Cleanup
    pbrtCleanup();
}
```

## Embree

Embree is an open-source library developed by Intel that provides high-performance ray tracing kernels. It is optimized for modern CPU architectures and supports features such as BVH construction, ray traversal, and intersection tests.

## Example of Using Embree

```
#include <embree3/rtcore.h>

void renderSceneWithEmbree(const Scene& scene) {
    // Initialize Embree device
```

```
RTCDevice device = rtcNewDevice(NULL);
// Create scene
RTCScene embreeScene = rtcNewScene(device);
loadSceneIntoEmbree(scene, embreeScene);
// Render scene
renderEmbreeScene(device, embreeScene);
// Cleanup
rtcReleaseScene(embreeScene);
rtcReleaseDevice(device);
}
```

## OptiX

OptiX is an API developed by NVIDIA for GPU-accelerated ray tracing. It provides a flexible framework for implementing ray tracing algorithms on NVIDIA GPUs and supports advanced features such as denoising, motion blur, and adaptive sampling.

## Example of Using OptiX

```
#include <optix.h>
void renderSceneWithOptiX(const Scene& scene) {
// Initialize OptiX context
OptixDeviceContext context;
optixDeviceContextCreate(0, 0, &context);
```

```
// Create pipeline and modules
OptixPipeline pipeline;
createOptiXPipeline(context, pipeline);
// Load scene and render
loadSceneIntoOptiX(scene, context, pipeline);
renderOptiXScene(context, pipeline);
// Cleanup
optixPipelineDestroy(pipeline);
optixDeviceContextDestroy(context);
}
```

## OSPRay

OSPRay is an open-source ray tracing library developed by Intel. It is designed for high-performance, scalable rendering on CPUs and supports features such as volume rendering, global illumination, and ambient occlusion.

## Example of Using OSPRay

```
#include <ospray/ospray.h>
void renderSceneWithOSPRay(const Scene& scene) {
// Initialize OSPRay
ospInit(NULL, NULL);
// Create renderer and load scene
```

```
OSPRenderer renderer = ospNewRenderer("scivis");

loadSceneIntoOSPRay(scene, renderer);

// Render scene

renderOSPRayScene(renderer);

// Cleanup

ospRelease(renderer);

ospShutdown();
}
```

## Radeon ProRender

Radeon ProRender is a high-performance ray tracing engine developed by AMD. It supports GPU and CPU rendering and provides features such as physically based materials, global illumination, and denoising.

## Example of Using Radeon ProRender

```
#include <RadeonProRender.h>

void renderSceneWithProRender(const Scene& scene) {

// Initialize ProRender context

rpr_context context;

rprCreateContext(RPR_API_VERSION, NULL, 0, RPR_CREATION_FLAGS_ENABLE_GPU0, NULL, NULL, &context);

// Create scene and load data
```

```
rpr_scene proScene;

rprContextCreateScene(context, &proScene);

loadSceneIntoProRender(scene, context, proScene);
// Render scene
renderProRenderScene(context, proScene);
// Cleanup
rprObjectDelete(proScene);

rprObjectDelete(context);
}
```

## Mitsuba

Mitsuba is a research-oriented ray tracing framework that supports a wide range of rendering algorithms and material models. It is designed for flexibility and extensibility, making it suitable for experimenting with new rendering techniques.

## Example of Using Mitsuba

```
#include <mitsuba/core/scene.h>

void renderSceneWithMitsuba(const Scene& scene) {
// Load Mitsuba scene
ref<Scene> mitsubaScene = loadScene(scene);
// Configure integrator and render
ref<Integrator> integrator = mitsubaScene->getIntegrator();
```

```
integrator->render(mitsubaScene);

// Save output

mitsubaScene->save("output.exr");

}
```

## LuxCoreRender

LuxCoreRender is an open-source physically based renderer that supports advanced features such as bidirectional path tracing, volumetric scattering, and spectral rendering. It is designed for high-quality, photorealistic rendering.

## Example of Using LuxCoreRender

```
#include <luxcore/luxcore.h>

void renderSceneWithLuxCore(const Scene& scene) {

// Initialize LuxCore

luxcore::Init();

// Create scene and load data

luxcore::Scene* luxScene = luxcore::Scene::Create();

loadSceneIntoLuxCore(scene, luxScene);

// Configure render settings and render

luxcore::RenderConfig* config = luxcore::RenderConfig::Create(luxScene);

luxcore::RenderSession* session = luxcore::RenderSession::Create(config);
```

```
session->Start();

// Save output

session->GetFilm().SaveOutputs();

}
```

## Conclusion

A variety of tools and libraries are available to assist developers in implementing and optimizing ray tracing algorithms. By leveraging these resources, developers can create high-performance, photorealistic ray tracing applications with advanced features and capabilities.

## 16.5. Open Source vs. Proprietary Solutions

Choosing between open source and proprietary solutions for ray tracing involves considering factors such as cost, flexibility, support, and performance. This section explores the advantages and disadvantages of both types of solutions.

### Advantages of Open Source Solutions

Open source solutions offer several benefits, including cost savings, flexibility, and a collaborative community. Developers can access the source code, customize it to their needs, and contribute to the project's development.

### Example of Open Source Solution: PBRT

```
#include <pbrt.h>

void renderSceneWithPBRT(const Scene& scene) {
```

```
// Initialize PBRT
PBRTOptions options;
pbrtInit(options);
// Load scene and render
pbrtScene(scene);
pbrtRender();
// Cleanup
pbrtCleanup();
}
```

## Advantages of Proprietary Solutions

Proprietary solutions often provide professional support, comprehensive documentation, and optimized performance. They may include advanced features and integrations that are not available in open source alternatives.

## Example of Proprietary Solution: OptiX

```
#include <optix.h>
void renderSceneWithOptiX(const Scene& scene) {
// Initialize OptiX context
OptixDeviceContext context;
optixDeviceContextCreate(0, 0, &context);
// Create pipeline and modules
```

```
OptixPipeline pipeline;
createOptiXPipeline(context, pipeline);
// Load scene and render
loadSceneIntoOptiX(scene, context, pipeline);
renderOptiXScene(context, pipeline);
// Cleanup
optixPipelineDestroy(pipeline);
optixDeviceContextDestroy(context);
}
```

## Cost Considerations

Open source solutions are typically free to use, making them an attractive option for individuals and small teams. Proprietary solutions often require licensing fees, which can be justified by the value of professional support and advanced features.

## Example of Cost Comparison

```
void compareCosts() {
// Open source solution
PBRT pbrt;
pbrt.render(scene);
// Proprietary solution
OptiX optix;
```

```
optix.render(scene);

// Cost comparison

std::cout << "PBRT: Free" << std::endl;

std::cout << "OptiX: License fee required" << std::endl;

}
```

## Flexibility and Customization

Open source solutions offer greater flexibility and customization options, allowing developers to modify the source code to fit their specific needs. Proprietary solutions may offer limited customization but often provide more polished and user-friendly interfaces.

## Example of Customization

```
void customizeOpenSourceSolution(Scene& scene) {

// Modify PBRT source code for custom shading model

pbrt.customizeShadingModel(customShadingModel);

pbrt.render(scene);

}
```

## Support and Community

Open source projects often rely on community support, which can be variable in quality and availability. Proprietary solutions typically offer professional support and comprehensive documentation, providing more reliable assistance for troubleshooting and development.

## Example of Community Support

```
void seekCommunitySupport() {
```
// Post question on PBRT forum

```
std::string question = "How to implement custom integrator in PBRT?";

postToForum("pbrt-users", question);
```
// Seek professional support for OptiX

```
std::string issue = "Error in pipeline creation";

optixSupport.requestAssistance(issue);

}
```

## Performance and Optimization

Proprietary solutions are often highly optimized for specific hardware and offer advanced performance features. Open source solutions may require additional optimization efforts by the developer.

## Example of Performance Optimization

```
void optimizePerformance() {
```
// Optimize PBRT performance

```
pbrt.optimize(scene);
```
// Use OptiX for hardware-accelerated performance

```
optix.optimize(scene);
```

}

## Conclusion

Choosing between open source and proprietary solutions for ray tracing involves weighing factors such as cost, flexibility, support, and performance. Both types of solutions offer unique advantages, and the choice depends on the specific needs and constraints of the project.

# Chapter 17: Real-Time Ray Tracing in Design and Architecture

## 17.1. Applications in Interior and Architectural Design

Real-time ray tracing has revolutionized interior and architectural design by enabling designers to create photorealistic renderings of spaces quickly and efficiently. This technology allows for accurate visualization of lighting, materials, and spatial relationships, enhancing the design process and client presentations.

### Enhancing Design Visualization

With real-time ray tracing, designers can visualize their concepts with unprecedented clarity. The ability to see how light interacts with different materials and surfaces helps in making informed design decisions.

### Example of Design Visualization

```
void visualizeDesign(const Scene& scene, Renderer& renderer) {

renderer.initialize();
```

renderer.loadScene(scene);

renderer.render();

}

## Interactive Design Adjustments

Real-time ray tracing allows for interactive adjustments to the design. Designers can modify lighting, materials, and geometry in real-time, seeing immediate results. This interactivity accelerates the design iteration process.

## Example of Interactive Adjustments

void adjustDesign(Renderer& renderer, Material& newMaterial) {

renderer.updateMaterial(newMaterial);

renderer.render();

}

## Accurate Lighting Simulation

One of the significant advantages of real-time ray tracing in design is its ability to simulate lighting accurately. This includes natural light, artificial light sources, and their interactions within a space.

## Example of Lighting Simulation

void simulateLighting(const Scene& scene, Light& sunlight, Light& artificialLight) {

scene.addLight(sunlight);

scene.addLight(artificialLight);

Renderer renderer;

renderer.render(scene);

}

## Material and Texture Realism

Real-time ray tracing provides realistic rendering of materials and textures, allowing designers to see the true appearance of surfaces. This includes reflections, refractions, and the interaction of light with different textures.

## Example of Material Realism

void renderMaterialRealism(const Scene& scene, Material& material) {

scene.addMaterial(material);

Renderer renderer;

renderer.render(scene);

}

## Client Presentations

The ability to present photorealistic renderings to clients enhances communication and helps in gaining client approval. Clients can better understand the design intent and provide feedback based on realistic visualizations.

## Example of Client Presentation

void presentToClient(const Scene& scene, Renderer& renderer) {

```
renderer.loadScene(scene);
renderer.render();
renderer.display();
}
```

## Virtual Reality Integration

Integrating real-time ray tracing with virtual reality (VR) provides immersive design experiences. Clients and designers can explore virtual spaces, experiencing the design at a one-to-one scale.

## Example of VR Integration

```
void integrateWithVR(const Scene& scene, VRDevice& vrDevice)
{
vrDevice.loadScene(scene);
vrDevice.render();
vrDevice.startSession();
}
```

## Efficient Design Iterations

Real-time ray tracing reduces the time required for design iterations. Designers can quickly test different configurations, materials, and lighting setups, leading to more refined and well-considered designs.

# Example of Efficient Iterations

```
void iterateDesign(Renderer& renderer, Scene& scene, Material& newMaterial) {

renderer.loadScene(scene);

scene.addMaterial(newMaterial);

renderer.render();

}
```

# Conclusion

Real-time ray tracing in interior and architectural design enhances visualization, improves client presentations, and accelerates the design process. Its ability to render realistic lighting, materials, and textures makes it an invaluable tool for modern designers.

## 17.2. Real-Time Visualization in Urban Planning

Real-time ray tracing is a powerful tool for urban planning, enabling planners to visualize large-scale projects with high accuracy and detail. This technology helps in understanding the impact of new developments on the urban environment.

### Large-Scale Visualization

Real-time ray tracing allows for the visualization of entire urban areas, including buildings, streets, and public spaces. This comprehensive view helps planners make informed decisions about urban development.

## Example of Urban Visualization

```
void visualizeUrbanArea(const Scene& urbanScene, Renderer& renderer) {
renderer.initialize();
renderer.loadScene(urbanScene);
renderer.render();
}
```

## Impact Analysis

By visualizing proposed developments, planners can analyze their impact on the surrounding environment. This includes evaluating shadows, traffic flow, and the visual integration of new buildings with existing structures.

## Example of Impact Analysis

```
void analyzeImpact(const Scene& urbanScene, Building& newBuilding) {
urbanScene.addBuilding(newBuilding);
Renderer renderer;
renderer.render(urbanScene);
}
```

## Public Engagement

Real-time ray tracing facilitates public engagement by providing clear and realistic visualizations of proposed projects. This helps in communicating the vision to the public and gathering feedback.

## Example of Public Engagement

```
void engagePublic(const Scene& urbanScene, Renderer& renderer) {

renderer.loadScene(urbanScene);

renderer.render();

renderer.displayForPublic();

}
```

## Interactive Urban Planning

Planners can interactively explore different design scenarios, making adjustments in real-time. This interactivity supports collaborative planning sessions and quick decision-making.

## Example of Interactive Planning

```
void planInteractively(Renderer& renderer, Scene& urbanScene, Building& newBuilding) {

renderer.loadScene(urbanScene);

urbanScene.addBuilding(newBuilding);

renderer.render();

}
```

## Sustainable Design

Real-time ray tracing supports sustainable urban planning by allowing for the analysis of environmental factors. Planners can evaluate solar exposure, wind patterns, and energy efficiency.

## Example of Sustainable Analysis

```
void analyzeSustainability(const Scene& urbanScene, EnvironmentalFactors& factors) {
    Renderer renderer;
    renderer.loadScene(urbanScene);
    renderer.analyze(factors);
}
```

## Traffic Simulation

Integrating traffic simulation with real-time ray tracing provides insights into the impact of new developments on traffic flow. Planners can test different road configurations and assess their effectiveness.

## Example of Traffic Simulation

```
void simulateTraffic(const Scene& urbanScene, TrafficData& trafficData) {
    Renderer renderer;
    renderer.loadScene(urbanScene);
    renderer.simulateTraffic(trafficData);
```

}

## Pedestrian Flow

Real-time visualization of pedestrian flow helps in designing walkable and accessible urban environments. Planners can assess the movement of people through public spaces and optimize pathways.

## Example of Pedestrian Flow Analysis

void analyzePedestrianFlow(const Scene& urbanScene, PedestrianData& pedestrianData) {

Renderer renderer;

renderer.loadScene(urbanScene);

renderer.simulatePedestrianFlow(pedestrianData);

}

## Conclusion

Real-time ray tracing in urban planning enhances visualization, supports public engagement, and enables interactive planning. By providing detailed and realistic visualizations, this technology helps in creating sustainable and well-planned urban environments.

## 17.3. Lighting Simulation for Architectural Spaces

Real-time ray tracing enables accurate lighting simulation for architectural spaces, enhancing the design and evaluation of lighting schemes. This technology allows designers to visualize how light interacts with different materials and surfaces.

## Accurate Daylighting Simulation

Real-time ray tracing simulates natural daylight, allowing designers to evaluate how sunlight enters and moves through a space. This helps in optimizing window placement and designing energy-efficient buildings.

## Example of Daylighting Simulation

void simulateDaylighting(const Scene& scene, Light& sunlight) {

scene.addLight(sunlight);

Renderer renderer;

renderer.render(scene);

}

## Artificial Lighting Design

Designing artificial lighting schemes is critical for creating functional and aesthetically pleasing spaces. Real-time ray tracing allows designers to experiment with different lighting fixtures and placements.

## Example of Artificial Lighting Design

void designArtificialLighting(const Scene& scene, Light& artificialLight) {

scene.addLight(artificialLight);

Renderer renderer;

renderer.render(scene);

}

## Light Interaction with Materials

The interaction of light with different materials affects the overall ambiance and visual appeal of a space. Real-time ray tracing accurately renders reflections, refractions, and shadows, providing a realistic representation of material properties.

## Example of Material Interaction

void renderMaterialInteraction(const Scene& scene, Material& material) {

scene.addMaterial(material);

Renderer renderer;

renderer.render(scene);

}

## Energy Efficiency Analysis

Real-time lighting simulation helps in analyzing the energy efficiency of a design. By evaluating daylighting and artificial lighting together, designers can optimize for energy savings while maintaining visual comfort.

## Example of Energy Efficiency Analysis

void analyzeEnergyEfficiency(const Scene& scene, Light& sunlight, Light& artificialLight) {

scene.addLight(sunlight);

scene.addLight(artificialLight);

```
Renderer renderer;

renderer.render(scene);

}
```

## Visual Comfort

Assessing visual comfort is essential for designing spaces that are pleasant to occupy. Real-time ray tracing allows for the evaluation of glare, brightness, and color rendering, ensuring a comfortable environment.

## Example of Visual Comfort Evaluation

```
void evaluateVisualComfort(const Scene& scene, Light& lighting) {

scene.addLight(lighting);

Renderer renderer;

renderer.render(scene);

}
```

## Dynamic Lighting Scenarios

Designers can create dynamic lighting scenarios that change over time, such as simulating different times of day or varying weather conditions. This helps in understanding the impact of lighting on the space throughout the day.

## Example of Dynamic Lighting

```
void simulateDynamicLighting(const Scene& scene, std::vector<Light>& lights) {
```

```
Renderer renderer;

for (auto& light : lights) {

scene.addLight(light);

renderer.render(scene);

}

}
```

## Conclusion

Real-time ray tracing provides accurate and detailed lighting simulations for architectural spaces. By visualizing natural and artificial lighting interactions, designers can create energy-efficient, visually appealing, and comfortable environments.

## 17.4. Interactive Design Tools

Interactive design tools powered by real-time ray tracing enable designers to explore and refine their concepts dynamically. These tools facilitate collaboration, enhance creativity, and streamline the design process.

### Real-Time Feedback

Interactive design tools provide real-time feedback on design changes, allowing designers to see the immediate impact of their decisions. This accelerates the design process and supports iterative refinement.

## Example of Real-Time Feedback

```
void provideRealTimeFeedback(Renderer& renderer, Scene& scene, Material& newMaterial) {
    scene.addMaterial(newMaterial);
    renderer.render();
}
```

## Collaborative Design

Real-time ray tracing tools support collaborative design sessions, where multiple stakeholders can interact with the design simultaneously. This enhances communication and ensures that all perspectives are considered.

## Example of Collaborative Design

```
void collaborateOnDesign(Renderer& renderer, Scene& scene, std::vector<Stakeholder>& stakeholders) {
    renderer.loadScene(scene);
    for (auto& stakeholder : stakeholders) {
        renderer.addStakeholder(stakeholder);
    }
    renderer.render();
}
```

## Design Exploration

Interactive tools allow designers to explore different design options quickly. By modifying materials, lighting, and geometry in real-time, designers can experiment with various configurations and identify the best solutions.

## Example of Design Exploration

```
void exploreDesignOptions(Renderer& renderer, Scene& scene, std::vector<Material>& materials) {

for (auto& material : materials) {

scene.addMaterial(material);

renderer.render();

}

}
```

## Parametric Design

Parametric design involves using algorithms and parameters to generate complex forms and structures. Real-time ray tracing tools can visualize parametric designs, allowing for dynamic adjustments and optimization.

## Example of Parametric Design

```
void visualizeParametricDesign(Renderer& renderer, Scene& scene, ParametricModel& model) {

model.generate(scene);

renderer.render();
```

}

## Conclusion

Interactive design tools powered by real-time ray tracing enhance creativity, collaboration, and efficiency in the design process. By providing real-time feedback, supporting collaborative sessions, and enabling dynamic exploration, these tools transform the way designers work.

## 17.5. Future of Design with Ray Tracing Technologies

The future of design with ray tracing technologies promises to bring even more advancements in realism, efficiency, and interactivity. This section explores potential developments and their impact on the design industry.

### Enhanced Realism

Future ray tracing technologies will continue to improve the realism of renderings. Advancements in hardware, algorithms, and AI will enable even more accurate simulations of light, materials, and environments.

### Example of Enhanced Realism

```
void renderWithEnhancedRealism(Renderer& renderer, Scene& scene, AdvancedMaterial& material) {

scene.addMaterial(material);

renderer.render();

}
```

## AI Integration

The integration of AI with ray tracing will revolutionize the design process. AI-driven tools will assist designers in generating and optimizing designs, predicting lighting effects, and automating repetitive tasks.

## Example of AI Integration

void integrateAIInDesign(Renderer& renderer, Scene& scene, AIModel& aiModel) {

aiModel.optimizeDesign(scene);

renderer.render(scene);

}

## Virtual and Augmented Reality

The use of virtual and augmented reality in design will become more prevalent, providing immersive experiences for designers and clients. Real-time ray tracing will enhance these experiences with photorealistic visuals.

## Example of VR/AR Integration

void integrateVRAR(Renderer& renderer, Scene& scene, VRDevice& vrDevice) {

vrDevice.loadScene(scene);

vrDevice.render();

}

## Real-Time Collaboration

Advancements in real-time collaboration tools will enable designers to work together seamlessly, regardless of their location. This will facilitate global collaboration and bring diverse perspectives to the design process.

## Example of Real-Time Collaboration

```
void collaborateGlobally(Renderer& renderer, Scene& scene, std::vector<Designer>& designers) {

renderer.loadScene(scene);

for (auto& designer : designers) {

renderer.addDesigner(designer);

}

renderer.render();

}
```

## Automated Design Optimization

Future tools will offer automated design optimization, where algorithms analyze various design parameters and suggest the best solutions. This will help in achieving optimal performance, aesthetics, and functionality.

## Example of Design Optimization

```
void optimizeDesignAutomatically(Renderer& renderer, Scene& scene, OptimizationModel& model) {

model.optimize(scene);
```

renderer.render(scene);

}

## Sustainable Design

Ray tracing technologies will support sustainable design by enabling detailed analysis of energy efficiency, material usage, and environmental impact. Designers will be able to create eco-friendly solutions with ease.

## Example of Sustainable Design

void designSustainably(Renderer& renderer, Scene& scene, SustainabilityModel& model) {

model.evaluateSustainability(scene);

renderer.render(scene);

}

## Conclusion

The future of design with ray tracing technologies holds exciting possibilities. Enhanced realism, AI integration, VR/AR experiences, real-time collaboration, automated optimization, and sustainable design are just a few of the developments that will transform the design industry.

# Chapter 18: Ethical and Environmental Considerations

## 18.1. Energy Consumption in High-Performance Ray Tracing

High-performance ray tracing requires significant computational power, leading to increased energy consumption. This section explores the impact of energy usage in ray tracing and potential solutions for reducing environmental impact.

### Energy Demands of Ray Tracing

Ray tracing algorithms involve complex calculations, often performed on powerful GPUs and CPUs. The energy demands of these computations can be substantial, especially for large-scale and real-time applications.

### Example of Energy Consumption Analysis

void analyzeEnergyConsumption(const Scene& scene, Renderer& renderer) {

renderer.loadScene(scene);

double energyUsage = renderer.calculateEnergyUsage();

std::cout << "Energy Usage: " << energyUsage << " kWh" << std::endl;

}

## Environmental Impact

The increased energy consumption associated with ray tracing contributes to carbon emissions and environmental degradation. It is crucial to address these impacts to promote sustainable practices in digital media.

## Example of Environmental Impact Evaluation

void evaluateEnvironmentalImpact(double energyUsage) {

double carbonFootprint = energyUsage * carbonFactor;

std::cout << "Carbon Footprint: " << carbonFootprint << " kg CO2" << std::endl;

}

## Optimization Techniques

Optimizing ray tracing algorithms and hardware can significantly reduce energy consumption. Techniques such as adaptive sampling, efficient memory management, and hardware acceleration play a vital role in this optimization.

## Example of Optimization

void optimizeRendering(Renderer& renderer, Scene& scene) {

renderer.enableAdaptiveSampling();

renderer.optimizeMemoryUsage();

renderer.render(scene);

}

## Renewable Energy Sources

Using renewable energy sources for powering data centers and rendering farms can mitigate the environmental impact of ray tracing. Solar, wind, and hydroelectric power are viable options for sustainable energy supply.

### Example of Renewable Energy Integration

void integrateRenewableEnergy(RenderingFarm& farm) {

farm.useRenewableEnergy(Solar);

farm.renderScene(scene);

}

## Future Directions

Future advancements in energy-efficient hardware and algorithms will continue to reduce the environmental impact of ray tracing. Innovations in quantum computing and AI-driven optimizations hold promise for further energy savings.

### Example of Future Innovations

void implementFutureInnovations(Renderer& renderer, QuantumModel& quantumModel) {

renderer.loadScene(scene);

quantumModel.optimizeEnergyUsage(renderer);

renderer.render(scene);

}

## Conclusion

Addressing the energy consumption of high-performance ray tracing is essential for promoting sustainable practices in digital media. By optimizing algorithms, utilizing renewable energy sources, and exploring future innovations, we can reduce the environmental impact of ray tracing.

## 18.2. Ethical Implications of Photorealism

The ability to create photorealistic images and animations with ray tracing raises ethical considerations. This section explores the potential issues and responsibilities associated with photorealism in digital media.

### Misinformation and Deepfakes

Photorealistic imagery can be used to create deepfakes and other forms of misinformation. These realistic manipulations can deceive viewers and spread false information, posing significant ethical challenges.

### Example of Deepfake Detection

```
void detectDeepfakes(const Image& image, AIModel& aiModel)
{
bool isDeepfake = aiModel.detectDeepfake(image);

std::cout << "Deepfake Detected: " << (isDeepfake ? "Yes" : "No") << std::endl;

}
```

## Copyright and Intellectual Property

Creating photorealistic digital content can lead to copyright and intellectual property issues. Ensuring that original creators are credited and compensated for their work is crucial for ethical media production.

## Example of Copyright Management

```
void manageCopyright(const Image& image, Metadata& metadata) {

metadata.addCopyrightInfo(image);

saveImageWithMetadata(image, metadata);

}
```

## Privacy Concerns

Photorealistic renderings can be used to create realistic representations of individuals without their consent, raising privacy concerns. Ethical guidelines should be established to protect individuals' rights.

## Example of Privacy Protection

```
void protectPrivacy(const Scene& scene, Renderer& renderer) {

renderer.anonymizeSensitiveData(scene);

renderer.render(scene);

}
```

## Responsible Use of Technology

It is essential to use photorealistic rendering technology responsibly, avoiding harm and promoting positive applications. This includes creating content that respects cultural, social, and ethical values.

## Example of Responsible Content Creation

void createResponsibleContent(const Scene& scene, Renderer& renderer) {

renderer.loadScene(scene);

renderer.ensureContentCompliance();

renderer.render(scene);

}

## Conclusion

The ethical implications of photorealism in ray tracing require careful consideration. Addressing issues such as misinformation, copyright, privacy, and responsible use is essential for promoting ethical practices in digital media.

# 18.3. Sustainable Practices in Ray Tracing Technology

Sustainable practices in ray tracing technology are essential for reducing environmental impact and promoting long-term viability. This section explores strategies for implementing sustainability in ray tracing.

## Energy-Efficient Hardware

Using energy-efficient hardware, such as GPUs and CPUs designed for low power consumption, can significantly reduce the energy footprint of ray tracing operations.

### Example of Energy-Efficient Hardware

```
void useEnergyEfficientHardware(Renderer& renderer, EnergyEfficientGPU& gpu) {

renderer.initializeWithGPU(gpu);

renderer.render(scene);

}
```

## Optimized Algorithms

Optimizing ray tracing algorithms to minimize computational requirements and maximize efficiency helps reduce energy consumption. Techniques such as adaptive sampling and parallel processing are effective optimization strategies.

### Example of Algorithm Optimization

```
void optimizeAlgorithm(Renderer& renderer, Scene& scene) {

renderer.enableAdaptiveSampling();

renderer.parallelizeRayTracing();

renderer.render(scene);

}
```

## Cloud Rendering

Using cloud rendering services with a focus on sustainability can help reduce the environmental impact of ray tracing. Many cloud providers offer eco-friendly data centers powered by renewable energy.

## Example of Cloud Rendering

```
void renderInCloud(Scene& scene, CloudRenderer& cloudRenderer) {

cloudRenderer.initialize();

cloudRenderer.loadScene(scene);

cloudRenderer.render();

}
```

## Recycling and Reuse

Promoting the recycling and reuse of hardware components can extend the lifecycle of equipment and reduce electronic waste. This includes refurbishing old GPUs and CPUs for use in less demanding applications.

## Example of Hardware Recycling

```
void recycleHardware(GPU& oldGPU, Renderer& secondaryRenderer) {

secondaryRenderer.initializeWithGPU(oldGPU);

secondaryRenderer.render(scene);

}
```

## Conclusion

Implementing sustainable practices in ray tracing technology is essential for reducing environmental impact. By using energy-efficient hardware, optimizing algorithms, leveraging cloud rendering, and promoting recycling, we can contribute to a more sustainable future for digital media.

## 18.4. The Role of Ray Tracing in Deepfakes

Ray tracing technology plays a significant role in the creation of deepfakes, which are realistic but fake digital representations of individuals. This section explores the implications and challenges associated with deepfakes.

### Creating Realistic Deepfakes

Ray tracing allows for the creation of highly realistic deepfakes by simulating light interactions with surfaces and materials. This realism makes it challenging to distinguish deepfakes from genuine content.

### Example of Deepfake Creation

```
void createDeepfake(Scene& scene, Renderer& renderer, FaceModel& faceModel) {
    renderer.loadScene(scene);
    scene.addFaceModel(faceModel);
    renderer.render(scene);
}
```

## Detecting Deepfakes

AI and machine learning techniques are essential for detecting deepfakes. These models analyze visual cues and inconsistencies that may indicate a digitally manipulated image or video.

## Example of Deepfake Detection

```
void detectDeepfake(const Image& image, AIModel& aiModel) {

bool isDeepfake = aiModel.detectDeepfake(image);

std::cout << "Deepfake Detected: " << (isDeepfake ? "Yes" : "No") << std::endl;

}
```

## Ethical Considerations

The use of ray tracing for creating deepfakes raises ethical concerns, including privacy violations, misinformation, and potential harm. Establishing guidelines and regulations is essential for ethical use of this technology.

## Example of Ethical Guidelines

```
void establishEthicalGuidelines(EthicsCommittee& committee) {

committee.createGuidelines();

committee.enforceGuidelines();

}
```

## Conclusion

Ray tracing technology significantly impacts the creation and detection of deepfakes. Addressing the ethical implications and developing robust detection methods are crucial for mitigating the risks associated with deepfakes.

## 18.5. Balancing Innovation with Responsibility

Balancing innovation in ray tracing technology with social and environmental responsibility is essential for sustainable development. This section explores strategies for achieving this balance.

### Responsible Innovation

Promoting responsible innovation involves developing technologies that benefit society while minimizing negative impacts. This includes considering ethical, social, and environmental factors in the development process.

### Example of Responsible Innovation

```
void promoteResponsibleInnovation(ResearchTeam& team, InnovationModel& model) {

model.includeEthicalConsiderations();

model.evaluateSocialImpact();

team.implementInnovations(model);

}
```

## Ethical Design

Incorporating ethical design principles ensures that ray tracing technologies are developed and used in ways that respect human rights and promote fairness and transparency.

### Example of Ethical Design

```
void implementEthicalDesign(DesignTeam& team, EthicalFramework& framework) {

framework.applyToDesignProcess(team);

team.evaluateDesignsForEthics();

}
```

## Environmental Sustainability

Ensuring environmental sustainability involves developing energy-efficient technologies, reducing waste, and promoting the use of renewable resources. This helps in mitigating the environmental impact of ray tracing.

### Example of Environmental Sustainability

```
void ensureSustainability(Renderer& renderer, SustainabilityModel& model) {

model.optimizeEnergyUsage(renderer);

model.promoteRecycling(renderer);

renderer.render(scene);

}
```

## Social Impact

Assessing the social impact of ray tracing technologies involves considering their effects on communities, cultures, and individuals. This helps in developing technologies that contribute positively to society.

### Example of Social Impact Assessment

```
void assessSocialImpact(DevelopmentTeam& team, ImpactModel& model) {

model.analyzeImpactOnCommunities(team);

model.recommendImprovements();

team.implementRecommendations();

}
```

## Conclusion

Balancing innovation in ray tracing technology with social and environmental responsibility is crucial for sustainable development. By promoting responsible innovation, ethical design, environmental sustainability, and positive social impact, we can ensure that technological advancements benefit society as a whole.

# Chapter 19: The Future of Real-Time Ray Tracing

## 19.1. Emerging Trends in Ray Tracing

The future of real-time ray tracing is shaped by several emerging trends that promise to revolutionize the field. These trends are driven by advancements in hardware, software, and integration with other technologies, leading to more realistic and efficient rendering.

## AI and Machine Learning Integration

AI and machine learning are increasingly being integrated into ray tracing workflows to optimize performance and enhance visual quality. AI-driven denoising, adaptive sampling, and predictive rendering are becoming standard practices.

## Example of AI-Driven Denoising

```
Image applyAIDenoising(const Image& noisyImage, AIDenoiser& denoiser) {
    return denoiser.denoise(noisyImage);
}
```

## Real-Time Global Illumination

Advancements in real-time global illumination techniques are making it possible to render complex lighting scenarios with high accuracy. Techniques like voxel cone tracing and real-time path tracing are at the forefront of this development.

## Example of Voxel Cone Tracing

```
void computeGlobalIllumination(Scene& scene, Renderer& renderer) {
    renderer.initializeVoxelConeTracing();
    renderer.computeGlobalIllumination(scene);
```

}

## Hybrid Rendering Techniques

Hybrid rendering combines rasterization and ray tracing to balance performance and quality. This approach leverages the strengths of both techniques, using rasterization for primary visibility and ray tracing for effects like reflections and shadows.

## Example of Hybrid Rendering

```
void renderSceneHybrid(Renderer& renderer, Scene& scene) {

renderer.rasterizeScene(scene);

renderer.applyRayTracingEffects(scene);

}
```

## Cloud-Based Ray Tracing

Cloud computing is becoming a crucial component in the future of ray tracing, offering scalable resources to handle complex rendering tasks. Cloud-based ray tracing services allow for high-quality rendering without the need for expensive local hardware.

## Example of Cloud-Based Rendering

```
void renderInCloud(Scene& scene, CloudRenderer& cloudRenderer) {

cloudRenderer.uploadScene(scene);

cloudRenderer.render();

cloudRenderer.downloadResults();
```

}

## Real-Time Ray Tracing in VR and AR

Real-time ray tracing is enhancing virtual and augmented reality experiences by providing realistic lighting and reflections. This integration significantly improves the immersion and realism of VR and AR applications.

### Example of VR Integration

void integrateRayTracingInVR(Scene& scene, VRDevice& vrDevice) {

vrDevice.loadScene(scene);

vrDevice.enableRayTracing();

vrDevice.render();

}

## Conclusion

Emerging trends in ray tracing, such as AI integration, real-time global illumination, hybrid rendering, cloud-based solutions, and VR/AR applications, are driving the future of real-time ray tracing. These advancements promise to deliver unprecedented levels of realism and efficiency in rendering.

## 19.2. The Convergence of Real-Time and Offline Rendering

The convergence of real-time and offline rendering is a significant trend in the field of ray tracing. This convergence aims to bring the quality of offline rendering to real-time applications, creating a seamless experience across different rendering contexts.

## Bridging the Gap

Historically, real-time rendering prioritized speed over quality, while offline rendering focused on achieving the highest possible visual fidelity. Advances in hardware and algorithms are now bridging this gap, enabling real-time rendering to approach the quality of offline methods.

## Example of Convergent Techniques

```
void combineRealTimeAndOffline(Renderer& realTimeRenderer, Renderer& offlineRenderer, Scene& scene) {

realTimeRenderer.render(scene);

offlineRenderer.render(scene);

combineResults(realTimeRenderer.getResults(), offlineRenderer.getResults());

}
```

## Unified Rendering Pipelines

Unified rendering pipelines are being developed to handle both real-time and offline rendering tasks. These pipelines allow for flexible switching between rendering modes based on the requirements of the application.

## Example of Unified Pipeline

```
void setupUnifiedPipeline(Renderer& renderer) {
```

```
renderer.initializeUnifiedPipeline();

renderer.configureForRealTime();

renderer.configureForOffline();
}
```

## Real-Time Ray Tracing Hardware

The development of dedicated ray tracing hardware, such as NVIDIA's RT Cores and AMD's Ray Accelerators, is facilitating the convergence by providing the necessary computational power to perform complex ray tracing tasks in real time.

## Example of Using Dedicated Hardware

```
void renderWithRayTracingHardware(Scene& scene, RayTracingHardware& hardware) {

hardware.initialize();

hardware.render(scene);
}
```

## AI-Driven Enhancements

AI-driven enhancements, such as denoising and upscaling, are playing a crucial role in achieving offline-quality rendering in real-time applications. These techniques reduce the computational load while maintaining high visual quality.

## Example of AI-Driven Upscaling

```
Image upscaleWithAI(const Image& lowResImage, AIUpscaler& upscaler) {
```

```
return upscaler.upscale(lowResImage);
}
```

## Case Studies

Several case studies demonstrate the successful convergence of real-time and offline rendering. Games, virtual production, and interactive design tools are benefiting from this trend, achieving higher visual fidelity without compromising performance.

## Example of a Case Study

```
void presentCaseStudy(Scene& scene, Renderer& renderer) {

renderer.loadScene(scene);

renderer.renderRealTime();

renderer.renderOffline();

renderer.compareResults();

}
```

## Conclusion

The convergence of real-time and offline rendering is transforming the way visual content is created and experienced. By combining the speed of real-time techniques with the quality of offline methods, this trend promises to deliver the best of both worlds.

## 19.3. Next-Generation Ray Tracing Technologies

Next-generation ray tracing technologies are set to revolutionize the field with new capabilities and higher performance. These advancements are driven by innovations in hardware, software, and algorithms.

### Quantum Computing

Quantum computing holds the potential to solve complex ray tracing problems that are currently infeasible with classical computing. Quantum algorithms can handle large datasets and complex calculations more efficiently.

### Example of Quantum Ray Tracing

```
void performQuantumRayTracing(Scene& scene, QuantumComputer& quantumComputer) {

quantumComputer.initialize();

quantumComputer.runRayTracingAlgorithm(scene);

}
```

### Neuromorphic Computing

Neuromorphic computing, inspired by the human brain, offers a new approach to processing information. This technology can potentially enhance ray tracing by providing efficient parallel processing and learning capabilities.

## Example of Neuromorphic Processing

```
void integrateNeuromorphicComputing(Scene& scene, NeuromorphicProcessor& processor) {
    processor.loadScene(scene);
    processor.performRayTracing();
}
```

## Photonic Computing

Photonic computing uses light instead of electrical signals to perform computations, offering the potential for ultra-fast processing speeds. This technology could dramatically reduce rendering times for complex scenes.

## Example of Photonic Computing

```
void applyPhotonicComputing(Scene& scene, PhotonicProcessor& processor) {
    processor.initialize();
    processor.renderScene(scene);
}
```

## Advanced Shading Models

Next-generation ray tracing will feature advanced shading models that accurately simulate complex light interactions, such as subsurface scattering, caustics, and global illumination.

## Example of Advanced Shading

```
void renderWithAdvancedShading(Scene& scene, Renderer& renderer) {
renderer.enableSubsurfaceScattering();
renderer.enableCaustics();
renderer.render(scene);
}
```

## Real-Time Path Tracing

Real-time path tracing is becoming more feasible with the advancement of hardware and optimization techniques. This method provides highly realistic lighting by simulating the paths of light rays as they bounce around a scene.

## Example of Real-Time Path Tracing

```
void performRealTimePathTracing(Scene& scene, PathTracer& pathTracer) {
pathTracer.initialize();
pathTracer.render(scene);
}
```

## Conclusion

Next-generation ray tracing technologies, including quantum computing, neuromorphic computing, photonic computing, advanced shading models, and real-time path tracing, promise to revolutionize the field. These advancements will enable more realistic and efficient rendering, pushing the boundaries of what is possible in visual computing.

## 19.4. Predictions for the Next Decade

The next decade promises significant advancements in ray tracing technology, driven by innovations in hardware, software, and integration with other fields. Here are some predictions for the future of ray tracing.

### Ubiquity of Real-Time Ray Tracing

Real-time ray tracing will become ubiquitous across various industries, from gaming and film to architecture and automotive design. This technology will be a standard feature in most visual applications.

### Example of Industry Adoption

```
void implementRayTracingInIndustry(Scene& scene, IndustryApplication& app) {
app.loadScene(scene);
app.enableRayTracing();
app.render();
}
```

### Enhanced AI Integration

AI integration will deepen, with machine learning models becoming more adept at optimizing ray tracing processes. AI will handle tasks like scene optimization, denoising, and even automating parts of the rendering process.

## Example of AI Optimization

void optimizeWithAI(Scene& scene, AIOptimizer& optimizer) {

optimizer.analyzeScene(scene);

optimizer.applyOptimizations();

}

## Increased Accessibility

Ray tracing technology will become more accessible, with tools and platforms designed for non-experts. This democratization will allow more creators to leverage the power of ray tracing in their projects.

## Example of User-Friendly Tools

void useAccessibleRayTracingTool(Scene& scene, EasyRenderer& renderer) {

renderer.loadScene(scene);

renderer.renderWithSimpleInterface();

}

## Sustainable Practices

Sustainable practices will be a significant focus, with energy-efficient hardware and algorithms becoming a priority. The environmental impact of ray tracing will be minimized through innovative solutions.

## Example of Sustainable Rendering

```
void renderSustainably(Scene& scene, GreenRenderer& renderer)
{
    renderer.initializeWithGreenTech();
    renderer.render(scene);
}
```

## Cross-Platform Integration

Ray tracing will seamlessly integrate across different platforms, including desktops, mobile devices, and cloud services. This integration will ensure consistent visual quality and performance regardless of the platform.

## Example of Cross-Platform Rendering

```
void renderAcrossPlatforms(Scene& scene, MultiPlatformRenderer& renderer) {
    renderer.loadScene(scene);
    renderer.renderOnDesktop();
    renderer.renderOnMobile();
    renderer.renderInCloud();
}
```

## Conclusion

The next decade will see ray tracing become more ubiquitous, AI-integrated, accessible, sustainable, and cross-platform. These advancements will transform industries and enable new possibilities in visual computing.

## 19.5. The Long-Term Impact of Ray Tracing on Digital Media

Ray tracing will have a profound long-term impact on digital media, reshaping the way visual content is created and experienced. This section explores the potential effects and opportunities arising from widespread adoption of ray tracing.

### Transforming Visual Storytelling

Ray tracing will enable new forms of visual storytelling by providing unprecedented levels of realism and detail. Filmmakers and game developers will create more immersive and emotionally engaging experiences.

### Example of Enhanced Storytelling

```
void createImmersiveStory(Scene& scene, StoryRenderer& renderer) {

renderer.loadScene(scene);

renderer.applyCinematicEffects();

renderer.render();

}
```

### Redefining Design and Architecture

The fields of design and architecture will be revolutionized by real-time ray tracing, allowing for accurate visualizations and simulations. This will lead to more efficient and innovative design processes.

## Example of Architectural Visualization

void visualizeArchitecturalDesign(Scene& scene, ArchRenderer& renderer) {

renderer.loadScene(scene);

renderer.applyRealisticLighting();

renderer.render();

}

## Enabling New Art Forms

Artists will explore new creative possibilities with ray tracing, pushing the boundaries of digital art. This technology will enable the creation of photorealistic and abstract works that were previously unimaginable.

## Example of Digital Art Creation

void createDigitalArt(Scene& scene, ArtRenderer& renderer) {

renderer.loadScene(scene);

renderer experimentWithLightAndMaterial();

renderer renderArtPiece();

}

### Enhancing Virtual Reality

Ray tracing will significantly enhance virtual reality experiences by providing realistic lighting, shadows, and reflections. This will lead to more immersive and believable virtual environments.

### Example of VR Enhancement

```
void enhanceVRExperience(Scene& scene, VRRenderer& renderer) {

renderer.loadScene(scene);

renderer enableRayTracing();

renderer renderInVR();

}
```

### Conclusion

The long-term impact of ray tracing on digital media will be transformative, enabling new forms of storytelling, design, art, and virtual experiences. As this technology continues to evolve, it will unlock unprecedented creative possibilities and reshape the landscape of digital media.

# Chapter 20: Case Studies and Practical Applications

## 20.1. In-Depth Analysis of Notable Real-Time Ray Tracing Projects

This section provides an in-depth analysis of notable real-time ray tracing projects that have set benchmarks in the industry. These case studies highlight the techniques, challenges, and solutions involved in achieving high-quality real-time ray tracing.

## Case Study: NVIDIA RTX Games

NVIDIA's RTX technology has brought real-time ray tracing to mainstream gaming, showcasing impressive visual effects like reflections, shadows, and global illumination.

## Example of RTX Implementation

```
void implementRTXInGame(Scene& scene, GameEngine& engine) {
engine.loadScene(scene);
engine.enableRTX();
engine.render();
}
```

## Case Study: Unreal Engine Ray Tracing

Unreal Engine has integrated ray tracing capabilities, allowing developers to create stunningly realistic environments. This case study explores the implementation and optimization techniques used in Unreal Engine.

## Example of Unreal Engine Ray Tracing

```
void useUnrealRayTracing(Scene& scene, UnrealEngine& engine) {
engine.loadScene(scene);
engine.enableRayTracing();
```

```
engine optimizePerformance();
}
```

## Case Study: Quake II RTX

Quake II RTX is a remastered version of the classic game, utilizing ray tracing to enhance its visuals. This project demonstrates how ray tracing can be applied to older titles to breathe new life into them.

## Example of Quake II RTX

```
void remasterQuakeIIWithRTX(Scene& scene, Renderer& renderer) {

renderer.loadScene(scene);

renderer.enableRayTracing();

renderer renderWithRTX();

}
```

## Conclusion

These case studies provide valuable insights into the application of real-time ray tracing in various projects. By examining the techniques and solutions used, developers can gain a deeper understanding of how to achieve high-quality ray tracing in their own work.

## 20.2. Comparative Study of Rendering Techniques

This section presents a comparative study of different rendering techniques, including rasterization, ray tracing, and hybrid methods. The study evaluates the strengths and weaknesses of each technique and their suitability for various applications.

### Rasterization

Rasterization is the traditional rendering method used in real-time graphics. It is fast and efficient but has limitations in simulating complex lighting interactions.

### Example of Rasterization

```
void renderWithRasterization(Scene& scene, Renderer& renderer) {
    renderer.initializeRasterization();
    renderer.render(scene);
}
```

### Ray Tracing

Ray tracing provides realistic lighting and reflections but is computationally intensive. It is ideal for applications requiring high visual fidelity, such as film and architectural visualization.

### Example of Ray Tracing

```
void renderWithRayTracing(Scene& scene, Renderer& renderer) {
    renderer.initializeRayTracing();
```

renderer.render(scene);

}

## Hybrid Rendering

Hybrid rendering combines the strengths of rasterization and ray tracing, using rasterization for primary visibility and ray tracing for effects like reflections and shadows.

## Example of Hybrid Rendering

void renderWithHybridTechnique(Scene& scene, Renderer& renderer) {

renderer.initializeHybridRendering();

renderer.rasterizeScene(scene);

renderer.applyRayTracingEffects(scene);

}

## Comparative Analysis

The comparative analysis evaluates the performance, visual quality, and computational requirements of each technique. This helps in determining the most suitable rendering method for specific applications.

## Example of Comparative Evaluation

void compareRenderingTechniques(Scene& scene, Renderer& rasterRenderer, Renderer& rayRenderer, Renderer& hybridRenderer) {

rasterRenderer.render(scene);

```
rayRenderer.render(scene);

hybridRenderer.render(scene);

compareResults(rasterRenderer.getResults(),
rayRenderer.getResults(), hybridRenderer.getResults());
}
```

## Conclusion

The comparative study highlights the trade-offs between different rendering techniques. By understanding the strengths and limitations of each method, developers can choose the most appropriate technique for their projects.

## 20.3. Lessons from Failed Ray Tracing Implementations

This section explores lessons learned from failed ray tracing implementations, examining common pitfalls and challenges. Understanding these lessons can help developers avoid similar issues in their own projects.

### Overestimating Hardware Capabilities

One common mistake is overestimating the capabilities of available hardware. Ray tracing is computationally intensive, and underpowered hardware can lead to poor performance and subpar visual quality.

### Example of Hardware Limitation

```
void   testHardwareCapabilities(Scene&   scene,   Renderer&
renderer) {
```

```
if (!renderer.isHardwareCapable()) {

    std::cerr << "Hardware not capable of real-time ray tracing." << std::endl;

    return;

}

renderer.render(scene);

}
```

## Insufficient Optimization

Failing to optimize ray tracing algorithms and scenes can result in excessive rendering times and resource consumption. Proper optimization is crucial for achieving real-time performance.

## Example of Optimization

```
void optimizeRayTracing(Scene& scene, Renderer& renderer) {

    renderer.enableAdaptiveSampling();

    renderer.optimizeMemoryUsage();

    renderer.render(scene);

}
```

## Ignoring Scene Complexity

Complex scenes with numerous objects and light sources can overwhelm ray tracing algorithms. Simplifying scenes and using techniques like level of detail (LOD) can help manage complexity.

### Example of Scene Simplification

```
void simplifyScene(Scene& scene) {
    scene.reduceComplexity();
    scene.applyLOD();
}
```

### Conclusion

Learning from failed ray tracing implementations provides valuable insights into avoiding common pitfalls. By addressing issues related to hardware capabilities, optimization, and scene complexity, developers can improve their chances of success.

## 20.4. Inspirational Success Stories in Ray Tracing

This section showcases inspirational success stories in ray tracing, highlighting projects that have set new standards in visual quality and performance. These stories serve as motivation and guidance for developers.

### Pixar's RenderMan

Pixar's RenderMan is renowned for its use in creating visually stunning films. The integration of ray tracing in RenderMan has enabled the production of photorealistic animations and special effects.

### Example of RenderMan Usage

```
void createAnimationWithRenderMan(Scene& scene, RenderMan& renderer) {
```

renderer.loadScene(scene);

renderer.render();

}

## Cyberpunk 2077

Cyberpunk 2077 is a groundbreaking game that utilizes real-time ray tracing to deliver immersive visuals. The game's use of ray tracing for reflections, shadows, and global illumination has set new benchmarks in gaming graphics.

## Example of Game Ray Tracing

void implementRayTracingInGame(Scene& scene, GameEngine& engine) {

engine.loadScene(scene);

engine.enableRayTracing();

engine render();

}

## Architectural Visualization by DBOX

DBOX is known for its high-quality architectural visualizations. The use of ray tracing in their projects has resulted in photorealistic representations that help clients visualize designs with exceptional clarity.

## Example of Architectural Visualization

void createArchitecturalRender(Scene& scene, ArchRenderer& renderer) {

renderer.loadScene(scene);

renderer.applyRealisticLighting();

renderer render();

}

## Conclusion

These success stories demonstrate the potential of ray tracing to transform visual media. By studying these examples, developers can gain inspiration and insights into achieving high-quality ray tracing in their own projects.

## 20.5. Guided Tutorial for a Basic Ray Tracing Project

This section provides a guided tutorial for creating a basic ray tracing project, covering essential steps and techniques. This hands-on approach helps developers understand the fundamentals of ray tracing implementation.

### Setting Up the Project

Begin by setting up the project environment. Choose a programming language and framework suitable for ray tracing, such as C++ with OpenGL or Vulkan.

### Example of Project Setup

void setupProjectEnvironment() {

initializeOpenGL();

createWindow();

}

## Defining the Scene

Define the scene by creating objects, materials, and light sources. This involves setting up geometric shapes, assigning materials, and positioning light sources.

## Example of Scene Definition

```
void defineScene(Scene& scene) {

scene.addObject(Sphere(Vector3(0, 0, -5), 1.0, Material(Color(1, 0, 0))));

scene.addLight(PointLight(Vector3(2, 2, 0), Color(1, 1, 1)));

}
```

## Implementing Ray Tracing

Implement the ray tracing algorithm by calculating intersections between rays and objects, determining shading, and rendering the final image.

## Example of Ray Tracing Implementation

```
void performRayTracing(Scene& scene, Image& output) {

for (int y = 0; y < output.height; ++y) {

for (int x = 0; x < output.width; ++x) {

Ray ray = generateRay(x, y, output.width, output.height);

Color color = traceRay(ray, scene);
```

output.setPixel(x, y, color);

}

}

}

## Adding Shading and Lighting

Enhance the ray tracing implementation by adding shading models and lighting calculations. This includes ambient, diffuse, and specular lighting components.

## Example of Shading and Lighting

Color shadeRay(const Ray& ray, const Scene& scene, const Intersection& hit) {

Color ambient = hit.material.ambient;

Color diffuse = hit.material.diffuse * max(0.0f, dot(hit.normal, scene.light.direction));

Color specular = hit.material.specular * pow(max(0.0f, dot(reflect(-scene.light.direction, hit.normal), hit.viewDirection)), hit.material.shininess);

**return** ambient + diffuse + specular;

}

## Rendering the Final Image

Render the final image by combining all the components and saving the output. This involves writing the image data to a file or displaying it on the screen.

## Example of Final Rendering

```
void renderFinalImage(Scene& scene, Image& output) {

performRayTracing(scene, output);

saveImage(output, "output.png");

}
```

## Conclusion

This guided tutorial provides a step-by-step approach to creating a basic ray tracing project. By following these steps, developers can gain practical experience and a deeper understanding of ray tracing implementation.